SIBERIA
and the Exile System

George Kennan

BY GEORGE KENNAN

SIBERIA

and the Exile System

ABRIDGED FROM THE FIRST EDITION OF 1891

With an Introduction
by
George Frost Kennan

THE UNIVERSITY OF CHICAGO PRESS

Siberia and the Exile System (New York, 1891) was originally published by the Century Company.

Library of Congress Catalog Number: 58-5618

THE UNIVERSITY OF CHICAGO PRESS, CHICAGO 37
Cambridge University Press, London, N.W. 1, England
The University of Toronto Press, Toronto 5, Canada

© *1958 by The University of Chicago. Published 1958. Composed and printed by* THE UNIVERSITY OF CHICAGO PRESS, *Chicago, Illinois, U.S.A.*

Contents

List of Illustrations

Introduction

O<small>N THE EVENING OF JUNE</small> 16, 1885, a heavy springless wagon, drawn by three small horses hitched abreast, lumbered through the eastern city gate of the Russian town of Ekaterinburg in the Urals and moved slowly off in the direction of Siberia. The driver was a bearded Russian peasant. Behind him, ensconced on their own baggage and clinging to the lurching sides, rode two American passengers, Mr. George Kennan, writer and lecturer of Norwalk, Ohio, and Mr. George A. Frost, artist of Boston.

Before returning to Ekaterinburg the following March these two travelers were destined to cover, by this means or ones still less comfortable, some eight thousand miles of Siberian territory. They would travel in the heat of summer and in the terrible blizzards of winter. Their route would lie either over dirt roads, often abominable, or over no roads at all. On occasion, they would have to traverse as much as a thousand miles at a stretch without finding a bed to sleep on, a place to take off their clothes, or a spot in which to escape from the vermin that swarmed over nearly all Siberian hostelries. Yet the physical discomfort of the journey, excruciating as it was, would be minor compared to the anguish of confronting the subject they had come to study: the penal and exile system of the Tsar's government, as it operated in Siberia.

The literary work reprinted in this volume represents Kennan's account of the extraordinary journey, together with what he saw of the treatment of convicts and administrative exiles in Siberia.

George Kennan came of a family of Scotch-Irish pioneers in the Western Reserve. He was born in Norwalk, Ohio, on February 16, 1845. His father kept the Western Union telegraph office at that place. At the age of twelve he was obliged to leave school, for financial reasons, and to go to work in his father's telegraph office. He never resumed his formal education. When people asked him in later life what his college was, he would reply: "Russia."

Too frail to serve in uniform during the Civil War, he continued as a telegrapher. He was transferred during the war to Cincinnati, where he served as assistant chief operator for Western Union and as military telegrapher for the Associated Press, working a fourteen-hour night shift in the office where Thomas Edison was later employed. One night in 1864 he was pleased to receive a message for himself from the company accepting his application for appointment as a member of an Alaskan-Siberian expedition. He was then nineteen years old.

The first attempt to lay an Atlantic cable had, at this juncture, only recently been made. Its failure had caused discouragement over the prospects for any underwater telegraph connection between Europe and America. The Western Union Company had turned, as an alternative, to the possibility of laying a telegraph line over Alaska and Siberia, to connect with the easternmost terminus of the Russian telegraph system, at Irkutsk. The expedition in which Kennan was to participate was mounted to implement this project. The young telegrapher had already invested his savings in the expedition before he applied for and received his appointment to it, and his pluck apparently impressed the superintendent of the company.

On July 1, 1865, Kennan and three companions set out from San Francisco in the Russian brig "Olga." Eight weeks later two of them, Kennan and a Russian major, were set ashore at Petropavlovsk, on the Kamchatka Peninsula. Their instructions were to make their way northward through the peninsula to the mainland of eastern Siberia, where they were to explore the two thousand miles of inhospitable territory lying between the Anadyrsk region on the Bering Sea and Nikolayevsk-on-the-Amur and to arrange for the laying of the telegraph line. They were to be picked up a year or so later, after surveying a line and having camps laid out and poles cut for the construction workers who would follow them. Meanwhile they would be on their own.

By a combination of good fortune, level-headedness, and physical courage young Kennan, then only twenty years old, survived this ordeal. Dressed like a native, leading the primitive and arduous life of the wandering tribes of that area, traveling at times, for weeks on end, alone with a Yakut dog team through the wastes of one of the world's most forbidding Arctic regions, he completed his assignment. When the relief ship finally arrived, it brought the news that the Atlantic cable had been laid and the entire project had been in vain.

After returning to the United States via European Russia (a journey that itself involved another four or five thousand miles by sleigh), Kennan took up in New York the struggle against poverty and against his own distaste for the humdrum routine of office work. He lectured on his Siberian experiences; he sold books for D. Appleton and Company; he worked in banks and law offices. Eventually, he moved to Washington, where he became night manager of the Associated Press. In 1870 he succeeded in getting G. P. Putnam's Sons to publish an account of the Siberian adventure under the title *Tent Life in Siberia*. It was a creditable literary achievement, especially for a young man without high school or college education. The style, like that of everything Kennan subsequently wrote, was straightforward, clear, and disciplined. Of today's college graduates, few indeed would be able to match it for literary quality. In its boyish freshness and humor, the story betrayed the author's tender years; but it was a good book, well-told, factual, and interesting.

With the proceeds from *Tent Life in Siberia*, Kennan, who had now acquired a taste for adventure, returned briefly to

Russia in 1870 for a further bout of exploratory travel, this time in the great Caucasian mountain range. The journey provided further substance for lectures and articles.

In the course of his work for the telegraph company in 1865–67, Kennan had seen relatively little of the Russian penal system in Siberia. His travels had for the most part taken him through uninhabited regions. He had come away, consequently, with a generally favorable impression of the Russian government and its administration. In the ensuing years he remained skeptical of the tales of police oppression and cruelty in Siberia that occasionally filtered through to the Western public. On the few occasions when he took part in public discussion of these matters, during those years, it was to defend the Tsar's government against what he thought were unjust attacks.

The intensification of the conflict between the Russian revolutionists and their government, beginning in the late 1870's and culminating in the murder of Tsar Alexander II in 1881, led to a new wave of sentences of political offenders to penal servitude or administrative exile in Siberia. Intrigued by the reports of these events, Kennan conceived the idea of an on-the-spot study of Siberia and the exile system; and the *Century Magazine* was eventually prevailed upon to sponsor and finance the expedition.

The sponsoring of journeys of exploration to remote parts of the globe was at that time a vogue of American journalism. Not long since, James Gordon Bennett, owner of the *New York Herald* had financed Stanley's sensational exploits in Africa. More recently, Bennett had given similar support to the ill-fated "Jeannette" expedition, an attempt to reach the North Pole from a vessel entering the Arctic Ocean through Bering Strait. The "Jeannette," after drifting two years in the ice, had finally been crushed and sunk off the northern coast of Siberia in 1882. The members of the expedition, taking to sleighs and small boats, had made for Siberian mainland. A portion of them had succeeded in reaching the Lena delta, itself one of the world's most desolate spots. Of these, only a few survived, to be repatriated through Siberia.

This tragic effort had drawn American attention once more to the eastern Siberian territory. It was not surprising in these circumstances that the *Century Magazine* should have supposed its readers would be interested in another visit to the interior regions of Siberia, to be carried out this time by a man who was an accomplished writer and an experienced Arctic traveler, with special knowledge of the Siberian area. The Tsar's government, aware of Kennan's favorable disposition, gave a somewhat hesitant assent to the undertaking. After a preliminary visit to St. Petersburg and Moscow to perfect the arrangements, Kennan set off on his journey in the early spring of 1885, accompanied by Frost, who was to serve as artist and photographer. What followed is so well told in Kennan's own words that it needs no recapitulation. Let it merely be noted here that only men of great stoutness of heart and of most unusual physical and moral courage could have persisted in so excruciatingly painful and depressing a journey as that related in this volume.

The account of the journey appeared serially, in the years 1888–89, in the *Century Magazine*. In 1891 it was published in book form under the title *Siberia and the Exile System* (a two-volume work of which the present book is a shortened version). Its effect was fortified by the lectures which Kennan, a forceful speaker, delivered in many parts of the country. The impression created by all this on the educated public of that day was profound. Few of its members remained ignorant of Kennan's experiences or unmoved by his tales. It was a time when America was coming of age, abandoning the egocentricity of its youth, and turning its eyes to the world beyond its borders. Tales of suffering and oppression elsewhere were particularly stirring to a generation which firmly believed in progress and which, still recovering from the trauma of the Civil War, was disinclined to any intensive introspective analysis of its own weaknesses. Kennan's book struck squarely and with great effect into that curious Victorian capacity for sympathy and indignation over evils that were far away.

On the Russian liberal public, too, Kennan's work, becoming available in the course of the 1890's in German and illegal Russian translations, made a deep impression. The gratitude of the entire opposition movement—moderates and extremists alike—went out to him for his profound understanding and effective public sponsorship of the opposition cause.

A word is in order here concerning the relationship of Kennan's work to the Russian political realities of the day. His journey was carried out in one of the first years of the reign of Alexander III, a period of extreme reaction and uninhibited police terror. The Marxist phase of the revolutionary movement was at that time only about to begin. Lenin was still a fifteen-year-old schoolboy, attending the *gymnasium* and reading Turgenev at his home in Simbirsk. It was still two years before Lenin's elder brother, Alexander, would be hung for his part in a conspiracy against the life of Tsar Alexander III. A few Russian revolutionists, led by Plekhanov, were already poring over Marxist texts and endeavoring to reconcile this new Western doctrine with the populist and utopian-socialist traditions of the Russian revolutionary movement. But years were to pass before Marxism would become an organized force in the ranks of the Russian opposition, and more years still before its protagonists, caught in the dragnets of police action, would become prominent among the prisoners and exiles in Siberia.

Kennan during his Siberian travels of the mid-eighties thus encountered representatives of the earlier generation of Russian oppositionists: the moderate idealists of the populist school, who had tried with such earnest faith and such pathetic lack of success to carry their ideas to the common people of Russia in the 1860's and 1870's; and the terrorists, mostly younger people who had turned in despair and impatience to organized assassination as a means of bringing home to the regime their bitter discontent and their insistence on change. In addition to this he met, among the administrative exiles in Siberian communities, many people who were innocent of any sort of real opposition activity but who had fallen foul in one way or another of the excesses and stupidities of the tsarist police. Often it was guilt by association, and in some cases (notably that of the well-known writer Korolenko) a refusal to give information about third parties, which had brought these latter people to the trials of a Siberian exile.

To all these, Kennan's sympathies went out generously. For the innocent ones he naturally felt deeply and with burning indignation. He was particularly moved, for example, by the fate of Prince Alexander Kropotkin, brother of the famous anarchist and writer, Peter. For the moderate oppositionists, such representatives of the older populist movement as Katherine Breshkovskaya (later to be known as the "Little Grandmother of the Russian Revolution") and Nikolas Chaikovsky, he also had complete respect and sympathy. With these people he formed enduring friendships, which he cultivated to the end of his life.

With respect to the terrorists the situation was somewhat different. Kennan himself had no sympathy for terrorism as a political method, and he could not remain wholly unaware of the particular responsibility borne by the terrorists for the violent measures of repression to which the regime resorted. But even to these young assassins, he could not deny his sympathy, nor could he refrain from attempting to tell the world their side of the story. "It is not my purpose," he stated in *Siberia and the Exile System* (p. 456 of the 1891 edition),

to justify the policy of the terrorists, nor to approve, even by implication, the resort to murder as a means of tempering despotism; but it is my purpose to explain, so far as I can, certain morbid social phenomena; and in making such explanation circumstances seem to lay upon me the duty of saying to the world for the Russian revolutionists and terrorists all that they might fairly say for themselves if the lips of the dead had not already moldered into dust, and if the voices of the living were not lost in the distance or stifled by prison walls. The Russian Government has its own press and its own representatives abroad; it can explain if it chooses, its methods and measures. The Russian revolutionists, buried alive in remote Siberian solitudes, can only tell their story to an occasional traveler from a freer country, and ask him to lay it before the world for judgment.

There is force in this statement; yet one wonders today whether Kennan, moved as he was by the sufferings which befell these people in Siberia, took full account of the preposterous and indiscriminate campaign of terrorism they had waged against the government and of the extent to which they, by these reckless and certainly criminal actions, had provoked the regime and its police establishment to extremism of which many others, besides the terrorists themselves, were the victims. One wonders what would have been the effect in the United States of a secretly organized campaign of assassination of public officials comparable to that which was launched in Russia in the late 1870's.

The Russian Marxists, for the reasons mentioned above, were never the particular objects of Kennan's sympathies or interests. For their doctrines he had no patience; and it is to be doubted that he ever understood very well the nature and history of their movement. Even they, however, were greatly affected by the illegal translations of *Siberia and the Exile System* that circulated in Russia in the 1890's; and they did not escape the general sense of appreciation to Kennan that dominated the revolutionary movement in general. Mikhail Kalinin, long-time member of Stalin's Politburo and Chairman of the Presidium of the Supreme Soviet of the U.S.S.R., told the writer of these lines that Kennan's work had been a veritable "Bible" for the early revolutionists; and others of the old-Bolshevik generation have made similar observations. Even the Russian Communist movement of the Stalin era was not wholly unaffected in its views toward the United States by the recollection that it had been, after all, an American who had once achieved so perceptive and informed an understanding of the Russian revolutionary movement and had carried its cause to the world public with such striking effectiveness.

With the appearance of *Siberia and the Exile System* in 1891, Kennan's reputation as a man of letters and as America's foremost authority on Russia was established. From this time on, he never swerved from his path as a writer and lecturer. He served as a war correspondent in the Spanish-American War. In 1903 he visited Russia once more but was abruptly expelled, this time by the Tsar's government, now aware of the full measure of his sympathy for the opposition movement and of his services to it. He never returned to Russia again. In the Russo-Japanese War he was again a correspondent, this time on the Japanese side.

When the Russian Revolution occurred, Kennan unhesitatingly welcomed and supported the Provisional Government of Lvov and Kerensky; but he was shocked at the Bolshevik seizure of power, in which he at once discerned a grievous setback to Russia's progress toward liberal self-government. Despite his feelings on this subject, he opposed any attempts on the part of the Allies to intervene by force in European Russia. He did favor an American action to stabilize the situation in Siberia, where Communist influence was initially tenuous and where, he believed, the bulk of the population was friendly to the United States and desirous of American help. Both President Wilson and Secretary of State Lansing respected Kennan as the soundest and most experienced of American authorities on Russia and sought his guidance in the difficult problems of policy posed for the United States by the Russian Revolution. Had it not been for Kennan's advanced age, it is very likely that he would have been given by Wilson the opportunity to carry his ideas into effect in 1918, as head of an American commission to Siberia.

Kennan died in 1924, mourned by a host of admirers both in Russia and in his own country. He has remained to this time without a biographer; and indeed the preparation of a real biography, revealing the inner man as well as his deeds, would be a difficult task. One of the outstanding features of Kennan's literary legacy is the extreme reserve that he showed at all times about his own person, his inner feelings, and his intimate life. Few men could have written so much and so well about other lands and other people—and so little about themselves. This same reserve must have carried into his daily life; for, although he had a vast number of acquaintances and well-wishers, he seems to have had few really intimate friends. In the entire body of biographical source material available to contemporary scholarship, one seeks in vain for a single critical or unfavorable observation. This points surely to a man of outstanding qualities, commanding a respect very close to universal among those who knew him at all; but it also suggests that there were none who really knew him very well—none, that is, who could penetrate below the surface to the deeper reality of the human soul, which is never without weakness and contradiction.

Whatever the weaknesses and contradictions may have been in Kennan's case, he was not a man who wore his heart on his sleeve. In the full-length account of his Siberian ordeal, the impeccable façade of a cheerful impersonality is broken only at two points. One is the account of a dream which overtook him during his uneasy slumbers on the floor of a remote Siberian post-station. To a modern psychologist its content would surely suggest the heavy uncertainties and exertions by which a shy and unschooled youngster worked his way, through his own efforts, to the top rank of the American literary world. The other is the reference to the feeling of utter desolation that overcame him after he had heard, on one occasion, a party of Siberian convicts sing the "begging song" as they passed through a remote and sordid Siberian village. When the sound had died away, he writes, "I felt a strange sense of dejection, as if the day had suddenly grown colder, darker, and more dreary, and the cares and sorrows of life more burdensome and oppressive."

Whatever the effects may have been on Kennan's inner world of the trials with which he had to contend in the course of his long life—loneliness, hardship, poverty, childlessness, and the sight of much human suffering—it can only be said that he never let his troubles become a burden to others; and the record of his life is unmarred by a single instance of faint-heartedness or ungenerosity. More than this, neither contemporaries nor posterity has a right to ask.

GEORGE FROST KENNAN

Preface to the First Edition

THE IDEA OF EXPLORING SOME OF
the less known parts of Siberia, and of making, in connection
with such exploration, a careful study of the exile system, first
took definite form in my mind in the year 1879. From such observations as I had been able to make during a residence of two
and a half years in the country, and a subsequent journey of
five thousand miles overland to St. Petersburg, it seemed to me
that Siberia offered to a competent investigator an extremely
interesting and promising field of research. To the Russians,
who had possessed it in whole or in part for nearly three centuries, it was, of course, comparatively familiar ground; but to
the average American, at that time, it was almost as much a
terra incognita as central Africa or Tibet. In 1881 the assassination of Alexander II, and the exile of a large number of Russian revolutionists to the mines of the Trans-Baikál, increased
my interest in Siberia and intensified my desire not only to
study the exile system on the ground, but to investigate the
Russian revolutionary movement in the only part of the empire where I thought such an investigation could successfully
be made—namely, in the region to which the revolutionists
themselves had been banished. It seemed to me a hopeless task
to look for nihilists in the cities of St. Petersburg and Moscow,
or to seek there an explanation of the political events and the
social phenomena that interested me. Most of the leading actors in the revolutionary drama of 1878–79 were already in Siberia; and if the imperial police could not discover the few
who still remained at large in European Russia, it was not at all

likely that I could. In Siberia, however, communication with exiled nihilists might perhaps be practicable; and there, if anywhere, was to be obtained the information that I desired.

Circumstances, and the want of time and means for such an extended journey as I wished to make, prevented me from taking any definite steps in the matter until the summer of 1884, when the editor of the *Century Magazine* became interested in my plans, and proposed to me that I should go to Siberia for that periodical and give to it the results of my work. I thereupon made a preliminary excursion to St. Petersburg and Moscow for the purpose of collecting material and ascertaining whether or not obstacles were likely to be thrown in my way by the Russian Government. I returned in October, fully satisfied that my scheme was a practicable one; that there was really nothing in Siberia which needed concealment; and that my literary record—so far as I had made a record—was such as to predispose the Russian Government in my favor, and to secure for me all the facilities that a friendly investigator might reasonably expect.

The opinions which I held at that time with regard to the Siberian exile system and the treatment of political offenders by the Russian Government were set forth fully and frankly in an address that I delivered before the American Geographical Society of New York, in 1882, and in the newspaper controversy to which that address gave rise. I then believed that the Russian Government and the exile system had been greatly misrepresented by such writers as Stépniak and Prince Kropotkin; that Siberia was not so terrible a country as Americans had always supposed it to be; and that the descriptions of Siberian mines and prisons in the just-published book of the Rev. Henry Lansdell were probably truthful and accurate. I also believed, although I did not say, that the nihilists, terrorists, and political malcontents generally, who had so long kept Russia in a state of alarm and apprehension, were unreasonable and wrong-headed fanatics of the anarchistic type with which we in the United States had become so familiar. In short, all my prepossessions were favorable to the Russian Government and unfavorable to the Russian revolutionists. I lay stress upon this fact, not because my opinions at that time had intrinsically any particular weight or importance, but because a just estimate of the results of an investigation cannot be formed without some knowledge of the preconceptions and personal bias of the investigator. I also lay stress upon it for the further reason that it partly explains the friendly attitude toward me which was taken by the Russian Government, the permission which was given me to inspect prisons and mines, and the comparative immunity from arrest, detention, and imprisonment which I enjoyed, even when my movements and associations were such as justly to render me an object of suspicion to the local Siberian authorities. It is very doubtful whether a traveler who had not already committed himself to views that the Government approved would have been allowed to go to Siberia for the avowed purpose of investigating the exile system, or whether, if permitted to go there, he would have escaped serious trouble when it was discovered that he was associating on terms of friendly intimacy with political criminals of the most dangerous class. In my frequent skirmishes with the police, and with suspicious local officials in remote Siberian villages, nothing but the letter which I carried from the Russian Minister of the Interior saved me from summary arrest and imprisonment, or from a search of my person and baggage which probably would have resulted in my expulsion from the empire under guard and in the loss of all my notes and documentary material. That letter, which was my sheet-anchor in times of storm and stress, would never, I think, have been given to me, if I had not publicly defended the Russian Government against some of its numerous assailants, and if it had not been believed that personal pride and a desire to seem consistent probably would restrain me from confessing error, even should I find the prison and exile system worse than I anticipated, and worse than I had represented it to be. How far this belief was well founded, and to what extent my preconceived ideas were in harmony with the facts, I purpose, in the present work, to show.

I wish it to be clearly understood, however, that I do not aim to present a complete and comprehensive picture of Russian society as a whole, nor to survey every part of the vast field occupied by the Russian Government, nor to set forth, in due order and proportion, all of the complex, heterogeneous and inter-related facts and phenomena that go to make up the composite national life of a hundred millions of people. A task of such magnitude would exceed my strength and would carry me far beyond the limits that I have set for myself. All that I aim to do is to give the reader a clear and vivid impression of the scenery, the people, and the customs of Siberia, to record the results of a careful study of the exile system, and to consider the attitude of the Russian Government toward its subjects so far—and only so far—as may be necessary to throw light upon the facts, the characters, or the events by me observed.

Some of the criticisms that have been made upon the articles on Siberia and the exile system published in the *Century Magazine* have been based apparently upon the assumption that a survey of any one particular department of national life must necessarily be incomplete and misleading, and that the fair-minded investigator should supplement it by taking into the field of vision a quantity of unrelated facts and phenomena from a dozen other departments.

"Your articles," certain critics have said, "give a false impression. Your statements with regard to Russian prisons, indiscriminate arrests, and the banishment of hundreds of people to Siberia without trial may all be true; but there are in Russia, nevertheless, thousands of peaceful, happy homes, where fathers and brothers are no more in danger of being arrested and exiled to Siberia than they would be if they lived in the United States. Russia is not a vast prison inhabited only by suspects, convicts, and jailors; it is full of cultivated, refined, kind-hearted people; and its Emperor, who is the embodiment of all the domestic virtues, has no higher aim in life than to promote the happiness and prosperity of his beloved subjects."

The obvious reply to such criticism as this is that it wholly mistakes the aim and scope of the work criticized. I did not go to Russia to observe happy homes, nor to make the acquaintance of congenial, kind-hearted people, nor to admire the domestic virtues of the Tsar. I went to Russia to study the working of a penal system, to make the acquaintance of exiles, outcasts, and criminals, and to ascertain how the Government treats its enemies in the prisons and mines of Eastern Siberia. Granted, for the sake of argument, that there *are* thousands of happy homes in Russia; that the empire *does* abound in cultivated and kind-hearted people, and that the Tsar *is* devotedly attached to his wife and children; what have these facts to do with the sanitary condition of a tumble-down *étape* in the province of Yakútsk, or with the flogging to death of a young and educated woman at the mines of Kará? The balancing of a happy and kind-hearted family in St. Petersburg against an epidemic of typhus fever in the exile forwarding prison at Tomsk is not an evidence of fairness and impartiality, but rather an evidence of an illogical mind. All that fairness and impartiality require of the investigator in any particular field is that he shall set forth, conscientiously, in due relative proportion and without prejudice, all the significant facts that he has been able to gather in that selected field, and then that he shall draw from the collected facts such conclusions as they may seem to warrant. His work may not have the scope of an encyclopedia, but there is no reason, in the nature of things, why it should not be full, accurate, and trustworthy as far as it goes. An investigation of the Indian question in the United States would necessarily deal with a very small part of the varied and complex life of the nation; but it might, nevertheless, be made as fair and complete, within its limits, as Bryce's *American Commonwealth*. It would, perhaps, present a dark picture; but to attempt to lighten it by showing that the President of the Republic is a moral man and good to his children, or that there are thousands of happy families in New York that have not been driven from their homes by gold-seekers, or that the dwellers on Commonwealth Avenue in Boston are refined and cultivated people who have never made a practice of selling intoxicating liquor to minors, would be not only illogical, but absurd. If the gloominess of the picture is to be relieved, the proper way to relieve it is to show what has been done to remedy the evils that make it gloomy, and not, by any means, to prove that in some other part of the country, under wholly different conditions, a picture might be drawn that would be cheerful and inspiriting.

In the present work I have tried to deal fairly both with the Government and with the exiles. If the Government's contention is not always set forth as fully as may seem to be desirable, it is simply because most of the Government officials to whom I applied for information, both in Siberia and St. Petersburg, either manifested such a disinclination to talk that I could not pursue the subject, or else made such transparent and preposterous attempts to deceive me that their statements were merely grotesque. It will be seen, however, that a large part—perhaps more than one-half—of my information with regard to Siberian prisons and the working of the exile system has been taken directly from official sources, and that a very small part of it—probably less than one-fifth—rests upon the statements of exiles or prisoners. I was assured by honest and intelligent officers of the exiled administration in Siberia that these statistics are often "cooked" in such a manner as to show a much more favorable state of affairs than that which in reality exists, but they are the best official evidence obtainable.

Before closing this preface I desire to tender my most sincere and hearty thanks to the many friends, acquaintances, and well-wishers throughout European Russia and Siberia who encouraged me in my work, coöperated in my researches, and furnished me with the most valuable part of my material. Some of them are political exiles, who imperiled even the wretched future that still remained to them by writing out for me histories of their lives; some of them are officers of the exile administration who, trusting to my honor and discretion, gave me without reserve the results of their long experience; and some of them are honest, humane prison officials who, after reporting again and again upon the evils and abuses of the prison system, finally pointed them out to me, as the last possible means of forcing them upon the attention of the Government and the world. Most of these people I dare not even mention by name. Although their characters and their services are such as to make their names worthy of remembrance and honor, it is their misfortune to live in a country where the Government regards a frankly expressed opinion as an evidence of "untrustworthiness," and treats an effort to improve the condition of things as an offense to be punished. To mention the names of such people, when they live under such a government, is simply to render them objects of suspicion and surveillance, and thus deprive them of the limited power they still exercise for good. All that I can do, therefore, to show my appreciation of their trust, their kindness, and their aid, is to use the information which they gave me as I believe they would wish it to be used—in the interest of humanity, freedom, and good government. For Russia and the Russian people I have the warmest affection and sympathy; and if, by a temperate and well-considered statement of the results of my Siberian investigations, I can make the country and the nation better known to the world, and ameliorate, even little, the lot of the "unfortunates" to whom "God is high above and the Tsar is far away," I shall be more than repaid for the hardest journey and the most trying experience of my life.

GEORGE KENNAN

CHAPTER ONE

St. Petersburg to the Volga

T HE SIBERIAN EXPEDITION OF THE
Century Magazine sailed from New York for Liverpool on
the second day of May, 1885. It consisted of Mr. George A.
Frost, an artist of Boston, and the author of this book. We
both spoke Russian, both had been in Siberia before, and I was
making to the empire my fourth journey. Previous association
in the service of the Russian-American Telegraph Company
had acquainted us with each other, and long experience in sub-
arctic Asia had familiarized us with the hardships and privations of Siberian travel. Our plan of operations had been approved by the *Century;* we had the amplest discretionary
power in the matter of ways and means; and although fully
aware of the serious nature of the work in hand, we were hope-
ful, if not sanguine, of success. We arrived in London on Sunday, May 10, and on Wednesday, the 13th, proceeded to St.
Petersburg by rail, via Dover, Ostend, Cologne, Hanover, Berlin, and Eydkuhnen. As the season was already advanced, and
as it was important that we should reach Siberia in time to
make the most of the summer weather and the good roads, I
decided to remain in the Russian capital only five days; but we
were unfortunate enough to arrive there just at the beginning
of a long series of church holidays, and were able to utilize in
the transaction of business only four days out of ten.

As soon as I could obtain an interview with Mr. Vlangálli,
the assistant Minister of Foreign Affairs, I presented my letters

of introduction and told him frankly and candidly what we desired to do. I said that in my judgment Siberia and the exile system had been greatly misrepresented by prejudiced writers; that a truthful description of the country, the prisons and the mines would, I thought, be advantageous rather than detrimental to the interests of the Russian Government; and that, inasmuch as I had already committed myself publicly to a defense of that Government, I could hardly be suspected of an intention to seek in Siberia for facts with which to undermine my own position. This statement, in which there was not the least diplomacy or insincerity, seemed to impress Mr. Vlangálli favorably; and after twenty minutes' conversation he informed me that we should undoubtedly be permitted to go to Siberia, and that he would aid us as far as possible by giving us an open letter to the governors of the Siberian provinces, and by procuring for us a similar letter from the Minister of the Interior. Upon being asked whether these letters would admit us to Siberian prisons, Mr. Vlangálli replied that they would not; that permission to inspect prisons must in all cases be obtained from provincial governors. As to the further question whether such permission would probably be granted, he declined to express an opinion. This, of course, was equivalent to saying that the Government would not give us *carte-blanche*, but would follow us with friendly observation, and grant or refuse permission to visit prisons as might, from time to time, seem expedient. I foresaw that this would greatly increase our difficulties, but I did not deem it prudent to urge any further concession; and after expressing my thanks for the courtesy and kindness with which we had been received I withdrew.

At another interview, a few days later, Mr. Vlangálli gave me the promised letters and, at the same time, said that he would like to have me stop in Moscow on my way to Siberia and make the acquaintance of Mr. Katkóff, the well-known editor of the *Moscow Gazette*. He handed me a sealed note of introduction to Baron Búhler, keeper of the imperial archives in Moscow, and said that he had requested the latter to present me to Mr. Katkóff, and that he hoped I would not leave Moscow without seeing him. I was not unfamiliar with the character and the career of the great Russian champion of autocracy, and was glad, of course, to have an opportunity of meeting him; but I more than suspected that the underlying motive of Mr. Vlangálli's request was a desire to bring me into contact with a man of strong personality and great ability, who would impress me with his own views of Russian policy, confirm my favorable opinion of the Russian Government, and guard me from the danger of being led astray by the specious misrepresentations of exiled nihilists, whom I might possibly meet in the course of my Siberian journey. This precaution—if precaution it was—seemed to me wholly unnecessary, since my opinion of the nihilists was already as unfavorable as the Government itself could desire. I assured Mr. Vlangálli, however, that I would see Mr. Katkóff if possible; and after thanking him again for his assistance I bade him good-by.

In reviewing now the representations that I made to high Russian officials before leaving St. Petersburg I have not to reproach myself with a single act of duplicity or insincerity. I did not obtain permission to go to Siberia by means of false pretenses, nor did I at any time assume a deceptive attitude for the sake of furthering my plans. If the opinions that I now hold differ from those that I expressed to Mr. Vlangálli in 1885, it is not because I was then insincere, but because my views have since been changed by an overwhelming mass of evidence.

On the afternoon of May 31, having selected and purchased photographic apparatus, obtained all necessary books and maps, and provided ourselves with about fifty letters of introduction to teachers, mining engineers, and Government officials in all parts of Siberia, we left St. Petersburg by rail for Moscow. The distance from the Russian capital to the Siberian frontier is about 1600 miles; and the route usually taken by travelers, and always by exiles, is that which passes through the cities of Moscow, Nízhni Nóvgorod, Kazán, Perm, and

Ekaterínburg. The eastern terminus of the Russian railway system is at Nízhni Nóvgorod, but, in summer, steamers ply constantly between that city and Perm on the rivers Volga and Káma; and Perm is connected with Ekaterínburg by an isolated piece of railroad about 180 miles in length, which crosses the mountain chain of the Ural, and is intended to unite the navigable waters of the Volga with those of the Ob.

Upon our arrival in Moscow I presented my sealed note of introduction to Baron Búhler, and called with him at the office of the *Moscow Gazette* for the purpose of making the acquaintance of its editor. We were disappointed, however, to find that Mr. Katkóff had just left the city and probably would be absent for two or three weeks. As we could not await his return, and as there was no other business to detain us in Moscow, we proceeded by rail to Nízhni Nóvgorod, reaching that city early on the morning of Thursday, June 4.

To a traveler visiting Nízhni Nóvgorod for the first time there is something surprising, and almost startling, in the appearance of what he supposes to be the city, and in the scene presented to him as he emerges from the railway station and walks away from the low bank of the Óka River in the direction of the Volga. The clean, well-paved streets; the long rows of substantial buildings; the spacious boulevard, shaded by leafy birches and poplars; the canal, spanned at intervals by graceful bridges; the picturesque tower of the water-works; the enormous cathedral of Alexánder Névski; the Bourse; the theaters; the hotels; the market places—all seem to indicate a great populous center of life and commercial activity; but of living inhabitants there is not a sign. Grass and weeds are growing in the middle of the empty streets and in the chinks of the travel-worn sidewalks; birds are singing fearlessly in the trees that shade the lonely and deserted boulevard; the countless shops and warehouses are all closed, barred, and padlocked; the bells are silent in the gilded belfries of the churches; and the astonished stranger may perhaps wander for a mile between solid blocks of buildings without seeing an open door, a vehicle, or a single human being. The city appears to have been stricken by a pestilence and deserted. If the newcomer remembers for what Nízhni Nóvgorod is celebrated, he is not long, of course, in coming to the conclusion that he is on the site of the famous fair; but the first realization of the fact that the fair is in itself a separate and independent city, and a city that during nine months of every year stands empty and deserted, comes to him with the shock of great surprise.

The fair-city of Nízhni Nóvgorod is situated on a low peninsula between the rivers Óka and Volga, just above their junction, very much as New York City is situated on Manhattan Island between East River and the Hudson. In geographical position it bears the same relation to the old town of Nízhni Nóvgorod that New York would bear to Jersey City if the latter were elevated on a steep, terraced bluff four hundred feet above the level of the Hudson. The Russian city, however, differs from New York City in that it is a mere temporary market—a huge commercial *caravansarái* where 500,000 traders assemble every year to buy and to sell commodities. In September it has frequently a population of more than 100,000 souls, and contains merchandise valued at $75,000,000; while in January, February, or March all of its inhabitants might be fed and sheltered in the smallest of its hotels, and all of its goods might be put into a single one of its innumerable shops. Its life, therefore, is a sort of intermittent commercial fever, in which an annual paroxysm of intense and unnatural activity is followed by a long interval of torpor and stagnation.

It seems almost incredible at first that a city of such magnitude—a city that contains churches, mosques, theaters, markets, banks, hotels, a merchants' exchange, and nearly seven thousand shops and inhabitable buildings, should have so ephemeral a life, and should be so completely abandoned every year after it has served the purpose for which it was created. When I saw this unique city for the first time, on a clear frosty night in January, 1868, it presented an extraordinary picture of loneliness and desolation. The moonlight streamed down into its long empty streets where the unbroken snow lay two feet deep upon the sidewalks; it touched with silver the white walls and swelling domes of the old fair-cathedral, from whose towers there came no clangor of bells; it sparkled on great snowdrifts heaped up against the doors of the empty houses, and poured a flood of pale light over thousands of snow-covered roofs; but it did not reveal anywhere a sign of a human being. The city seemed to be not only uninhabited, but wholly abandoned to the arctic spirits of solitude and frost. When I saw it next, at the height of the annual fair in the autumn of 1870, it was so changed as to be almost unrecognizable. It was then surrounded by a great forest of shipping; its hot, dusty atmosphere thrilled with the incessant whistling of steamers; merchandise to the value of 125,000,000 rubles lay on its shores or was packed into its 6000 shops; every building within its limit was crowded; 60,000 people were crossing every day the pontoon bridge that connected it with the old town; a military band was playing airs from Offenbach's operas on the great boulevard in front of the governor's house; and through all the streets of the reanimated and reawakened city poured a great tumultuous flood of human life.

I did not see the fair-city again until June, 1885, when I found it almost as completely deserted as on the occasion of my first visit, but in other ways greatly changed and improved. Substantial brick buildings had taken the place of the long rows of inflammable wooden shops and sheds; the streets in many parts of the city had been neatly paved; the number of stores and warehouses had largely increased; and the lower end of the peninsula had been improved and dignified by the erection of the great Alexánder Névski cathedral, which now forms the most prominent and striking architectural feature of the fair.

It was supposed that, with the gradual extension of the Russian railway system, and the facilities afforded by it for the distribution of merchandise throughout the empire in small quantities, the fair of Nízhni Nóvgorod would lose most of its importance; but no such result has yet become apparent. During the most active period of railway construction in Russia, from 1868 to 1881, the value of the merchandise brought annually to the fair rose steadily from 126,000,000 to 246,000,000 rubles, and the number of shops and stores in the fair-city increased from 5738 to 6298. At the present time the volume of business transacted during the two fair-months amounts to something like 225,000,000 rubles, and the number of shops and stores in the fair exceeds 7000.

The station of the Moscow and Nízhni Nóvgorod railway is situated within the limits of the fair-city, on the left bank of the river Óka, and communication between it and the old town on the other side is maintained in summer by means of a steam ferry, or a long floating bridge consisting of a roadway supported by pontoons. As the bridge, at the time of our arrival, had not been put in position for the season, we crossed the river on a low, flat barge in tow of a small steamer.

The view that one gets of the old fortified city of Nízhni Nóvgorod while crossing the Óka from the fair is both striking and picturesque. The long steep bluff upon which it is situated rises abruptly almost from the water's edge to the height of four hundred feet, notched at intervals by deep V-shaped cuts through which run the ascending roads to the upper plateau, and broken here and there by narrow terraces upon which stand white-walled and golden-domed cathedrals and monasteries half buried in groves of trees. In the warm, bright sunshine of a June day the snowy walls of the Byzantine churches scattered along the crest of the bluff; the countless domes of blue, green, silver, and gold rising out of dark masses of foliage on the terraces; the smooth, grassy slopes which descend here and there almost to the water's edge; and the river front, lined with steamers and bright with flags—all make up a picture that is hardly surpassed in northern Russia. Fronting the Volga, near what seems to be the eastern end of the ridge, stands the ancient *krémlin*,[1] or stronghold of the city, whose high, crenelated walls descend the steep face of the bluff toward the river in a series of titanic steps, and whose arched gateways and massive round towers carry the imagination back to the Middle Ages. Three hundred and fifty years ago this great walled enclosure was regarded as an absolutely impregnable fortress, and for more than a century it served as a secure place of refuge for the people of the city when the fierce Tatars of Kazán invaded the territories of the Grand Dukes. With the complete subjugation of the Tatar khanate, however, in the sixteenth century, it lost its importance as a defensive fortification, and soon began to fall into decay. Its thirteen towers, which were originally almost a hundred feet in height, are now half in ruins; and its walls, which have a circuit of about a mile and a quarter, would probably have fallen long ago had they not been extraordinarily thick, massive, and deeply founded. They make upon one an impression of even greater solidity and strength than do the walls of the famous *krémlin* in Moscow.

Upon landing from the ferry-boat in the old town of Nízhni Nóvgorod, we drove to a hotel in the upper part of the city, and after securing rooms and sending our passports to the chief of police, we walked down past the *krémlin* to the river front. Under the long bluff upon which the city and the *krémlin* stand, and between the steep escarpment and the river, there is a narrow strip of level ground which is now given up almost wholly to commerce and is known as the "lower bazaar." Upon this strip of land are huddled together in picturesque

1. A *krémlin*, or, to use the Russian form of the word, a *kreml*, is merely a walled enclosure with towers at the corners, situated in a commanding position near the center of a city, and intended to serve as a stronghold, or place of refuge, for the inhabitants in time of war. It differs from a castle or fortress in that it generally encloses a larger area, and contains a number of buildings, such as churches, palaces, treasuries, etc., which are merely protected by it. It is popularly supposed that the only *krémlin* in Russia is that of Moscow; but this is a mistake. Nízhni Nóvgorod, Kazán, and several other towns in the part of Russia that was subject to Tatar invasion, had strongholds of this kind.

confusion a multitude of buildings of the most heterogeneous character and appearance. Pretentious modern stores, with gilded signs and plate-glass windows, stand in neighborly proximity to wretched hucksters' stalls of rough, unpainted boards; banks, hotels, and steamship offices are sandwiched in among ship-chandlers' shops, old-clothes stalls, and *traktírs* [teahouses]; fantastic, highly colored churches of the last century appear in the most unexpected places, and give an air of sanctity to the most disreputable neighborhoods; and the entire region, from the river to the bluff, is crowded with wholesale, retail, and second-hand shops, where one can buy anything and everything—from a paper of pins, a wooden comb, or a string of dried mushrooms, to a ship's anchor, a church bell, or a steam-engine. In a single shop of the lower bazaar I saw exposed for sale a set of parlor chairs, two wicker-work baby-carriages, a rustic garden seat, two cross-cut log saws, half a dozen battered *samovárs*, a child's cradle, a steam-engine, one half of a pair of elk horns, three old boilers, a collection of telescopes, an iron church-cross four feet in height, six or eight watches, a dilapidated carriage-top, feather dusters, opera-glasses, log chains, watch charms, two blacksmith's anvils, measuring tapes, old boots, stove cover, a Caucasian dagger, turning lathes, sleigh bells, pulleys and blocks from a ship's rigging, fire-engine nozzles, horse collars, an officer's sword, axe helves, carriage cushions, gilt bracelets, iron barrel-hoops, trunks, accordions, three or four soup plates filled with old nails and screws, carving-knives, vises, hinges, revolvers, old harnesses, half a dozen odd lengths of rusty stove-pipe, a tin can of "mixed biscuits" from London, and a six-foot bath tub. This list of articles, which I made on the spot, did not comprise more than a third part of the dealer's heterogeneous stock in trade; but I had not time for a careful and exhaustive enumeration. In a certain way this shop was illustrative and typical of the whole lower bazaar, since nothing, perhaps, in that quarter of the city is more striking than the heterogeneity of buildings, people, and trades. The whole river front is lined with landing-stages and steamers; it is generally crowded with people from all parts of the empire, and it always presents a scene of great commercial activity. Steamers are departing almost hourly for the lower Volga, the frontier of Siberia, and the far-away Caspian; huge black barges, which lie here and there at the landing-stages, are being loaded or unloaded by gangs of swarthy Tatar stevedores; small, unpainted one-horse *telégas*, which look like longitudinal halves of barrels mounted on four wheels, are carrying away bags, boxes, and crates from the piles of merchandise on the shore; and the broad, dusty street is thronged all day with traders, peddlers, peasants, longshore-men, pilgrims, beggars, and tramps.

Even the children seem to feel the spirit of trade that con-trols the city; and as I stood watching the scene on the river front, a ragged boy, not more than eight or nine years of age, whose whole stock in trade consisted of a few strings of dried mushrooms, elbowed his way through the crowd with all the assurance of an experienced peddler, shouting in a thin, childish treble, "Mushrooms! Fine mushrooms! Sustain commerce, gentlemen! Buy my mushrooms and sustain commerce!"

The diversity of popular types in the lower bazaar is not perhaps so great in June as it is in September, during the fair, but the peculiarities of dress are such as to make almost every figure in the throng interesting and noteworthy to a foreign observer. There are swarthy Tatars in round skull caps and long, loose *khaláts* [coats]; Russian peasants in greasy sheep-skin coats and huge wicker-work shoes, with their legs swathed in dirty bandages of coarse linen cloth and cross-gartered with hempen cords; disreputable-looking, long-haired, long-bearded monks, who solicit alms for hospitals or churches, receiving contributions on small boards covered with black velvet and transferring the money deposited thereon to big tin boxes hung from their necks and secured with enormous iron padlocks; strolling dealers in *kvas* [a drink made from fermented rye], mead, sherbert, and other seductive bright-colored drinks; brazen-throated peddlers proclaiming aloud the vitues of brass jewelry, salted cucumbers, strings of dried mushrooms, and cotton handkerchiefs stamped with railroad maps of Russia; and, finally, a surging crowd of wholesale and retail traders from all parts of the Volga River basin.

The first thing that strikes the traveler on the threshold of southeastern Russia is the *greatness* of the country—that is, the enormous extent of its material resources, and the intense commercial activity manifested along its principal lines of communication. The average American thinks of southeastern Russia as a rather quiet, semi-pastoral, semi-agricultural country, which produces enough for the maintenance of its own half-civilized and not very numerous population, but which, in point of commercial activity, cannot bear comparison for a moment with even the most backward of our States. He is not a little astonished, therefore, at Nízhni Nóvgorod, to find the shipping of the Volga occupying six or eight miles of river front; to learn that for its regulation there is in the city a shipping court with special jurisdiction; that the *pristan*, or, as a Western steamboatman would say, the levee, is under control of an officer appointed by the Minister of Ways and Communications and aided by a large staff of subordinates; that the number of steamers plying on the Volga and its tributaries is greater than the number on the Mississippi;[2] that $15,000,000 worth of products come annually down a single tributary of the Volga—namely, the Káma, a stream of which few Americans have ever heard; and, finally, that the waters of the Volga River system float annually nearly 5,000,000 tons of merchandise, and furnish employment to 7000 vessels and nearly 200,000 boatmen. It may be that an ordinarily well-educated American ought to know all these things; but I certainly did not know them, and they came to me with the shock of a complete surprise.

On the morning of Saturday, June 6, after having visited the fair-city and the *krémlin* and made as thorough a study of

2. In 1880 there were on the upper and the lower Mississippi 681 steamers. The number on the Volga and its tributaries is about 700.

Nízhni Nóvgorod as the time at our disposal would permit, we embarked on one of the Kámenski Brothers' steamers for a voyage of nearly a thousand miles down the Volga and up the Káma to Perm.

It has been said that Egypt is the creation of the Nile. In a different sense, but with equal truth, it may be said that eastern Russia is the creation of the Volga. The ethnological composition of its population was mainly determined by that river; the whole history of the country has been intimately connected with it for more than a thousand years; the character and pursuits of all the east-Russian tribes have been greatly modified by it; and upon it now depend, directly or indirectly, the welfare and prosperity of more than 10,000,000 people. From any point of view, the Volga must be regarded as one of the great rivers of the world. Its length, from the Váldai hills to the Caspian Sea, is nearly 2300 miles; its width below Tsarítsin, in time of high water, exceeds 30 miles, so that a boatman, in crossing it, loses sight entirely of its low banks and is virtually at sea; it washes the borders of nine provinces, or administrative divisions of the empire, and on its banks stand 39 cities and more than 1000 villages and settlements. The most important part of the river, commercially, is that lying between Nízhni Nóvgorod and the mouth of the Káma, where there ply, during the season of navigation, about 450 steamers. As far down as the so-called "Samára bend," the river presents almost everywhere a picture of busy life and activity, and is full of steamers, barges, and great hulks, like magnified canal-boats, loaded with goods from eastern Russia, Siberia, and Central Asia. The amount of merchandise produced, even in the strip of country directly tributary to the Volga itself, is enormous. Many of the agricultural villages, such as Lískovo, which the steamer swiftly passes between Nízhni Nóvgorod and Kazán, and which seem, from a distance, to be insignificant clusters of unpainted wooden houses, load with grain 700 vessels a year.

The scenery of the upper Volga is much more varied and

picturesque than one would expect to find along a river running through a flat and monotonous country. The left bank, it is true, is generally low and uninteresting; but on the other side the land rises abruptly from the water's edge to a height of 400 or 500 feet, and its boldly projecting promontories, at intervals of two or three miles, break up the majestic river into long, still reaches, like a series of placid lakes opening into one another and reflecting in their tranquil depths the dense foliage of the virgin forest on one side and the bold outlines of the half-mountainous shore on the other. White-walled churches with silver domes appear here and there on the hills, surrounded by little villages of unpainted wooden houses, with elaborately carved and decorated gables; deep valleys, shaggy with hazel bushes, break through the wall of bluffs on the right at intervals, and afford glimpses of a rich farming country in the interior; and now and then, in sheltered nooks half up the mountain-side overlooking the river, appear the cream-white walls and gilded domes of secluded monasteries, rising out of masses of dark-green foliage. Sometimes, for half an hour together, the steamer plows her way steadily down the middle of the stream, and the picturesque right bank glides past like a magnificent panorama with a field of vision ten miles wide; and then suddenly, to avoid a bar, the vessel sweeps in toward the land, until the wide panorama narrows to a single vivid picture of a quaint Russian hamlet which looks like an artistically contrived scene in a theater. It is so near that you can distinguish the features of the laughing peasant girls who run down into the foreground to wave their handkerchiefs at the passing steamer; or you can talk in an ordinary tone of voice with the *muzhiks* in red shirts and black velvet trousers who are lying on the grassy bluff in front of the green-domed village church. But it lasts only a moment. Before you have fairly grasped the details of the strange Russian picture it has vanished, and the steamer glides swiftly into a new reach of the river, where there is not a sign of human habitation, and where the cliffs on one side and the forest on the other seem to be parts of a vast primeval wilderness.

Fascinated by the picturesque beauty of the majestic Volga and the ever-changing novelty of the scenes successively presented to us as we crossed from side to side, or swept around great bends into new landscapes and new reaches of tranquil water, we could not bear to leave the hurricane deck until long after dark. The fresh, cool air was then filled with the blended fragrance of flowery meadows and damp forest glens; the river lay like an expanse of shining steel between banks whose impenetrable blackness was intensified rather than relieved by a few scattered spangles of light; and from some point far away in the distance came the faint voice of a timber rafter, or a floating fisherman, singing that song dear to the heart of every Russian boatman—*V'nis po mátushke po Vólge* ["Down the Mother Volga"].

CHAPTER TWO

The Tiumén Forwarding Prison

Tiumén, WHERE WE VIRTUALLY began our Siberian journey as well as our investigation of the exile system, is a town of 19,000 inhabitants, situated 1700 miles east of St. Petersburg, on the right bank of the river Túra just above the junction of the latter with the Toból. The chief interest that the place had for us lay in the fact that it contains the most important exile forwarding prison in Siberia, and the *Prikáz o Sílnikh*, or Chief Bureau of Exile Administration. Through the Tiumén prison pass all persons condemned to banishment, colonization, or penal servitude in Siberia, and in the Tiumén *prikáz* are kept all the records and statistics of the exile system.

Russian exiles began to go to Siberia very soon after its discovery and conquest—as early probably as the first half of the seventeenth century. The earliest mention of exile in Russian legislation is in a law of the Tsar Alexéi Mikháilovich in 1648. Exile, however, at that time, was regarded not as a punishment in itself, but as a means of getting criminals who had already been punished out of the way. The Russian criminal code of that age was almost incredibly cruel and barbarous. Men were impaled on sharp stakes, hanged, and beheaded by the hundred for crimes that would not now be regarded as capital in any civilized country in the world; while lesser offenders were flogged with the *knut* and bastinado, branded with hot irons, mutilated by amputation of one or more of their limbs, deprived of their tongues, and suspended in the air by hooks passed under two of their ribs until they died a lingering and miserable death. When criminals had been thus *knuted*, bastinadoed, branded, or crippled by amputation, Siberian exile was resorted to as a quick and easy method of getting them out of the way; and in this attempt to rid society of criminals who were both morally and physically useless Siberian exile had its origin. The amelioration, however, of the Russian criminal code, which began in the latter part of the seventeenth century, and the progressive development of Siberia itself gradually brought about a change in the view taken of Siberian exile. Instead of regarding it, as before, as a means of getting rid of disabled criminals, the Government began to look upon it as a means of populating and developing a new and promising part of its Asiatic territory. Toward the close of the seventeenth century, therefore, we find a number of *ukázes* abolishing personal mutilation as a method of punishment, and substituting for it, and in a large number of cases even for the death penalty, the banishment of the criminal to Siberia with all his family. About the same time exile, as a punishment, began to be extended to a large number of crimes that had previously been punished in other ways; as, for example, desertion from the army, assault with intent to kill, and vagrancy when the vagrant was unfit for military service and no land-owner or village commune would take charge of him. Men were exiled, too, for almost every conceivable sort of minor offense, such, for instance, as fortune-telling, prize-fighting, snuff-taking,[1] driving with reins,[2] begging with a pretense of being in distress, and setting fire to property accidentally.

In the eighteenth century the great mineral and agricultural resources of Siberia began to attract to it the serious and earnest attention of the Russian government. The discovery

1. The snuff-taker was not only banished to Siberia, but had the septum between his nostrils torn out.
2. This was punished as a Western or European innovation. The old Russian driver had been accustomed to ride his horse or run beside it.

of the Daúrski silver mines, and the rich mines of Nérchinsk in the Siberian territory of the Trans-Baikál, created a sudden demand for labor, which led the government to promulgate a new series of *ukázes* providing for the transportation thither of convicts from the Russian prisons. In 1762 permission was given to all individuals and corporations owning serfs, to hand the latter over to the local authorities for banishment to Siberia whenever they thought they had good reason for so doing. With the abolition of capital punishment in 1753, all criminals that, under the old law, would have been put to death, were condemned to perpetual exile in Siberia with hard labor.

In the reign of Catherine II the demand for laborers in Siberia became more and more imperative, by reason of the discovery of the rich and important mines of Ekaterínburg, and the establishment of large manufactories in Irkútsk; and the list of crimes and offenses punishable by exile grew larger and larger. Jews were exiled for refusing or neglecting to pay their taxes for three successive years; serfs were exiled for cutting down trees without leave; noncommissioned officers of the army were exiled for second offenses of various kinds, and bad conduct of almost any sort became a sufficient warrant for deportation to Siberia.

Up to the close of the eighteenth century, very little attention was paid to the treatment of the exiles *en route*, and still less to the proper organization and control of the exile system. *Kolódniks*, as the exiles were then called, were simply driven in troops, like cattle, from one provincial town to another, sometimes begging their way because no provision had been made for their subsistence, and sometimes starving to death on the road. No one knew who they were, whence they had come, what crimes they had committed, or whither they were going. Hardened murderers, who should have been sent to the mines for life, were set at liberty in Siberia as colonists; while unfortunate peasants who had merely lost their passports, or incurred the resentment of some hot-tempered land-owner, were kept at hard labor in the mines until they perished from privation and cruel treatment. The exile system, in short, was nothing but a chaos of disorder, in which accident and caprice played almost equally important parts.

Early in the nineteenth century, steps were taken by the Government to remedy some of the evils that had become apparent under this lax system of administration, and to subject the methods of exile to stricter control. In 1811 a suitable force of regular guards was organized to convoy exile parties, and all exiles were furnished with identifying documents, called *statéini spíski,* to show who they were and whither they were bound. In 1817 *étapes* [or way stations for convicts being marched into Siberia], were erected along the most important routes; and in 1823, upon the initiative of the great Russian reformer Count Speránski, the present *Prikáz o Sílnikh,* or Bureau of Exile Administration, was established in Tobólsk. It has since been removed to Tiumén. The duties of this bureau are of a two-fold nature. In the first place it sorts and classifies all exiles, upon their arrival in Tiumén, and keeps a full and accurate record of them, and in the second it watches and controls, through six subordinate bureaus, their transportation and distribution throughout Siberia. These subordinate bureaus, which are known as *expedítsii o sílnikh,* are situated in Kazán, Perm, Tobólsk, Tomsk, Krasnoyársk, and Irkútsk. They are aided in their work of supervision and control by three inspectors of exile transportation, each of whom looks after one division of the great exile route. At the time of our journey, Colonel Vinokúrof was inspector of exile transportation for Western Siberia with headquarters at Tiumén, while Colonel Zagárin occupied a similar position in Eastern Siberia with headquarters at Krasnoyársk.

Since the organization of the *Prikáz o Sílnikh* in 1823, a careful and accurate record has been kept of all the exiles that have crossed the Siberian frontier; and from the books of this great central bureau may now be obtained the fullest statistical information with regard to the working of the exile system. The first questions that naturally rise in one's mind in connection with this subject are, "How many persons are banished to Siberia annually, and how many have been sent there in all?" From the records of the *Prikáz o Sílnikh* it appears that between the years 1823 and 1887 inclusive there were sent to Siberia 772,979 exiles.

Exiles to Siberia may be grouped, according to the nature of their sentences, into four great classes, namely:

1. *Kátorzhniki,* or hard-labor convicts.

2. *Poseléntsi,* or penal colonists.

3. *Sílni,* or persons simply banished.

4. *Dobrovólni,* or women and children that go to Siberia voluntarily with their exiled husbands or parents. Persons belonging to the first two classes, who are always supposed to be criminals, are deprived of all civil rights and must remain in Siberia for life. Persons belonging to the third class, who are not necessarily criminals, retain some of their civil rights and may return to European Russia at the expiration of their terms of banishment. Convicts and penal colonists go to their places of destination in five-pound leg-fetters and with half-shaven heads, while simple exiles wear no fetters and are not personally disfigured. Exiles of the third class comprise:

a. Vagrants (persons without passports who refuse to disclose their identity).

b. Persons banished by sentence of a court.

c. Persons banished by the village communes to which they belong.

d. Persons banished by order of the Minister of the Interior.

An analysis shows in the first place that the largest single class of exiles (5536 out of 15,766) is composed of women and children who go to Siberia voluntarily with their husbands and fathers. It shows, in the second place, that out of the 10,230 persons sent to Siberia as criminals, only 4392, or less than a half, have had a trial by a court, while 5838 are exiled by "administrative process"— that is, by a mere order from the Minister of the Interior. Finally, it shows that more than one-third of the involuntary exiles (3751 out of 10,230) were sent to Siberia by village communes, and not by the Government.

Every *mir*, or village commune, in Russia has the right to banish any of its members who, through bad conduct or general worthlessness, have rendered themselves obnoxious to their fellow-citizens and burdensome to society. It has also the right to refuse to receive any of its members who, after serving out terms of imprisonment for crime, return to the *mir* and ask to be readmitted. Released prisoners whom the *mir* will not thus readmit are exiled to Siberia by administrative process.

The political offenders that are exiled to Siberia do not constitute a separate penal class or grade, but are distributed among all of the classes above enumerated. I was not able to obtain full and trustworthy statistics with regard to them from any source of information open to me. A fragmentary record of them has been kept recently by the inspectors of exile transportation, but this record covers only a few years, and includes only "administratives," or persons banished by executive order for political "untrustworthiness." All the rest are classed, both in the reports of the inspectors and in the books of the *prikáz*, as either hard-labor convicts or penal colonists, and in these classes there is no means of distinguishing state criminals from common felons. There can be no doubt, however, that the number of political offenders is much smaller than it is generally supposed to be. From the annual reports of Colonel Vinokúrof, inspector of exile transportation for Western Siberia, it appears that the number of politicals banished by administrative process from 1879 to 1884 is 749.

This is at an average rate of 125 per annum. If twenty-five more per annum be added for politicals sent to Siberia as hard-labor convicts and penal colonists, the whole number deported will make a little less than 1 per cent of the total number of exiles; which is probably an approximation to the truth. This estimate, however, does not include Polish insurgents, and it may not hold good for years anterior to 1879. First and last, about 100,000 Poles have been banished, and first and last, a great many thousands of political conspirators. My estimate relates only to the years between 1879 and 1885.

As a general rule, exile to Siberia, under the severer sentences and for felony, involves first, deprivation of all civil rights; second, forfeiture of all property, which, upon the conviction of the criminal, descends to his heirs as if he were dead; and third, severance of all family relations, unless the criminal's family voluntarily accompanies him to his place of exile. If a prisoner's wife and children wish to go with him, they are allowed to do so, and are furnished by the Government with transportation; but if not, the authority of the criminal over his family ceases with his exile, and his wife is at liberty to marry again precisely as if he were dead.

Exiles of all classes are now brought from Kazán to Tiumén either in convict railway trains or in convict barges. The route is precisely the same one that we followed, viz., down the Volga and up the Káma by steamer to Perm, and thence across the mountains of the Ural to Ekaterínburg and Tiumén by rail. At Tiumén all exiles go into the Tiumén forwarding prison, and lie there, on an average, about two weeks. They are then sent in convict barges down the Írtish and up the Ob to the city of Tomsk.

We naturally felt some doubt as to the result of an application for leave to inspect the forwarding prison of Tiumén; but upon presenting my letters of introduction to Mr. Bóris Krásin, the *isprávnik* or chief police officer of the district, I was received with a cordiality that was as pleasant as it was unexpected. Mr. Krásin invited us to lunch, said that he had already been informed by private and official letters from St. Petersburg of our projected journey through Siberia, and that he would gladly be of service to us in any way possible. He granted without hesitation my request to be allowed to visit the forwarding prison, and promised to go thither with us on the following day. We would find the prison, he said, greatly overcrowded and in bad sanitary condition; but, such as it was, we should see it.

Mr. Krásin was unfortunately taken sick Monday, but, mindful of his promise, he sent us on Tuesday a note of introduction to the warden which he said would admit us to the prison; and about ten o'clock Wednesday morning, accompanied by Mr. Ignátof, a former member of the prison committee, we presented ourselves at the gate. The Tiumén forwarding prison is a rectangular three-story brick building, 75 feet in length by 40 or 50 in width, covered with white stucco and roofed with painted tin. It is situated in a large yard formed by a whitewashed brick wall 12 or 15 feet in height, at each corner of which stands a black-and-white zig-zag-barred sentry-box, and along each face of which paces a sentry carrying a loaded Berdan rifle with fixed bayonet. Against this wall, on the right-hand side of the gate, is a small building used as a prison office, and in front of it stands a post surmounted by a small A-shaped roof under which hangs a bell. A dozen or more girls and old women were sitting on the ground in front of the prison with baskets full of black rye-bread, cold meat, boiled eggs, milk, and fish-pies for sale to the imprisoned exiles. The Tiumén prison was originally built to hold 550 prisoners, but was subsequently enlarged by means of detached barracks so that it could accommodate 850. On the day of our visit, as we were informed by a small blackboard hanging beside the office door, it contained 1741. As we approached the entrance we were stopped by an armed sentry, who, upon being informed that we desired admittance, shouted through a square port-hole in the heavy gate, "Star-she-e-e!" (the usual call for the officer of the day). A corporal or sergeant, with a saber at his side and a Colt's revolver in a holster on his hip, answered the summons, carried our note to the warden, and in a moment we were admitted to the prison yard. Fifty or sixty exiles and convicts were walking aimlessly back and forth in front of the main prison building, or sitting idly in groups here and there on the ground. They were all dressed from head to foot in a costume of gray, consisting of a visorless Scotch cap, a shirt and trousers of coarse homespun linen, and a long gray overcoat with one or two diamond-shaped patches of black or yellow cloth sewn upon the back between the shoulders. Nearly all of them wore leg-fetters, and the air was filled with a peculiar clinking of chains which suggested the continuous jingling of innumerable bunches of keys.

The first *kámera*, or cell, that we entered was situated in a one-story log barrack standing against the wall on the left of the gate, and built evidently to receive the overflow from the crowded main building. The room was about 35 feet in length by 25 in width and 12 feet high; its walls of hewn logs were covered with dirty whitewash; its rough plank floor was black with dried mud and hard-trodden filth; and it was lighted by three grated windows looking out into the prison yard. Down the center of the room, and occupying about half its width, ran the sleeping-bench—a wooden platform 12 feet wide and 30 feet long, supported at a height of 2 feet from the floor by stout posts. Each longitudinal half of this low platform sloped a little, roof-wise, from the center, so that when the prisoners slept upon it in two closely packed transverse rows, their heads in the middle were a few inches higher than their feet at the edges. These sleeping-platforms are known as *nári*, and a Siberian prison cell contains no other furniture except a large wooden tub for excrement. The prisoners have neither pillows, blankets, nor bed-clothing, and must lie on these hard plank *nári* with no covering but their overcoats. As we entered the cell, the convicts, with a sudden jingling of chains, sprang to their feet, removed their caps, and stood silently in a dense throng around the *nári*. "Zdrástvuitye rebiáta!" ("How do you do, boys?") said the warden. "Zdrávie zheláiem váshe vuisóki blagaródie" ("We wish you health, your high nobility"), shouted a hundred voices in a hoarse chorus. "The prison," said the warden, "is terribly overcrowded. This cell, for example, is only 35 feet long by 25 feet wide, and has air space for 35, or at most 40 men. How many men slept here last night?" he inquired, turning to the prisoners.

"A hundred and sixty, your high nobility," shouted half a dozen hoarse voices

"You see how it is," said the warden, again addressing me. "This cell contains more than four times the number of prisoners that it was intended to hold, and the same condition of things exists throughout the prison." I looked around the cell. There was practically no ventilation whatever, and the air was so poisoned and foul that I could hardly force myself to breathe it. We visited successively in the yard six *kámeras* or cells essentially like the first, and found in every one of them three or four times the number of prisoners for which it was intended, and five or six times the number for which it had adequate air space. In most of the cells there was not room enough on the sleeping-platforms for all of the convicts, and scores of men slept every night on the foul, muddy floors, under the *nári*, and in the gangways between them and the walls. Three or four pale, dejected, and apparently sick prisoners crawled out from under the sleeping-platform in one of the cells as we entered.

From the log barracks in the prison yard we went into the main building, which contained the kitchen, the prison workshops, and the hospital, as well as a large number of *kámeras*, and which was in much worse sanitary condition than the barracks. It was, in fact, a building through which Mr. Ignátof—a former member of the prison committee—declined to accompany us. On each side of the dark, damp, and dirty corridors were heavy wooden doors, opening into cells which varied in size from 8 feet by 10 to 10 by 15, and contained from half a dozen to thirty prisoners. They were furnished with *nári*, like those in the cells that we had already inspected; their windows were small and heavily grated, and no provision whatever had been made for ventilation. In one of these cells were eight or ten *dvoryáne*, or "nobles," who seemed to be educated men, and in whose presence the warden removed his hat. Whether any of them were "politicals" or not I do not know; but in this

COURTYARD OF TIUMÉN PRISON

FAMILY KÁMERA IN TOMSK FORWARDING PRISON

part of the prison the politicals were usually confined. The air in the corridors and cells, particularly in the second story, was indescribably and unimaginably foul. Every cubic foot of it had apparently been respired over and over again until it did not contain an atom of oxygen; it was laden with fever germs from the unventilated hospital wards, fetid odors from diseased human lungs and unclean human bodies, and the stench arising from unemptied excrement buckets at the ends of the corridors. I breathed as little as I possibly could, but every respiration seemed to pollute me to the very soul, and I became faint from nausea and lack of oxygen. It was like trying to breathe in an underground hospital-drain. The *smatrítel*, or warden, noticing perhaps that my face had grown suddenly pale, offered me his cigarette case, and said: "You are not accustomed to prison air. Light a cigarette: it will afford some relief, and we will get some wine or vodka presently in the dispensary." I acted upon this suggestion and we continued our investigations. The prison workshops, to which we were next taken, consisted of two small cells in the second story, neither of them more than eight feet square, and neither of them designed for the use to which it had been put. In one, three or four convicts were engaged in cobbling shoes, and in the other an attempt was being made to do a small amount of carpenter's work. The workmen, however, had neither proper tools nor suitable appliances, and it seemed preposterous to call the small cells which they occupied "workshops."

We then went to the prison kitchen, a dark, dirty room in the basement of the main building, where three or four half-naked men were baking black rye-bread in loaves about as large as milk-pans, and boiling soup in huge iron kettles on a sort of brick range. I tasted some of the soup in a greasy wooden bowl which a convict hastily cleaned for me with a wad of dirty flax, and found it nutritious and good. The bread was rather sour and heavy, but not worse than that prepared and eaten by Russian peasants generally. The daily ration of the prisoners consisted of two and a half pounds of this black bread, about six ounces of boiled meat, and two or three ounces of coarsely ground barley or oats, with a bowl of *kvas* morning and evening for drink.

After we had examined the workshops, the kitchen, and most of the *kámeras* in the first and second stories, the *smatrítel* turned to me and said, "Do you wish to go through the hospital wards?" "Certainly," I replied; "we wish to see everything that there is to be seen in the prison." The warden shrugged his shoulders, as if he could not understand a curiosity which was strong enough to take travelers into a Siberian prison hospital; but, without making any remarks, he led the way up another flight of stone steps to the third story, which was given up entirely to the sick. The hospital wards, which numbered five or six, were larger and lighter than any of the cells that we had previously examined in the main building, but they were wholly unventilated, no disinfectants apparently were used in them, and the air was polluted to the last possible degree. It did not seem to me that a well man could live there a week without becoming infected with disease, and that a sick man should ever recover in that awful atmosphere was inconceivable. In each ward were twelve or fifteen small iron bedsteads, set with their heads to the walls round three sides of the room, and separated one from another by about five feet of space. Each bedstead was furnished with a thin mattress consisting of a coarse gray bed-tick filled with straw, a single pillow, and either a gray blanket or a ragged quilt. Mr. Frost thought that some of the beds were supplied with coarse gray linen sheets and pillow-cases, but I did not notice anything of the kind. Over the head of each bedstead was a small blackboard, bearing in Russian and Latin characters the name of the prisoner's disease and the date of his admission to the hospital. The most common disorders seemed to be scurvy, typhus fever, typhoid fever, acute bronchitis, rheumatism, and syphilis. Prisoners suffering from malignant typhus fever were isolated in a single ward; but with this exception no attempt apparently had been made to group the patients in classes according to the nature of their diseases. Women were separated from the men, and that was all. Never before in my life had I seen faces so white, haggard, and ghastly as those that lay on the gray pillows in these hospital cells. The patients, both men and women, seemed to be not only desperately sick, but hopeless and heart-broken. I could not wonder at it. As I breathed that heavy, stifling atmosphere, poisoned with the breaths of syphilitic and fever-stricken patients, loaded and saturated with the odor of excrement, disease germs, exhalations from unclean human bodies, and foulness inconceivable, it seemed to me that over the hospital doors should be written, "All hope abandon, ye who enter here."

After we had gone through the women's lying-in ward and the ward occupied by patients suffering from malignant typhus fever, I told the *smatrítel* that I had seen enough; all I wanted was to get out of doors where I could once more breathe. He conducted us to the dispensary on the ground floor, offered us alcoholic stimulants, and suggested that we allow ourselves to be sprayed with carbolic acid and water. We probably had not been in the prison long enough, he said, to take any infection; but we were unaccustomed to prison air, the hospital was in bad condition, we had visited the malignant typhus fever ward, and he thought the measure that he suggested was nothing more than a proper precaution. We of course assented, and were copiously sprayed from head to foot with dilute carbolic acid, which, after the foulness of the prison atmosphere, seemed to us almost as refreshing as spirits of cologne.

At last, having finished our inspection of the main building, we came out into the prison yard, where I drew a long, deep breath of pure air with the delicious sense of relief that a half-drowned man must feel when he comes to the surface of the water.

"How many prisoners," I asked the warden, "usually die in that hospital in the course of the year?"

"About 300," he replied. "We have an epidemic of typhus

almost every fall. What else could you expect when buildings that are barely adequate for the accommodation of 800 persons are made to hold 1800? A prison so overcrowded cannot be kept clean, and as for the air in the cells, you know now what it is like. In the fall it is sometimes much worse. During the summer the windows can be left open, and some ventilation can be secured in that way; but when the weather becomes cold and stormy the windows must be closed, and then there is no ventilation at all. We suffer from it as well as the prisoners. My assistant has only recently recovered from an attack of typhus fever which kept him in bed for six weeks, and he caught the disease in the prison. The local authorities here have again and again urged the Government to make adequate provision for the large number of exiles crowded into this prison during the season of navigation, but thus far nothing has been done beyond the building of two log barracks."

The warden spoke naturally and frankly, as if the facts that he gave me were known to everybody in Tiumén, and as if there was no use in trying to conceal them even from a foreign traveler when the latter had been through the prison and the prison hospital.

From the main prison building we went to the women's prison, which was situated on the other side of the road in a courtyard formed by a high stockade of closely set and sharpened logs. It did not differ much in external appearance from the men's barracks inside the prison-wall, which we had already examined. The *kámeras* varied in size from 10 feet by 12 to 30 feet by 45, and contained from three to forty women each. They were all clean and well lighted, the floors and sleeping-platforms had been scrubbed to a snowy whiteness, strips of coarse carpet had been laid down here and there in the gangways between the *nári*, and one cell even had potted plants in the window. The women, like the men, were obliged to sleep in rows on the hard platforms without pillows or blankets, but their cells were not so overcrowded as were those of the men, and the air was infinitely purer. Most of the women seemed to belong to the peasant class; many of them were accompanied by children, and I saw very few hard or vicious faces.

From the women's prison we went to the prison for exiled families, another stockaded log barrack about 75 feet in length which had no cell partitions and which contained nearly 300 men, women, and children. Here again the sleeping-platforms were overcrowded; the air was heavy and foul; dozens of children were crying from hunger or wretchedness; and the men and women looked tired, sleepless, and dejected. None of the women in this barrack were criminals. All were voluntarily going into banishment with their criminal husbands, and most of them were destined for points in Western Siberia.

About one o'clock in the afternoon, after having made as thorough an examination as possible of all the prison buildings, Mr. Frost and I went with Mr. Ignátof to lunch. Knowing that our host was the contractor for the transportation of exiles eastward by barge, and that he had been a prominent member of the Tiumén prison committee, I asked him if the Government in St. Petersburg was aware of the condition of the Tiumén forwarding prison, and of the sickness and misery in which it resulted. He replied in the affirmative. The local authorities, the prison committee, and the inspector of exile transportation for Western Siberia had reported upon the condition of the Tiumén prison, he said, every year; but the case of that prison was by no means an exceptional one. New prisons were needed all over European Russia, as well as Siberia, and the Government did not yet feel able financially to make sweeping prison reforms, nor to spend perhaps ten million rubles in the erection of new prison buildings. The condition of the Tiumén prison was, he admitted, extremely bad, and he himself had resigned his place as a member of the prison committee because the Government would not authorize the erection of a new building for use as a hospital. The prison committee had strongly recommended it, and when the Government disapproved the recommendation, he resigned.

CHAPTER THREE

First Meeting with Political Exiles

OUR FIRST MEETING WITH POLIT-
ical exiles in Siberia was brought about by a fortunate accident,
and, strangely enough, through the instrumentality of the
Government. Among the many officers whose acquaintance
we made in Semipalátinsk was an educated and intelligent gentleman named Pávlovski, who had long held an important position in the Russian service, and who was introduced to us as a
man whose wide and accurate knowledge of Siberia, especially
of the steppe territories, might render him valuable to us, both
as an adviser and as a source of trustworthy information. Although Mr. Pávlovski impressed me from the first as a cultivated, humane, and liberal man, I naturally hesitated to apply
to him for information concerning the political exiles. The advice given me in St. Petersburg had led me to believe that the
Government would regard with disapprobation any attempt
on the part of a foreign traveler to investigate a certain class
of political questions or to form the acquaintance of a certain
class of political offenders; and I expected, therefore, to have
to make all such investigations and acquaintances stealthily and
by underground methods. I was not at that time aware of the
fact that Russian officials and political exiles are often secretly
in sympathy, and it would never have occurred to me to seek
the aid of the one class in making the acquaintance of the other.
In all of my early conversations with Mr. Pávlovski, therefore,
I studiously avoided the subject of political exile, and gave him,

I think, no reason whatever to suppose that I knew anything about the Russian revolutionary movement, or felt any particular interest in the exiled revolutionists.

In the course of a talk one afternoon about America, Mr. Pávlovski, turning the conversation abruptly, said to me, "Mr. Kennan, have you ever paid any attention to the movement of young people into Siberia?"

I did not at first see the drift nor catch the significance of this inquiry, and replied, in a qualified negative, that I had not, but that perhaps I did not fully understand the meaning of his question.

"I mean," he said, "that large numbers of educated young men and women are now coming into Siberia from European Russia; I thought perhaps the movement might have attracted your attention."

The earnest, significant way in which he looked at me while making this remark, as if he were experimenting upon me or sounding me, led me to conjecture that the young people to whom he referred were the political exiles. I did not forget, however, that I was dealing with a Russian officer; and I replied guardedly that I had heard something about this movement, but knew nothing of it from personal observation.

"It seems to me," he said, looking at me with the same watchful intentness, "that it is a remarkable social phenomenon, and one that would naturally attract a foreign traveler's attention."

I replied that I was interested, of course, in all the social phenomena of Russia, and that I should undoubtedly feel a deep interest in the one to which he referred if I knew more about it.

"Some of the people who are now coming to Siberia," he continued, "are young men and women of high attainments—men with a university training and women of remarkable character."

"Yes," I replied, "so I have heard; and I should think that they might perhaps be interesting people to know."

"They are," he assented. "They are men and women who, under other circumstances, might render valuable services to their country; I am surprised that you have not become interested in them."

In this manner Mr. Pávlovski and I continued to fence cautiously for five minutes, each trying to ascertain the views of the other, without fully disclosing his own views concerning the unnamed, but clearly understood, subject of political exile. Mr. Pávlovski's words and manner seemed to indicate that he himself regarded with great interest and respect the "young people now coming to Siberia"; but that he did not dare make a frank avowal of such sentiments until he should feel assured of my discretion, trustworthiness, and sympathy. I, on my side, was equally cautious, fearing that the uncalled-for introduction of this topic by a Russian official might be intended to entrap me into an admission that the investigation of political exile was the real object of our Siberian journey. The adoption of a quasi-friendly attitude by an officer of the Government toward the exiled enemies of that Government seemed to me an extraordinary and unprecedented phenomenon, and I naturally regarded it with some suspicion.

At last, tired of this conversational beating around the bush, I said frankly, "Mr. Pávlovski, are you talking about the political exiles? Are they the young people to whom you refer?"

"Yes," he replied; "I thought you understood. It seems to me that the banishment to Siberia of a large part of the youth of Russia is a phenomenon that deserves a traveler's attention."

"Of course," I said, "I am interested in it, but how am I to find out anything about it? I don't know where to look for political exiles, nor how to get acquainted with them; and I am told that the Government does not regard with favor intercourse between foreign travelers and politicals."

"Politicals are easy enough to find," rejoined Mr. Pávlovski. "The country is full of them, and there is nothing, so far as I know, to prevent you from making their acquaintance if you feel so disposed. There are thirty or forty of them here in Semipalátinsk, and they walk about the streets like other people: why shouldn't you happen to meet them?"

Having once broken the ice of reserve and restraint, Mr. Pávlovski and I made rapid advances toward mutual confidence. I soon became convinced that he was not making a pretense of sympathy with the politicals in order to lead me into a trap; and he apparently became satisfied that I had judgment and tact enough not to get him into trouble by talking to other people about his opinions and actions. Then everything went smoothly. I told him frankly what my impressions were with regard to the character of nihilists generally, and asked him whether, as a matter of fact, they were not wrong-headed fanatics and wild social theorists, who would be likely to make trouble in any state.

"On the contrary," he replied, "I find them to be quiet, orderly, reasonable human beings. We certainly have no trouble with them here. Governor Tseklínski treats them with great kindness and consideration; and, so far as I know, they are good citizens."

In the course of further conversation, Mr. Pávlovski said that there were in Semipalátinsk, he believed, about forty political exiles, including four or five women. They had all been banished without judicial trial, upon mere executive orders, signed by the Minister of the Interior and approved by the Tsar. Their terms of exile varied from two to five years; and at the expiration of such terms, if their behavior meanwhile had been satisfactory to the local Siberian authorities, they would be permitted to return, at their own expense, to their homes. A few of them had found employment in Semipalátinsk and were supporting themselves; others received money from relatives or friends; and the remainder were supported—or rather kept from actual starvation—by a Government allowance, which amounted to six rubles ($3.00) a month for exiles belonging to the noble or privileged class, and two rubles and seventy kopeks ($1.35) a month for non-privileged exiles.

"Of course," said Mr. Pávlovski, "such sums are wholly inadequate for their support. Nine kopeks [four and a half cents] a day won't keep a man in bread, to say nothing of providing him with shelter; and if the more fortunate ones who get employment or receive money from their relatives did not help the others, there would be much more suffering than there is. Most of them are educated men and women, and Governor Tseklínski, who appreciates the hardships of their situation, allows them to give private lessons, although, according to the letter of the law, teaching is an occupation in which political exiles are forbidden to engage. Besides giving lessons, the women sew and embroider, and earn a little money in that way. They are allowed to write and receive letters, as well as to have unobjectionable books and periodicals; and although they are nominally under police surveillance, they enjoy a good deal of personal freedom."

"What is the nature of the crimes for which these young people were banished?" I inquired. "Were they conspirators? Did they take part in plots to assassinate the Tsar?"

"Oh, no!" said Mr. Pávlovski with a smile; "they were only 'untrustworthy.' Some of them belonged to forbidden societies, some imported or were in possession of forbidden books, some had friendly relations with other more dangerous offenders, and some were connected with disorders in the higher schools and the universities. The greater part of them are administrative exiles—that is, persons whom the Government, for various reasons, has thought it expedient to remove from their homes and put under police surveillance in a part of the empire where they can do no harm. The real conspirators and revolutionists—the men and women who have actually been engaged in criminal activity—are sent to more remote parts of Siberia and into penal servitude. Banishment to the steppe territories is regarded as a very light punishment; and, as a rule, only administrative exiles are sent here."

In reply to further questions with regard to the character of these political exiles, Mr. Pávlovski said, "I don't know anything to their discredit; they behave themselves well enough here. If you are really interested in them, I can, perhaps, help you to an acquaintance with some of them, and then you can draw your own conclusions as to their character."

Of course I assured Mr. Pávlovski that an introduction to the politicals would give me more pleasure than any other favor he could confer upon me. He thereupon suggested that we should go at once to see a young political exile named Lobonófski, who was engaged in painting a drop-curtain for the little town theater.

"He is something of an artist," said Mr. Pávlovski, "and has a few Siberian sketches. You are making and collecting such sketches: of course you want to see them."

"Certainly," I replied with acquiescent diplomacy. "Sketches are my hobby, and I am a connoisseur in drop-curtains. Even although the artist be a nihilist and an exile, I must see his pictures."

Mr. Pávlovski's *dróshky* was at the door, and we drove at once to the house where Mr. Lobonófski was at work.

I find it extremely difficult now, after a whole year of intimate association with political exiles, to recall the impressions that I had of them before I made the acquaintance of the exile colony in Semipalátinsk. I know that I was prejudiced against them, and that I expected them to be wholly unlike the rational, cultivated men and women whom one meets in civilized society; but I cannot, by any exercise of will, bring back the unreal, fantastic conception of them that I had when I crossed the Siberian frontier. As nearly as I can now remember, I regarded the people whom I called nihilists as sullen, and more or less incomprehensible "cranks," with some education, a great deal of fanatical courage, and a limitless capacity for self-sacrifice, but with the most visionary ideas of government and social organization, and with only the faintest trace of what an American would call "hard common-sense." I did not expect to have any more ideas in common with them than I should have in common with an anarchist like Louis Lingg; and although I intended to give their case against the Government a fair hearing, I believed that the result would be a confirmation of the judgment I had already formed. Even after all that Mr. Pávlovski had said to me, I think I more than half expected to find in the drop-curtain artist a long-haired, wild-eyed being who would pour forth an incoherent recital of wrongs and outrages, denounce all governmental restraint as brutal tyranny, and expect me to approve of the assassination of Alexander II.

The log house occupied by Mr. Lobonófski as a workshop was not otherwise tenanted, and we entered it without announcement. As Mr. Pávlovski threw open the door, I saw, standing before a large square sheet of canvas which covered one whole side of the room, a blond young man, apparently about thirty years of age, dressed from head to foot in a suit of cool brown linen, holding in one hand an artist's brush, and in the other a plate or palette covered with freshly mixed colors. His strongly built figure was erect and well-proportioned; his bearing was that of a cultivated gentleman; and he made upon me, from the first, a pleasant and favorable impression. He seemed, in fact, to be an excellent specimen of the blond type of Russian young manhood. His eyes were clear and blue; his thick, light-brown hair was ill cut, and rumpled a little in a boyish way over the high forehead; the full blond beard gave manliness and dignity to his well-shaped head, and his frank, open, good-tempered face, flushed a little with heat and wet with perspiration, seemed to me to be the face of a warm-hearted and impulsive but, at the same time, strong and well-balanced man. It was, at any rate, a face strangely out of harmony with all my preconceived ideas of a nihilist.

Mr. Pávlovski introduced me to the young artist as an American traveler, who was interested in Siberian scenery, who had heard of his sketches, and who would like very much to see some of them. Mr. Lobonófski greeted me quietly but cordially, and at once brought out the sketches—apologizing, however, for their imperfections, and asking us to remember that they had been made in prison, on coarse writing-paper, and that the outdoor views were limited to landscapes that could be seen from prison and *étape* windows. The sketches were evidently the work of an untrained hand, and were mostly representations of prison and *étape* interiors, portraits of political exiles, and such bits of towns and villages as could be seen from the windows of the various cells that the artist had occupied in the course of his journey to Siberia. They all had, however, a certain rude force and fidelity.

My conversation with Mr. Lobonófski at this interview did not touch political questions, and was confined, for the most part, to topics suggested by the sketches. He described his journey to Siberia just as he would have described it if he had made it voluntarily, and, but for an occasional reference to a prison or an *étape*, there was nothing in the recital to remind one that he was a nihilist and an exile. His manner was quiet, modest, and frank; he followed any conversational lead with ready tact, and although I watched him closely I could not detect the slightest indication of eccentricity or "crankiness." He must have felt conscious that I was secretly regarding him with critical curiosity—looking at him, in fact, as one looks for the first time at an extraordinary type of criminal—but he did not manifest the least awkwardness, embarrassment, or self-consciousness. He was simply a quiet, well-bred, self-possessed gentleman.

When we took our leave, after half an hour's conversation, Mr. Lobonófski cordially invited me to bring Mr. Frost to see him that evening at his house, and said that he would have a few of his friends there to meet us. I thanked him and promised that we would come.

"Well," said Mr. Pávlovski, as the door closed behind us, "what do you think of the political exile?"

"He makes a very favorable impression upon me," I replied. "Are they all like him?"

"No, not precisely like him; but they are not bad people. There is another interesting political in the city whom you ought to see—a young man named Leátief. He is employed in the office of Mr. Makovétski, a justice of the peace here, and is engaged with the latter in making anthropological researches among the Kírghis. I believe they are now collecting material for a monograph upon Kírghis customary law. Why shouldn't you call upon Mr. Makovétski? I have no doubt that he would introduce Mr. Leántief to you, and I am sure that you would find them both to be intelligent and cultivated men."

This seemed to me a good suggestion; and as soon as Mr. Pávlovski had left me I paid a visit to Mr. Makovétski, ostensibly for the purpose of asking permission to sketch some of the Kírghis implements and utensils in the town library, of which he was one of the directors. Mr. Makovétski seemed pleased to learn that I was interested in their little library, granted me permission to sketch the specimens of Kírghis handiwork there exhibited, and finally introduced me to his writing-clerk, Mr. Leántief, who, he said, had made a special study of the Kírghis, and could give me any desired information concerning the natives of that tribe.

Mr. Leántief was a good-looking fellow, apparently about twenty-five years of age, rather below the medium height, with light-brown hair and beard, intelligent gray eyes, a slightly aquiline nose, and a firm, well-rounded chin. His head and face were suggestive of studious and scientific tastes, and if I had met him in Washington and had been asked to guess his profession from his appearance, I should have said that he was probably a young scientist connected with the United States Geological Survey, the Smithsonian Institution, or the National Museum. He was, as I subsequently learned, the son of an army officer who at one time commanded the Cossack garrison in this same city of Semipalátinsk. As a boy he was enrolled in the corps of imperial pages and began his education in the large school established by the Government for the training of such pages in the Russian capital. At the age of eighteen or nineteen he entered the St. Petersburg University, and in the fourth year of his student life was arrested and exiled by "administrative process" to Western Siberia for five years, upon the charge of having had secret communication with political prisoners in the fortress of Petropávlovsk.

Although Mr. Leántief's bearing was somewhat more formal and reserved than that of Mr. Lobonófski, and his attitude toward me one of cool, observant criticism, rather than of friendly confidence, he impressed me very favorably; and when, after half an hour's conversation, I returned to my hotel, I was forced to admit to myself that if all nihilists were like the two whom I had met in Semipalátinsk, I should have to modify my opinions with regard to them. In point of intelligence and education Mr. Lobonófski and Mr. Leántief seemed to me to compare favorably with any young men of my aquaintance.

At eight o'clock that evening Mr. Frost and I knocked at Mr. Lobonófski's door and were promptly admitted and cordially welcomed. We found him living in a small log house not far from our hotel. The apartment into which we were shown, and which served in the double capacity of sitting-room and bed-room, was very small—not larger, I think, than ten feet in width by fourteen feet in length. Its log walls and board ceiling were covered with dingy whitewash, and its floor of rough unmatched planks was bare. Against a rude, unpainted partition to the right of the door stood a small single bedstead of stained wood, covered with neat but rather scanty bed-clothing, and in the corner beyond it was a triangular table, upon which were lying, among other books, Herbert Spencer's *Essays: Moral, Political, and Esthetic*, and the same author's *Principles of Psychology*. The opposite corner of the room was occupied by a what-not, or étagère, of domestic manufacture, upon the shelves of which were a few more books, a well-filled herbarium of coarse brown wrapping-paper, an opera-glass, and an English New Testament. Between two small deeply set windows opening into the courtyard stood a large, unpainted wooden table, without a cloth, upon which was lying, open, the book that Mr. Lobonófski had been reading when we entered—a French translation of Balfour Stewart's *Conservation of Energy*. There was no other furniture in the apartment except three or four unpainted wooden chairs. Everything was scrupulously neat and clean; but the room looked like the home of a man too poor to afford anything more than the barest essentials of life.

After Mr. Lobonófski had made a few preliminary inquiries with regard to the object of our journey to Siberia, and had expressed the pleasure which he said it afforded him to meet and welcome Americans in his own house, he turned to me with a smile and said, "I suppose, Mr. Kennan, you have heard terrible stories in America about the Russian nihilists?"

"Yes," I replied; "we seldom hear of them except in connection with a plot to blow up something or to kill somebody, and I must confess that I have had a bad opinion of them. The very word 'nihilist' is understood in America to mean a person who does not believe in anything and who advocates the destruction of all existing institutions."

" 'Nihilist' is an old nickname," he said; "and it is no longer applicable to the Russian revolutionary party, if, indeed, it was ever applicable. I don't think you will find among the political exiles in Siberia any 'nihilists,' in the sense in which you use the word. Of course there are, in what may be called the anti-Government class, people who hold all sorts of political opinions. There are a few who believe in the so-called policy of 'terror'—who regard themselves as justified in resorting even to political assassination as a means of overthrowing the Government; but even the terrorists do not propose to destroy all existing institutions. Every one of them, I think, would lay down his arms, if the Tsar would grant to Russia a constitutional form of government and guarantee free speech, a free press, and freedom from arbitrary arrest, imprisonment, and exile. Have you ever seen the letter sent by the Russian revolutionists to Alexander III upon his accession to the throne?"

"No," I replied; "I have heard of it, but have never seen it."

"It sets forth," he said, "the aims and objects of the revolutionary party, and contains a distinct promise that if the Tsar will grant freedom of speech and summon a national assembly the revolutionists will abstain from all further violence, and will agree not to oppose any form of government which such assembly may sanction. You can hardly say that people who express a willingness to enter into such an agreement as this are in favor of the destruction of all existing institutions. I suppose you know," he continued, "that when your President Garfield was assassinated, the columns of 'The Will of the People'" (the organ of the Russian revolutionists in Geneva) "were bordered with black as a token of grief and sympathy, and that the paper contained an eloquent editorial condemning political assassination as wholly unjustifiable in a country where there are open courts and a free press, and where the officers of the government are chosen by a free vote of the people?"

"No," I replied; "I was not aware of it."

"It is true," he rejoined. "Of course at that time Garfield's murder was regarded as a political crime, and as such it was condemned in Russia, even by the most extreme terrorists."

Our conversation was interrupted at this point by the entrance of three young men and a lady, who were introduced to us as Mr. Lobonófski's exiled friends. In the appearance of the young men there was nothing particularly striking or noticeable. One of them seemed to be a bright university student, twenty-four or twenty-five years of age, and the other two looked like educated peasants or artisans, whose typically Russian faces were rather heavy, impassive, and gloomy, and whose manner was lacking in animation and responsiveness. Life and exile seemed to have gone hard with them, and to have left them depressed and embittered. The lady, whose name was Madame Dicheskúla, represented apparently a different social class and had a more buoyant and sunny disposition. She was about thirty years of age, tall and straight, with a well-proportioned but somewhat spare figure, thick, short brown hair falling in a soft mass about the nape of her neck, and a bright, intelligent, mobile face, which I thought must once have been extremely pretty. It had become, however, a little too thin and worn, and her complexion had been freckled and roughened by exposure to wind and weather and by the hardships of prison and *étape* life. She was neatly and becomingly dressed in a Scotch plaid gown of soft dark serge, with little ruffles of white lace at her throat and wrists; and when her face lighted up in animated conversation, she seemed to me to be a very attractive and interesting woman. In her demeanor there was not a suggestion of the boldness, hardness, and eccentricity that I had expected to find in women exiled to Siberia for political crime. She talked rapidly and well; laughed merrily at times over reminiscences of her journey to Siberia; apologized for the unwomanly shortness of her hair, which, she said, had all been cut off in prison; and related with a keen sense of humor her adventures while crossing the Kírghis steppe from Akmolá to Semipalátinsk. That her natural buoyancy of disposition was tempered by deep feeling was evident from the way in which she described some of the incidents of her Siberian experience. She seemed greatly touched, for example, by the kindness shown to her party by the peasants of Kamishlóva, a village through which they passed on their way from Ekaterínburg to Tiumén. They happened to arrive there on Trinity Sunday, and were surprised to find that the villagers, as a manifestation of sympathy with the political exiles, had thoroughly scoured out and freshened up the old village *étape,* and had decorated its gloomy cells with leafy branches and fresh wildflowers. It seemed to me that tears came to her eyes as she expressed her deep and grateful appreciation of this act of thoughtfulness and good-will on the part of the Kamishlóva peasants.

About nine o'clock Mr. Lobonófski brought in a steaming *sámovar,* Madame Dicheskúla made tea, and throughout the remainder of the evening we sat all around the big pine table as if we had been acquainted for months instead of hours, talking about the Russian revolutionary movement, the exile system, literature, art, science, and American politics. The cool, reasonable way in which these exiles discussed public affairs, problems of government, and their personal experience impressed me very favorably. There was none of the bitterness of feeling and extravagance of statement that I had anticipated, and I did not notice in their conversation the least tendency to exaggerate or even to dwell upon their own sufferings as a means of exciting our sympathy. Madame Dicheskúla, for instance, had been robbed of most of her clothing and personal effects by the police at the time of her arrest; had spent more than a year in solitary confinement in the Moscow forwarding prison; had then been banished, without trial, to a dreary settlement in the Siberian province of Akmolínsk; and, finally, had been brought across the great Kírghis steppe in winter to the city of Semipalátinsk. In all this experience there must have been a great deal of intense personal suffering; but she did not lay half as much stress upon it in conversation as she did upon the decoration of the old *étape* with leafy branches and flowers by the people of Kamishlóva, as an expression of sympathy with her and her exiled friends. About eleven o'clock, after a most pleasant and interesting evening, we bade them all good-night and returned to our hotel.

On the following morning Mr. Lobonófski, Madame Dicheskúla, Mr. Frost, and I took *dróshkies* and drove down the right bank of the Írtish a mile or two, to a small grove of poplars and aspens near the water's edge, where six or eight political exiles were spending the summer in camp. A large Kírghis *yurt* of felt, and two or three smaller cotton tents, had been pitched on the grass under the trees, and in them were living two or three young women and four or five young men, who had taken this means of escaping from the heat, glare, and sand of the verdureless city. Two of the women were mere girls, seventeen or eighteen years of age, who looked as if they ought to be pursuing their education in a high school or a female seminary, and why they had been exiled to Siberia I could not imagine. It did not seem to me possible that they could be regarded in any country, or under any circumstances, as a dangerous menace to social order or to the stability of the Government. As I shook hands with them and noticed their shy, embarrassed behavior, and the quick flushes of color which came to their cheeks when I spoke to them, I experienced for the first time something like a feeling of contempt for the Russian Government. "If I were the Tsar," I said to Mr. Frost, "and had an army of soldiers and police at my back, and if, nevertheless, I felt so afraid of timid, half-grown school-girls that I couldn't sleep in peaceful security until I had banished them to Siberia, I think I should abdicate in favor of some stronger and more courageous man." The idea that a powerful Government like that of Russia could not protect itself against seminary girls and Sunday-school teachers without tearing them from their families, and isolating them in the middle of a great Asiatic desert, seemed to me not only ludicrous, but absolutely preposterous.

We spent in the pleasant shady camp of these political exiles nearly the whole of the long, hot summer day. Mr. Frost made sketches of the picturesquely grouped tents, while I talked with the young men, read Irving aloud to one of them who was studying English, answered questions about America, and asked questions in turn about Siberia and Russia. Before the day ended we were upon as cordial and friendly a footing with the whole party as if we had known them for a month.

Late in the afternoon we returned to the city, and in the evening went to the house of Mr. Leántief, where most of the political exiles whom we had not yet seen had been invited to meet us. The room into which we were ushered was much larger and better furnished than that in which Mr. Lobonófski lived; but nothing in it particularly attracted my attention except a portrait of Herbert Spencer, which hung on the wall over Mr. Leántief's desk. There were twelve or fifteen exiles present, including Mr. Lobonófski, Madame Dicheskúla, Dr. Bogomólets—a young surgeon whose wife was in penal servitude at the mines of Kará—and the two Prisédski sisters, to whom reference was made in my article upon the "Prison Life of the Russian Revolutionists," in the *Century Magazine* for December, 1887. The general conversation which followed our introduction to the assembled company was bright, animated, and informal. Mr. Leántief, in reply to questions from me, related the history of the Semipalátinsk library, and said that it had not only been a great boon to the political exiles, but had noticeably stimulated the intellectual life of the city. "Even the Kírghis," he said, "occasionally avail themselves of its privileges. I know a learned old Kírghis here, named Ibrahim Konobai, who not only goes to the library, but reads such authors as Buckle, Mill, and Draper."

"You don't mean to say," exclaimed a young university student, "that there is any old Kírghis in Semipalátinsk who actually reads Mill and Draper!"

"Yes, I do," replied Mr. Leántief, coolly. "The very first time I met him he astonished me by asking me to explain to him the difference between induction and deduction. Some time afterward I found out that he was really making a study of English philosophy, and had read Russian translations of all the authors that I have named."

"Do you suppose that he understood what he read?" inquired the university student.

"I spent two whole evenings in examining him upon Draper's *Intellectual Development of Europe*," replied Mr. Leántief; "and I must say that he seemed to have a very fair comprehension of it."

"I notice," I said, "that a large number of books in the library—particularly the works of the English scientists—have been withdrawn from public use, although all of them seem once to have passed the censor. How does it happen that books are at one time allowed and at another time prohibited?"

"Our censorship is very capricious," replied one of the exiles. "How would you explain the fact that such a book as Adam Smith's *Wealth of Nations* is prohibited, while Darwin's *Origin of Species* and *Descent of Man* are allowed? The latter are certainly more dangerous than the former."

"It has been suggested," said another, "that the list of prohibited books was made up by putting together, without examination, the titles of all books found by the police in the quarters of persons arrested for political offenses. The *Wealth*

of Nations happened to be found in some unfortunate revolutionist's house, therefore the *Wealth of Nations* must be a
dangerous book."

"When I was arrested," said Mr. Lobonófski, "the police
seized and took away even a French history that I had bor-
rowed from the public library. In looking hastily through it
they noticed here and there the word 'revolution,' and that
was enough. I tried to make them understand that a French
history must, of course, treat of the French Revolution, but
it was of no use. They also carried off, under the impression
that it was an infernal machine, a rude imitation of a steam-
engine which my little brother had made for amusement out of
some bits of wood and metal and the tubes of an old opera-
glass." Amidst general laughter, a number of the exiles related
humorous anecdotes illustrating the methods of the Russian
police, and then the conversation drifted into other channels.

As an evidence of the intelligence and culture of these political
exiles, and of the wide range of their interests and sympathies,
it seems to me worth while to say that their conversation
showed more than a superficial acquaintance with the best English and American literature, as well as a fairly accurate knowledge of American institutions and history. Among the authors
referred to, discussed, or quoted by them that evening were
Shakespeare, Mill, Spencer, Buckle, Balfour Stewart, Heine,
Hegel, Lange, Irving, Cooper, Longfellow, Bret Harte, and
Harriet Beecher Stowe. They knew the name and something of
the record of our newly elected President, discussed intelli-
gently his civil-service reform policy and asked pertinent questions with regard to its working, and manifested generally an
acquaintance with American affairs that one does not expect to
find anywhere on the other side of the Atlantic, and least of
all in Siberia.

After a plain but substantial supper, with delicious overland
tea, the exiles sang for us in chorus some of the plaintive popular melodies of Russia, and Mr. Frost and I tried, in turn, to
give them an idea of our college songs, our war songs, and the

music of the American negroes. It must have been nearly midnight when we reluctantly bade them all good-by and returned
to the Hotel Sibir.

It is impossible, of course, to give even the substance of the
long conversations concerning the Russian Government and
the Russian revolutionary movement which I had with the
political exiles in Semipalátinsk. All that I aim to do at present
is to describe, as fairly and accurately as possible, the impression that these exiles made upon me. If I may judge others by
myself, American readers have had an idea that the people who
are called nihilists stand apart from the rest of mankind in a
class by themselves, and that there is in their character something fierce, gloomy, abnormal, and, to a sane mind, incomprehensible, which alienates from them, and which should alienate
from them, the sympathies of the civilized world. If the political exiles in Semipalátinsk be taken as fair representatives of
the class thus judged, the idea seems to me to be a wholly mistaken one. I found them to be bright, intelligent, well-informed
men and women, with warm affections, quick sympathies,
generous impulses, and high standards of honor and duty. They
are, as Mr. Pávlovski said to me, "men and women who, under
other circumstances, might render valuable services to their
country." If, instead of thus serving their country, they are
living in exile, it is not because they are lacking in the virtue
and the patriotism that are essential to good citizenship, but
because the Government, which assumes the right to think and
act for the Russian people, is out of harmony with the spirit
of the time.

CHAPTER FOUR

Exile by Administrative Process

E XILE BY ADMINISTRATIVE PROC-
ess means the banishment of an obnoxious person from one part
of the empire to another without the observance of any of the
legal formalities that, in most civilized countries, precede the
deprivation of rights and the restriction of personal liberty. The
obnoxious person may not be guilty of any crime, and may not
have rendered himself amenable in any way to the laws of the
state, but if, in the opinion of the local authorities, his presence
in a particular place is "prejudicial to public order," or "in-
compatible with public tranquillity," he may be arrested without a warrant, may be held from two weeks to two years in
prison, and may then be removed by force to any other place
within the limits of the empire and there be put under police
surveillance for a period of from one year to ten years. He may
or may not be informed of the reasons for this summary pro-
ceeding, but in either case he is perfectly helpless. He cannot
examine the witnesses upon whose testimony his presence is
declared to be "prejudicial to public order." He cannot summon friends to prove his loyalty and good character, without
great risk of bringing upon them the same calamity that has be-
fallen him. He has no right to demand a trial, or even a hearing.
He cannot sue out a writ of habeas corpus. He cannot appeal
to his fellow-citizens through the press. His communications
with the world are so suddenly severed that sometimes even
his own relatives do not know what has happened to him. He

is literally and absolutely without any means whatever of self-defense. To show the nature of the evidence upon which certain classes of Russians are banished to Siberia, and to illustrate the working of the system generally, I will give a few cases of administrative exile from the large number recorded in my notebooks.

Some of the readers of this chapter will perhaps remember a young naval officer named Constantine Staniukóvich, who was attached to the staff of the Grand Duke Alexis at the time of the latter's visit to the United States. From the fact that I saw in Mr. Staniukóvich's house in Tomsk the visiting cards of people well known in New York and San Francisco, I infer that he went a good deal into society here and that he may still be recalled to mind by persons who met him. He was the son of a Russian admiral, was an officer of great promise, and had before him the prospect of a brilliant career in the Russian naval service. He was, however, a man of broad and liberal views, with a natural taste for literary pursuits, and after his return from America he resigned his position in the navy and became an author. He wrote a number of novels and plays which were fairly successful, but which, in the language of the censor, "manifested a pernicious tendency," and in 1882 or 1883 he purchased a well-known Russian magazine in St. Petersburg called the *Diélo* and became its editor and proprietor. He spent a considerable part of the summer of 1884 abroad, and in the latter part of that year left his wife and children at Baden-Baden and started for St. Petersburg. At the Russian frontier station of Vérzhbolof he was suddenly arrested, was taken thence to St. Petersburg under guard, and was there thrown into the fortress of Petropávlovsk. His wife, knowing nothing of this misfortune, continued to write to him at St. Petersburg without getting any answers to her letters, until finally she became alarmed, and telegraphed to the editorial department of the *Diélo*, asking what had happened to her husband and why he did not write to her. The managing editor of the magazine replied that Mr. Staniukóvich was not there, and that they had supposed him to be still in Baden-Baden. Upon the receipt of this telegram, Mrs. Staniukóvich, thoroughly frightened, proceeded at once with her children to St. Petersburg. Nothing whatever could be learned there with regard to her husband s whereabouts. He had not been seen at the editorial rooms of the *Diélo,* and none of his friends had heard anything of or from him in two weeks. He had suddenly and mysteriously disappeared. At last, after days of torturing anxiety, Mrs. Staniukóvich was advised to make inquiries of General Órzhefski, the chief of gendarmes. She did so, and found that her husband was a prisoner in one of the casemates of the Petropávlovsk fortress. The police, as it afterward appeared, had for some time been intercepting and reading his letters, and had ascertained that he was in correspondence with a well-known Russian revolutionist who was then living in Switzerland. The correspondence was perfectly innocent in its character, and related solely to the business of the magazine; but the fact that an editor, and a man of known liberal views, was in communication with a political refugee was regarded as sufficient evidence that his presence in St. Petersburg would be "prejudicial to public order," and his arrest followed. In May, 1885, he was exiled for three years by administrative process to the city of Tomsk in Western Siberia. The publication of the magazine was of course suspended in consequence of the imprisonment and ultimate banishment of its owner, and Mr. Staniukóvich was financially ruined. If the Russian Government deals in this arbitrary way with men of rank, wealth, and high social position in the capital of the empire, it can be imagined what treatment is accorded to authors, physicians, students, and small landed proprietors whose presence is regarded as "prejudicial to public order" in the provinces.

In the year 1880 the well-known and gifted Russian novelist Vladímir Korolénko, two of whose books have recently been translated into English and published in Boston, was exiled to Eastern Siberia as a result of what the Government itself finally admitted to be an official mistake. Through the influence of

Prince Imeretínski, Mr. Korolénko succeeded in getting this mistake corrected before he reached his ultimate destination and was released in the West Siberian city of Tomsk. Hardly had he returned, however, to European Russia, when he was called upon to take the oath of allegiance to Alexander III, and to swear that he would betray every one of his friends or acquaintances whom he knew to be engaged in revolutionary or anti-Government work. No honorable and self-respecting man could take such an oath as that, and of course Mr. Korolénko declined to do so. He was thereupon exiled by administrative process to the East Siberian territory of Yakútsk, where, in a wretched native *ulús*, he lived for about three years.

Mr. Boródin, another Russian author and a well-known contributor to the Russian magazine *Annals of the Fatherland*, was banished to the territory of Yakútsk on account of the alleged "dangerous" and "pernicious" character of a certain manuscript found in his house by the police during a search. This manuscript was a spare copy of an article upon the economic condition of the province of Viátka, which Mr. Boródin had written and sent to the above-named magazine, but which, up to that time, had not been published. The author went to Eastern Siberia in a convict's gray overcoat with a yellow ace of diamonds on his back, and three or four months after his arrival in Yakútsk he had the pleasure of reading in the *Annals of the Fatherland* the very same article for which he had been exiled. The Minister of the Interior had sent him to Siberia merely for having in his possession what the police called a "dangerous" and "pernicious" manuscript, and then the St. Petersburg committee of censorship had certified that another copy of that same manuscript was perfectly harmless, and had allowed it to be published, without the change of a line, in one of the most popular and widely circulated magazines in the empire.

A gentleman named Achkín, in Moscow, was exiled to Siberia by administrative process in 1885 merely because, to adopt the language of the order that was issued for his arrest, he was "suspected of an intention to put himself into an illegal situation." The high crime which Mr. Achkín was "suspected of an intention" to commit was the taking of a fictitious name in the place of his own. Upon what ground he was "suspected of an intention" to do this terrible thing he never knew.

Another exile of my acquaintance, Mr. Y——, was banished merely because he was a friend of Mr. Z——, who was awaiting trial on the charge of political conspiracy. When Mr. Z——'s case came to a judicial investigation he was found to be innocent and was acquitted; but in the meantime Mr. Y——, merely for being a friend of this innocent man, had gone to Siberia by administrative process.

In another case a young student, called Vladímir Sidórski (I use a fictitious name), was arrested by mistake instead of another and a different Sidórski named Victor, whose presence in Moscow was regarded by somebody as "prejudicial to public order." Vladímir protested that he was not Victor, that he did not know Victor, and that his arrest in the place of Victor was the result of a stupid blunder; but his protestations were of no avail. The police were too much occupied in unearthing what they called "conspiracies" and looking after "untrustworthy" people to devote any time to a troublesome verification of an insignificant student's identity. There must have been something wrong about him, they argued, or he would not have been arrested, and the safest thing to do with him was to send him to Siberia, whoever he might be—and to Siberia he was sent. When the convoy officer called the roll of the out-going exile party, Vladímir Sidórski failed to answer to Victor Sidórski's name, and the officer, with a curse, cried "Victor Sidórski! Why don't you answer to your name?"

"It is not my name," replied Vladímir, "and I won't answer to it. It's another Sidórski who ought to be going to Siberia."

"What is your name, then?"

Vladímir told him. The officer coolly erased the name "Victor" in the roll of the party, inserted the name "Vladímir," and remarked cynically, "It doesn't make a ——— bit of difference!"

In the years 1877, 1878, and 1879, no attempt was made, apparently, by the Government to ascertain whether an arrested person was deserving of exile or not, nor even to ascertain whether the man or woman exiled was the identical person for whom the order of banishment had been issued. The whole system was a chaos of injustice, accident, and caprice. Up to November, 1878, as appears from an official circular to provincial governors, the local authorities did not even take the trouble to make a report of political arrests to the Minister of the Interior. If a man was taken into custody as a political offender, that, in many cases, was the end of it so far as an investigation was concerned. The fact that he had been arrested by mistake, or in the place of some other person, did not necessarily insure his release. The local authorities reversed the humane rule of Catherine II and acted, in political cases, upon the principle that it is better to punish ten innocent persons than to allow one criminal to escape.

The above-cited case of the student Sidórski is by no means exceptional. In the open letter to the Tsar for which Madame Tsébrikova has recently been exiled to the province of Vólogda, the reader will find a brief statement of a similar case in which two brothers were banished by mistake in place of two other brothers of like name but of different family. The banished young men were the sole support of their widowed mother and a fifteen-year-old sister. When, at last, the blunder was discovered and the innocent brothers were permitted to return to their home, they found that their mother had died of grief and privation, and that, after her death, their child-sister had been sold by a boarding-house keeper into a house of prostitution. "What must have been the feeling of those young men toward the Government," Madame Tsébrikova asks, "when they came back and were informed of their mother's death and their sister's shame?" In the light of such facts ter-

rorism ceases to be an unnatural or an inexplicable phenomenon. Wrong a man in that way, deny him all redress, exile him
again if he complains, gag him if he cries out, strike him in the
face if he struggles, and at last he will stab and throw bombs.
It is useless to say that the Russian Government does not exas-
perate men and women in this way. The case of Madame
Tsébrikova herself is a recent case in point. For merely writing
out the above story of injustice and other stories like it, and
sending them to Alexander III with an earnest and respectful
letter imploring him to right such wrongs, Madame Tsébrikova
has been exiled by administrative process to a remote village in
the province of Vólogda. The only results of her letter were a
decree of banishment and a contemptuous inquiry from the
Tsar, "What business is it of hers?"

The two things that are most exasperating to a liberal and
warm-hearted young Russian are, first, official lawlessness in
the sphere of personal rights, and second, the suffering brought
by such lawlessness upon near relatives and dear friends. In exile by administrative process these two exasperating agencies
operate conjointly. The suffering of a loved wife, or the loss
of an affectionate child, is hard enough to bear when it comes
in the ordinary course of nature and seems to be inevitable;
but when it comes as the direct result of unnecessary causes,
such as injustice, tyranny, and official caprice, it has more than
the bitterness of death, and it arouses fiercer passions than
those that carry men into the storm of battle. As an illustration
of this I will relate briefly the story of a young Russian surgeon who is known to a number of persons in the United
States.

In the year 1879 there was living in the town of Ivángorod,
in the province of Chernígof, a skilful and accomplished young
surgeon named Dr. Biéli. Although he was a man of liberal
views, he was not an agitator nor a revolutionist, and had taken
no active part in political affairs. Some time in the late winter
or early spring of 1879 there came to him, with letters of introduction, two young women who had been studying in one of

the medical schools for women in St. Petersburg, and had been expelled and ordered to return to their homes in central Russia on account of their alleged political "untrustworthiness." They were very anxious to complete their education and to fit themselves for useful work among the peasants; and they begged Dr. Biéli to aid them in their studies, to hear their recitations, and to allow them to make use of his library and the facilities of his office. As they were both in an "illegal" position—that is, were living in a place where, without permission from the authorities, they had no right to be—it was Dr. Biéli's duty as a loyal subject to hand them over to the police, regardless of the fact that they had come to him with letters of introduction and a petition for help. He happened, however, to be a man of courage, independence, and generous instincts; and, instead of betraying them, he listened with sympathy to their story, promised them his aid, introduced them to his wife, and began to give them lessons. The year 1879 in Russia was a year of intense revolutionary activity. Attempts were constantly being made by the terrorists to assassinate high Government officials; and the police, in all parts of the empire, were more than usually suspicious and alert. The visits of the young girls to Dr. Biéli's house and office soon attracted the attention of the local authorities in Ivángorod, and they took steps to ascertain who they were and where they had come from. An investigation showed that one of them was living on a forged passport, while the other had none, and that both had been expelled from St. Petersburg for political "untrustworthiness." Their unauthorized appearance in Ivángorod, when they should have been at their homes, and their half-secret visits—generally at night—to the house of Dr. Biéli were regarded as evidence of a political conspiracy, and on the 10th of May, 1879, both they and the young surgeon were arrested and exiled by administrative process to Siberia. Dr. Biéli eventually was sent to the arctic village of Verkhoyánsk, latitude 67.30°, in the province of Yakútsk, where he was seen in 1882 by Engineer Melville, Lieutenant Danenhower, Mr. W. H. Gilder, and all the survivors of the arctic exploring steamer "Jeannette." At the time of Dr. Biéli's banishment, his wife, a beautiful young woman, twenty-four or twenty-five years of age, was expecting confinement, and was therefore unable to go to Siberia with him. As soon as possible, however, after the birth of her child, and before she had fully recovered her strength, she left her nursing baby with relatives and started on a journey of more than 6000 miles to join her husband in a village situated north of the arctic circle and near the Asiatic pole of cold. She had not the necessary means to make such a journey by rail, steamer, and post, as Lieutenant Schuetze made it in 1885–86, and was therefore forced to ask permission of the Minister of the Interior to travel with a party of exiles.[1] As far as the city of Tomsk in Western Siberia both political and common-criminal exiles are transported in convict trains or barges. Beyond that point the common criminals walk, and the politicals are carried in *telégas*, at the rate of about sixty miles a week, stopping in an *étape* every third day for rest. At this rate of progress Mrs. Biéli would have reached her husband's place of exile only after sixteen months of incessant hardship, privation, and suffering. But she did not reach it. For many weeks her hope, courage, and love sustained her, and enabled her to endure without complaint the jolting, the suffocating dust, the scorching heat, and the cold autumnal rains on the road, the bad food, the plank sleeping-benches, the vermin, and the pestilential air of the *étapes;* but human endurance has its limits. Three or four months of this unrelieved misery, with constant anxiety about her husband and the baby that, for her husband's sake, she had abandoned in Russia, broke down her health and her spirit. She sank into deep despondency and eventually began to show signs of mental aberration. After passing Krasnoyársk her condition became such that any sudden shock was likely completely to overthrow her reason—and the shock soon

1. By Russian law a wife may go to her exiled husband at the expense of the Government, provided she travels with an exile party, lives on the exile ration, sleeps in the roadside *étapes,* and submits generally to prison discipline.

came. There are two villages in Eastern Siberia whose names are almost alike—Verkholénsk and Verkhoyánsk. The former is situated on the river Léna, only 180 miles from Irkútsk, while the latter is on the headwaters of the Yána, and is distant from Irkútsk nearly 2700 miles. As the party with which she was traveling approached the capital of Eastern Siberia, her hope, strength, and courage seemed to revive. Her husband she thought was only a few hundred miles away, and in a few more weeks she would be in his arms. She talked of him constantly, counted the verst-posts which measured her slow progress towards him, and literally lived upon the expectation of speedy reunion with him. A few stations west of Irkútsk she accidentally became aware, for the first time, that her husband was not in Verkholénsk, but in Verkhoyánsk; that she was still separated from him by nearly 3000 miles of mountain, steppe, and forest; and that in order to reach his place of banishment that year she would have to travel many weeks on dog or reindeer sledges, in terrible cold, through the arctic solitudes of northeastern Asia. The sudden shock of this discovery was almost immediately fatal. She became violently insane, and died insane a few months later in the Irkútsk prison hospital, without ever seeing again the husband for whose sake she had endured such mental and physical agonies.

I have been compelled to restrict myself to the barest outline of this terrible tragedy; but if the reader could hear the story, as I heard it, from the lips of exiles who traveled with Mrs. Biéli, and who saw the flickering spark of her reason go out, in an East Siberian *étape*, he would not wonder that exile by administrative process makes terrorists, but rather that it does not make a nation of terrorists.

A recent writer in the German periodical *Unsere Zeit* of Leipzig, who signs himself "A Russian Resident of Eastern Siberia," and who is, apparently, a sincere and earnest man, attempts to lay the whole responsibility for exile by administrative process upon the Russian revolutionists. He admits the truth of all I have said on the subject, and acknowledges that "no man knows at what moment he may be seized and cast into prison or doomed to exile without even a hearing"; but he declares that "all this has been brought upon us by a band so vile—so horribly vile—that their crimes are without parallel. . . . But for the nihilists of Kará there would have never been any administrative exile." The "Russian Resident of Eastern Siberia," however, is as much mistaken in the explanation that he gives of the origin of administrative exile, as in the character that he attributes to the Russian revolutionists. Exile by administrative process is not a new thing in Russia, nor was it first resorted to by the Russian Government as an extraordinary and exceptional measure of self-defense in the struggle with the revolutionists. It is older than nihilism, it is older than the modern revolutionary movement, it is older than the imperial house of Románof. It has been practiced for centuries as a short and easy method of dealing with people who happen to be obnoxious or in the way, but who cannot conveniently be tried or convicted in a court of justice. If the "Russian Resident of Eastern Siberia" will read attentively the works of Tarásof, Sergéyefski, Maxímof, and Anúchin, he will find that administrative exile has been not only a recognized, but a well established, method of dealing with certain classes of offenders ever since the seventeenth century. In the reign of the Emperor Nicholas, for example, nihilism had not been so much as heard of—the very word was unknown—and yet men and women were being exiled to Siberia by administrative process, not in hundreds merely, but in thousands, and not only by order of the Tsar, but by order of the administrative authorities, by order of the ecclesiastical authorities, by order of the village communes, and even by order of private landowners. Most of them, it is true, were not political offenders; but they were none the less entitled to a trial, and they were all victims of the system that the "Russian Resident" says was brought into existence half a century later, "in a time of terrible necessity, as the only possible means to counteract the nefarious doings of those dark conspirators," the nihilists.

MARCHING EXILE PARTY

A Break for Liberty

The careful and exhaustive researches of Anúchin in the archives of the chief exile bureau at Tobólsk, show that between 1827 and 1846 there was not a year in which the number of persons sent to Siberia by administrative process fell below three thousand, and that it reached a maximum, for a single year, of more than six thousand. The aggregate number for the twenty-year period is 79,909. It can hardly be contended, I think, that the nihilists or the terrorists are responsible for a system that had sent eighty thousand persons to Siberia without judicial trial, long before such a thing as a nihilist or a terrorist was known, and before most of the modern Russian revolutionists were born. The "Russian Resident of Eastern Siberia" has simply put the cart before the horse. It was administrative exile, administrative caprice, and the absence of orderly and legal methods in political cases generally, that caused terrorism, and not terrorism that necessitated official lawlessness. The wolf always contends, with a show of virtuous indignation, that while he was peacefully drinking as usual, the lamb muddied the brook, and thus compelled him to "take exceptional measures for the reëstablishment of public tranquillity"; but his statement is very properly discredited when it appears that he was above the lamb on the brook, and that, for years, he had been taking "exceptional measures" of the same kind with other lambs that had not been near the brook. To defend or to justify the crimes of the terrorists is not the object of my work; but when the history of the nineteenth century in Russia shall have been written by someone having access to the secret archives of the Ministry of the Interior and the Third Section of the Tsar's Chancellery, it will appear, I think, to the satisfaction of all men, that most of the so-called terroristic crimes in Russia were committed, not, as the "Russian Resident" asserts, by "bloodthirsty tigers in human form at the prompting of presumptuous fancies," but by ordinary men and women exasperated to the pitch of desperation by administrative suppression of free speech and free thought, administrative arrest without warrant, administrative imprisonment for years upon suspicion, administrative banishment to the arctic regions without trial, and, to crown all, administrative denial of every legal remedy and every peaceful means of redress.

It is true that in 1879, as a result of the criminal activity of the terrorists, martial law was declared throughout European Russia, unlimited discretionary power was given to governors-general, and exile by administrative process, as a quick and convenient method of dealing with political suspects, was expressly authorized by the Tsar; but the imperial authorization was nothing more than a formal sanction of a preëxisting measure, and an intimation that it might, thenceforth, be given a wider scope. To say that this form of exile was previously unknown, and that it was forced upon the Government by the crimes of the terrorists, is to set chronology at naught and to ignore all the historical facts of the case. The first attempt on the part of the terrorists to assassinate a Government official was the attempt of Véra Zasúlich to kill General Trepof, the St. Petersburg chief of police, on the 5th of February, 1878. Administrative exile for political reasons had then been common for almost a decade. If I mistake not, Véra Zasúlich herself had been one of its victims seven or eight years before. I think she was one of twenty or thirty persons who were tried before a special session of the Governing Senate in 1871 upon the charge of complicity in the Necháief conspiracy, who were judicially declared to be not guilty, but who were immediately rearrested, nevertheless, and exiled by administrative process, in defiance of all law and in contemptuous disregard of the judgment of the highest court in the empire. A government that acts in this way sows dragons' teeth and has no right to complain of the harvest. The so-called "propagandists" of 1870–74 did not resort to violence in any form, and did not even make a practice of resisting arrest, until after the Government had begun to exile them to Siberia for life with ten or twelve years of penal servitude, for offenses that were being punished at the very same time in Austria with only a few days—or at most a few weeks—of personal detention. It was not terrorism that necessitated administrative exile in Russia; it was merciless severity and banishment without due process of law that provoked terrorism.

In the latter part of the reign of Alexander II, and particularly between the years 1870 and 1880, administrative exile was resorted to, in political cases, upon a scale never before known, and with a recklessness and cynical indifference to personal rights that were almost unparalleled. In Odessa, General Todleben, by virtue of the unlimited discretionary power given him in the Imperial *ukáz* of April 17, 1879, proceeded to banish, without inquiry or discrimination, the whole "politically untrustworthy" class—that is, to exile every person whose loyalty to the existing Government was even doubtful. The mere fact that a man had been registered as a suspect in the books of the secret police, or had been accused, even anonymously, of political disaffection, was a sufficient reason for his deportation to the remotest part of the empire. Parents who had never had a disloyal thought were exiled because their children had become revolutionists; schoolboys who happened to be acquainted with political offenders were exiled because they had not betrayed the latter to the police; teachers were exiled for circulating copies of the Russian magazine *Annals of the Fatherland;* members of provincial assemblies were exiled because they insisted upon their right to petition the crown for the redress of grievances; and university students who had been tried for political crime and duly acquitted by the courts were immediately rearrested and exiled by administrative process, in violation of the most elementary principles of justice.

In December, 1879, a young revolutionist—a Jew—named Maidánski, was hanged in Odessa by sentence of a court-martial for having taken part in a conspiracy to assassinate a Government spy named Gorinóvich. His old father and mother, who lived in Elizabethgrad, came to Odessa to have a last interview with him before he should be put to death; but the authorities, instead of allowing the aged parents to see their condemned son, promptly arrested them both and sent them to

Eastern Siberia by administrative process. They were nothing but poor illiterate peasants, and there was not the least evidence to show that they had encouraged their son's criminal activity, or even that they had been aware of it; but the opinion of the Government seemed to be that they deserved punishment for having brought such a son into the world. It may be thought, in the light of more recent events, that they were treated in this merciless way because they were Jews; but the Government, at that time, was dealing in precisely the same manner with orthodox Russians belonging to the educated and privileged classes.

In the late summer or early fall of 1879 two educated young women from Nikoláief—the sisters Livandófskaya—were exiled for political reasons to different parts of Eastern Siberia. One of them, named, Véra, was banished by administrative process to Mínusínsk in the province of Yeniséisk, while the other was sentenced by a court-martial to forced colonization in the little town of Kírensk on the river Léna. If the Government had been satisfied with the deportation of these two young women only, there would have been nothing unusual or particularly noteworthy in the case; but it went much further than this. The family of the two exiled girls consisted of a father aged about seventy, a mother aged fifty-five or sixty, and two younger sisters fifteen and sixteen years of age respectively.

After the banishment of Véra and the other elder sister to Eastern Siberia, all the remaining members of the family were exiled by administrative process for a term of three years to a village near the sub-arctic coast of the White Sea in the province of Archangel. As long as their term of banishment lasted they received a small monthly allowance from the Government for their maintenance, and so managed to exist; but when, in 1882, they were informed that they were at liberty to return to Nikoláief, and that their allowance would no longer be paid to them, they were left without any means of support in the place where they were, and had no money with which to get back to their home. They wrote a piteous letter to Véra in

Mínusínsk, describing their sufferings and their almost helpless situation, and Véra, upon receipt of it, determined to make her escape, return to European Russia, and there, under an assumed name, earn money enough, if possible, to bring her aged parents and her two younger sisters back to their home in Nikoláief. Her attempt to escape was successful, she reached European Russia in safety, and began, in the city of Kiev, her search for employment. Failing to get anything to do, she used up, little by little, the small sum of money that she had brought with her from Siberia, and at last, to escape starvation, she was forced, in despair, to give herself up to the police. She lay for some months in prison, while the authorities were investigating her story, and was then sent back to Mínusínsk. In the meantime her aged father and mother had succeeded in obtaining from friends money enough to get as far south as Moscow, and when the unfortunate daughter passed through that city on her way to Eastern Siberia, her parents and sisters, whom she had hoped to help, came to see her in prison and were permitted to have a brief interview with her. Véra subsequently married, in Mínusínsk, the talented young author, publicist, and political exile, Iván Petróvich Belokónski, and lived there with him until the termination of her period of banishment. She then returned to European Russia in order that she might help take care of her aged father, who had gone insane, and her feeble and almost heart-broken mother. At the time when we left Siberia, she, herself, was living with her parents in the city of Kiev, her exiled husband was more than three thousand miles away in Mínusínsk, and her exiled sister was more than four thousand miles away on the head-waters of the river Léna.

To one who lives in a country where personal rights are secured by all sorts of legal and constitutional guarantees, it may seem, perhaps, that nothing could be more unjust and tyrannical than the banishment of an infirm father, an aged mother, and two helpless children, merely because certain other members of the family had become disloyal; but in the history of administrative exile in Russia there are things even more extraordinary and unreasonable than this.

Toward the close of the Russo-Turkish war of 1877–78, when the conspicuous gallantry of General Skóbelef had attracted to him the attention of the world, and had made him the idol of enthusiastic young men throughout Russia, a large number of students in the university of Kiev undertook to give formal expression to their feeling of admiration for the great popular hero by getting up an address to him. There happened, at that time, to be more or less political excitement among a certain class of the Kiev university students, and the meetings that were held for the purpose of drafting and discussing the proposed address to Skóbelef were thought by the Government to have in view another and a more dangerous end. They were soon prohibited, therefore, by the authorities, and several of the students who had taken a prominent part in them were arrested on suspicion, held for a time in prison, and then sent by administrative process to the northern province of Vólogda. Among the students thus exiled was Ivan N——, the son of a wealthy landed proprietor in Khersón. When the young man had spent three or four months in the northern village to which he had been banished, his father, by means of a liberal expenditure of money, succeeded in getting him transferred to the province of Khersón, where the climate is milder than in Vólogda, and where the young exile was nearer his home. He was still kept, however, under police surveillance, and was regarded by the authorities as "politically untrustworthy." In April, 1879, General Todlében was appointed governor-general of Odessa, with unlimited discretionary power, and as soon as he reached his post he proceeded to extirpate "sedition" in the provinces under his jurisdiction by banishing to Siberia, without trial or hearing, every man, woman, or child who was registered as a suspect in the books of the secret police, or who happened at that time to be under police surveillance. Among such persons was the unfortunate Kiev student Ivan N——. His transfer from the province of Vólogda to the province of Khersón had brought him within the limits of the territory subject to the authority of Governor-General Todlében, and had thus rendered his situation worse instead of better. It was of no use for him to plead that the Government, in consenting to his transfer from a northern to a southern province, had intended to show him mercy, and that to send him to Siberia would be to punish him a second time, and with redoubled severity, for an action that was wholly innocent in the first place, and that ought not to have been punished at all. The chinóvniks in the office of the governor-general had no time to investigate or to make discriminations. The orders were to banish to Siberia all persons then under police surveillance; and if they should once begin to inquire, and investigate, and grant hearings, they would never get anybody banished at all. If he felt aggrieved he could send a petition to the Minister of the Interior from Siberia. All the young man's efforts to get his case reconsidered on its merits were fruitless, and in the summer of 1879 he was sent to Eastern Siberia by administrative process. In the prison of Krasnoyársk, where the exile party to which he belonged was detained for a few days, a misunderstanding of some sort arose between the prison officials and the politicals, in the course of which the latter became insubordinate and turbulent. The inspector of exile transportation came to the prison in a state of semi-intoxication to quiet the disturbance, and while he was haranguing and threatening the politicals, one of them exclaimed ironically, "Vazhno!" which may be rendered in English, "How important we are!" The inspector was beside himself with fury, and, not being able to find out who had uttered the offensive exclamation, he caused all the prisoners in that *kámera* to be sent to the sub-arctic territory of Yakútsk. The young student from Kiev was not a political and had taken no active part in the disorder, but he happened to be in the cell from which the ironical cry, "Vazhno!" came, and that circumstance alone was sufficient to send him to the arctic regions. In the next five years of enforced solitude he had ample time to reflect upon the danger of falling under suspicion in a country where the will of a *chinóvnik* is the law of the land, and where patriotic admiration for a great general may be punished as severely as an assault with intent to kill. The Persian poet Saadi, who evidently saw practiced at Bagdad in the twelfth century the same governmental methods that prevail in Russia now, tells a story in the *Gulistan* of a terror-stricken fox who was seen limping and running away, and who, upon being asked what he was afraid of, replied, "I hear they are going to press a camel into the service."

"Well, what of it?" said the interrogator; "what relationship is there between that animal and you?"

"Be silent!" rejoined the fox. "If the malignant, out of evil design, should say, 'This is a camel,' who would be so solicitous for my relief as to order an inquiry into my case? and 'before the antidote can be brought from Irak he who has been bitten by the serpent may be dead.'"

In the year 1879 there was living in the Russian city of Pultáva a poor apothecary named Schiller, who desired for some reason to change the location of his place of business. As druggists in Russia are not allowed to migrate from one town to another without the permission of the Government, Schiller wrote to the Minister of the Interior, stating his desire to move and the reasons for it, and asking that he be authorized to close his shop in Pultáva and open another in Kharkóf. Week after week passed without bringing any answer to his request. At last, the Minister of the Interior happened to stop in Pultáva for a day or two on one of his journeys from St. Petersburg to the Crimea, and Schiller, regarding this as a providential opportunity, attempted to get an interview with him for the purpose of presenting his petition in person. Of course the guard at the door of the house occupied by the Minister refused to admit a poor apothecary with a paper, and Schiller, indignant at what he thought was an injustice, wrapped his petition around a stone, to give it weight, and threw it into the window of the Minister's room. He was at once arrested and imprisoned, and a few months later, upon the charge of having behaved in a disorderly manner and shown gross disrespect to the higher authorities, he was banished by administrative process, as a political offender, to the village of Varnavin in the province of Kostromá. This was not regarded by the authorities as a particularly severe punishment; but Schiller, finding enforced residence in an unfamiliar village to be irksome and tedious, and having no further confidence in petitions, changed his location between sunset and dawn without asking leave of anybody—in other words, ran away. About this time the Tsar issued a *poveléinie*, or command, directing that all administrative exiles found absent from their places of banishment without leave should be sent to the East Siberian province of Yakútsk.[2] When, therefore, a few months later, Schiller was rearrested in a part of the empire where he had no right to be, he was sent by *étape* to Irkútsk, and the governor-general of Eastern Siberia was requested to put him under police surveillance in some part of the territory named in the Imperial command. Governor-General Anúchin, who had then recently come to Irkútsk, and who had not had time, apparently, to familiarize himself with the vast region intrusted to his care, directed that Schiller be sent to the district town of Zashíversk, which was supposed to be situated on the river Indigírka, a few miles

2. This Imperial command was issued on the 2d of April, 1880, and was intended to discourage attempts on the part of political exiles to escape. In the hands of local police officials it was soon made an instrument for the punishment of politicals who incurred their hostility. The first time, for example, that an obnoxious exile went two hundred yards beyond the limits of the village—perhaps only into a neighboring forest to gather flowers or berries—he was arrested upon the charge of attempting to escape and immediately banished to the province of Yakútsk— the wildest part of northeastern Asia. It made little difference whether the charge rested upon any basis of fact or not. In the latter part of the year 1880, a political named Peter Mikháilovich Volokhóf—an acquaintance of the Russian novelist Kololénko—was banished to the province of Yakútsk for an alleged attempt to escape from Archangel. As a matter of fact he had never even been in Archangel, much less attempted to escape from there.

south of the arctic circle.[3] A century or a century and a half
ago, this town of Zashíversk was a place of considerable local
importance; but, for some reason, it lost its preëminence as a
fur-trading center, fell gradually into decay, and finally ceased
to exist. Its location was still marked with two concentric cir-
cles on all the maps, its name continued to appear annually in
the records of the governor-general's office, and I have no
doubt that a coterie of *chinóvniks* in Irkútsk were dividing and
pocketing every year the money appropriated for repairs to
its public buildings; but, as a matter of fact, it had not contained a building nor an inhabitant for more than half a century, and forest trees were growing on the mound that marked
the site of its *ostróg*. Poor Schiller, after having been carried
three or four thousand miles up and down the rivers Léna and
Indigírka in a vain search for a non-existent arctic town, was
finally brought back to Yakútsk; and a report was made to the
governor-general that Zashíversk, apparently, had ceased to
exist. The governor-general thereupon ordered that the prisoner
be taken to Srédni Kolímsk, another "town" of forty-five
houses, situated on the river Kolymá north of the arctic circle,
3700 miles from Irkútsk and 7500 miles from the capital of the
empire. When, after more than a year of *étape* life, the unfortunate druggist from Pultáva reached the last outpost of Russian power in northeastern Asia and was set at liberty, he made
his way to the little log church, entered the belfry, and proceeded to jangle the church bells in a sort of wild, erratic
chime. When the people of the town ran to the belfry in alarm
and inquired what was the matter, Schiller replied with dignity
that he wished the whole population to know that by the grace
of God, Herman Augustóvich Schiller, after long and perilous
wanderings, had reached in safety the town of Srédni Kolímsk.
Whether the mind of the exile had given way under the pro-

3. Eastern Siberia has an area considerably greater than that of the
United States and Alaska taken together, and most of the vast territory
of Yakútsk is as wild and unsettled as the northern part of British North
America.

longed strain of hardship and suffering, or whether, as some assert, he had become intoxicated and rang the church bells merely as a drunken freak, I do not know; but the local police reported to the governor-general that the "political" exile Schiller was disorderly and turbulent, and that he had caused a public scandal before he had been in Srédni Kolímsk twenty-four hours. Upon this report the governor-general indorsed an order to remove the offender to some place at least twelve versts distant from the town. His idea probably was to have Schiller sent to some small suburban village in the general neighborhood of Srédni Kolímsk, but far enough away so that he could not easily get into the town to make a disturbance. Unfortunately there was no suburban village within a hundred versts in any direction, and the local authorities, not knowing what else to do, carried the wretched druggist about twelve versts out into the primeval wilderness, erected a log cabin for him, and left him there—assuring him cheerfully, as they bade him good-by, that *káknibúd* ("somehow or other") he would get along. With a little help occasionally from wandering Chúkchi and Tongusí he did get along, catching fish, gathering berries, and snaring ptarmigan for his subsistence, and living, for several years, the life of a continental Crusoe. What eventually became of him I do not know.

Of course cases of this kind are exceptional. The Russian Government does not make a practice of sending to the arctic regions druggists who wish to change their places of business, neither does it regularly banish to the territory of Yakútsk students who express admiration for Skóbelef. Nevertheless, under a system of administration that allows an irresponsible official to punish at his own discretion, such results are not only possible but probable.

In the year 1874, a young student named Egór Lázaref was arrested in one of the southeastern provinces of European Russia upon the charge of carrying on a secret revolutionary propaganda. He was taken to St. Petersburg and kept in solitary confinement in the House of Preliminary Detention and in the fortress of Petropávlovsk for about four years. He was then tried with one hundred and ninety-two other political suspects before the Governing Senate, found to be not guilty, and acquitted. As there still existed, however, a possibility that he might be guilty on some future occasion, he was punished in advance by being sent as a soldier to a regiment then engaged in active service in the Trans-Caucasus.[4] One would suppose that to be arrested without cause, to be held four years in solitary confinement, to be declared innocent by the highest court in the empire, and then to be punished with compulsory military service in Asia Minor for an offense prophetically fore-seen, but not yet committed, would make a revolutionist, if not a terrorist, out of the most peaceable citizen; but Mr. Lázaref, as soon as he had been released from the army, quietly com-pleted his education in the university, studied law, and began the practice of his profession in the city of Sarátof on the Vólga. He had no more trouble with the Government until the summer of 1884, when a police officer suddenly appeared to him one morning and said that the governor of the province would like to see him. Mr. Lázaref, who was on pleasant per-sonal terms with the governor, went at once to the latter's office, where he was coolly informed that he was to be exiled by administrative process to Eastern Siberia for three years. Mr. Lázaref stood aghast.

"May I ask your high excellency for what reason?" he final-ly inquired.

4. This was a favorite method of Nicholas for the punishment of liter-ary men and students whose opinions were too liberal for his taste. He compelled the gifted Russian poet Shevchénko to serve ten years as a common soldier, and kept him most of that time in the hottest and most desolate part of Central Asia—the district of Mángishlák. The talented novelist Dostoevski was also forced to serve as a common soldier after the expiration of his term of hard labor in the Omsk convict prison. I cannot now recall any case in which Nicholas insulted his own courts by punishing administratively persons whom they had just declared to be innocent, but such cases were common in the reign of Alexander II. Most of the prisoners acquitted by the Senate in the trial of "the 193" were immediately rearrested and banished by administrative process, or sent as common soldiers into the ranks.

"I do not know," replied the governor. "I have received orders to that effect from the Ministry of the Interior, and that is all I know about it."

Through the influence of friends in St. Petersburg, Mr. Lázaref obtained a respite of two weeks in which to settle up his affairs, and he was then sent as a prisoner to Moscow. He reached that city after the last party of political exiles had been despatched for the season, and had to live in the Moscow forwarding prison until the next spring. While there he wrote a respectful letter to the Department of Imperial Police, asking, as a favor, that he might be informed for what reason he was to be exiled to Eastern Siberia. The reply that he received was comprised in two lines, and was as follows: "You are to be put under police surveillance in Eastern Siberia because you have not abandoned your previous criminal activity." In other words, he was to be banished to the Trans-Baikál because he had not "abandoned" the "previous criminal activity" of which a court of justice had found him not guilty! In the Moscow forwarding prison, soon after Mr. Lázaref's arrival, a number of the political prisoners were comparing experiences one day, and asking one another for what offenses they had been condemned to banishment. One said that forbidden books had been found in his house; another said that he had been accused of carrying on a revolutionary propaganda; and a third admitted that he had been a member of a secret society. Finally Mr. Lázaref's turn came, and upon being asked why he was on his way to Siberia, he replied simply, "I don't know."

"Don't know!" exclaimed one of his comrades. "Didn't your father have a black-and-white cow?"

"Very likely," said Mr. Lázaref. "He had a lot of cows."

"Well!" rejoined his comrade triumphantly, "what more would you have? That's enough to exile twenty men—and yet he says he doesn't know!"

On the 10th of May, 1885, Mr. Lázaref left Moscow with an exile party for Siberia, and on the 10th of October, 1885, after twenty-two weeks of travel "by *étape*," reached the town of Chíta, in the Trans-Baikál, where I had the pleasure of making his acquaintance.

The grotesque injustice, the heedless cruelty, and the preposterous "mistakes" and "misunderstandings" that make the history of administrative exile in Russia seem to an American like the recital of a wild nightmare are due to the complete absence, in the Russian form of government, of checks upon the executive power, and the almost equally complete absence of official responsibility for unjust or illegal action. The Minister of the Interior, in dealing with politicals, is almost wholly unrestrained by law; and as it is utterly impossible for him personally to examine all of the immense number of political cases that come to him for final decision, he is virtually forced to delegate a part of his irresponsible power to chiefs of police, chiefs of gendarmes, governors of provinces, and subordinates in his own ministry. They in turn are compelled, for similar reasons, to intrust a part of their authority and discretion to officers of still lower grade; and the latter, who often are stupid, ignorant, or unscrupulous men, are the persons who really make the investigations, the searches, and the examinations upon which the life or liberty of an accused citizen may depend. Theoretically, the Minister of the Interior, aided by a council composed of three of his own subordinates and two officers from the Ministry of Justice, reviews and reëxamines the cases of all political offenders who are dealt with by administrative process; but practically he does nothing of the kind, and it is impossible that he should do anything of the kind for the very simple reason that he has not the time.

In the years 1886 and 1887 there came before the Department of Justice 1883 political cases, involving no less than 2972 persons. A very large proportion of these cases were dealt with by administrative process, and if the Minister of the Interior had given to each one of them a half, or one-quarter, of the study which was absolutely essential to a clear comprehension of it, he would have had no time to attend to anything else. As a matter of fact he did not give the cases such study, but, as a rule, simply signed the papers that came up to him from below. Of course he would not have signed the order for the exile of Mr. Korolénko to the province of Yakútsk if he had known that the whole charge against the young novelist was based on a mistake; nor would he have signed the order for the exile of Mr. Boródin if he had been aware that the magazine article for which the author was banished had been approved by the St. Petersburg Committee of Censorship. He accepted the statements passed up to him by a long line of subordinate officials, and signed his name merely as a formality and as a matter of course. How easy it is in Russia to get a high official's signature to any sort of a document may be illustrated by an anecdote that I have every reason to believe is absolutely true. A *stóla-nachálnik*, or head of a bureau, in the provincial administration of Tobólsk, while boasting one day about his power to shape and direct governmental action, made a wager with another *chinóvnik* that he could get the governor of the province—the late Governor Lisogórski—to sign a manuscript copy of the Lord's Prayer. He wrote the prayer out in the form of an official document on a sheet of stamped paper, numbered it, attached the proper seal to it, and handed it to the governor with a pile of other papers which required signature. He won his wager. The governor duly signed the Lord's Prayer, and it was probably as harmless an official document as ever came out of his office.

How much of this sort of careless and reckless signing there was in the cases of political offenders dealt with by administrative process may be inferred from the fact that, when the liberal minister Loris-Melikof came into power in 1880, he found it necessary to appoint a revisory commission, under the presidency of General Cherévin, to investigate the cases of persons who had been exiled and put under police supervision by administrative process, and to correct, so far as possible, the "mistakes," "misunderstandings," and "irregularities" against which the sufferers in all parts of the empire began to protest as soon as the appointment of a new Minister of the Interior gave them some reason to hope that their complaints would be heeded. There were said to be at that time 2800 political offenders in Siberia and in various remote parts of European Russia who had been exiled and put under police surveillance by administrative process. Up to the 23d of January, 1881, General Cherévin's commission had examined the cases of 650 such persons, and had recommended that 328, or more than half of them, be immediately released and returned to their homes.

Of course the only remedy for such a state of things as this is to take the investigation of political offenses out of the hands of an irresponsible police, put it into the courts, where it belongs, and allow the accused to be defended there by counsel of their own selection. This remedy, however, the Government persistently refuses to adopt. The Moscow Assembly of Nobles, at the suggestion of Mr. U. F. Samárin, one of its members, sent a respectful but urgent memorial to the Crown, recommending that every political exile who had been dealt with by administrative process should be given the right to demand a judicial investigation of his case. The memorial went unheeded, and the Government, I believe, did not even make a reply to it.

Before the year 1882 the rights, privileges, and obligations of political offenders exiled to Siberia by administrative process were set forth only in secret circular-letters, sent from time to time by the Minister of the Interior to the governors of the different Siberian provinces. Owing to changes in the ministry, changes in circumstances, and changes of ministerial policy, these circular-letters of instruction ultimately became so contradictory, or so inconsistent one with another, and led to so many "misunderstandings," "irregularities," and collisions between the exiles and the local authorities in the Siberian towns and villages, that on the 12th of March, 1882, the Minister of the Interior drew up, and the Tsar approved, a set of rules for the better regulation of police surveillance and administrative exile. An official copy of this paper, which I brought back with me from Siberia, lies before me as I write. It is entitled: "Rules Relating to Police Surveillance." The first thing that strikes the reader in a perusal of this document is the fact that it declares exile and police surveillance to be, not *punishments* for crimes already committed, but measures of precaution to prevent the commission of crimes that evil-minded men may contemplate. The first section reads as follows: "Police surveillance," which includes administrative exile, "is a means of preventing crimes against the existing imperial order; and it is applicable to all persons who are prejudicial to public tranquillity." The power to decide when a man is "prejudicial to public tranquillity," and when exile and surveillance shall be resorted to as a means of "preventing crime," is vested in the governors-general, the governors, and the police; and in the exercise of that power they pay quite as much attention to the opinions that a man holds as to the acts that he commits. They can hardly do otherwise. If they should wait in all cases for the commission of criminal acts, they would not be *preventing* crime," but merely watching and waiting for it, while the object of administrative exile is to *prevent* crime by anticipation. Clearly, then, the only thing to be done is to nip crime in the bud by putting under restraint, or sending to Siberia, every man whose political opinions are such as to raise a presumption that he *will* commit a crime "against the existing imperial order" if he sees a favorable opportunity for so doing. Administrative exile, therefore, is directed against ideas and opinions from which criminal acts may come, rather than against the criminal acts themselves. It is designed to anticipate and prevent the acts by suppressing or discouraging the opinions; and, such being the case, the document which lies before me should be called, not "Rules Relating to Police Surveillance," but "Rules for the Better Regulation of Private Opinion." In the spirit of this latter title, the "Rules" are interpreted by most of the Russian police.

The pretense that administrative exile is not a punishment, but only a precaution, is a mere juggle with words. The Government says, "We do not exile a man and put him under police surveillance as a punishment for holding certain opinions, but only as a means of preventing him from giving such opinions outward expression in criminal acts." If the banishment of a man to the province of Yakútsk for five years is not a "punishment," then the word "punishment" must have in Russian jurisprudence a very peculiar and restricted signification. In the case of women and young girls a sentence of banishment to Eastern Siberia is almost equivalent to a sentence of death, on account of the terrible hardships of the journey and the bad sanitary conditions of the *étapes*—and yet the Government says that exile by administrative process is not a punishment!

In 1884 a pretty and intelligent young girl named Sophia Nikítina, who was attending school in Kiev, was banished by administrative process to one of the remote provinces of Eastern Siberia. In the winter of 1884–85, when she had accomplished about 3000 miles of her terrible journey, she was taken sick, on the road between Tomsk and Áchinsk, with typhus fever, contracted in one of the pestilential *étapes*. Physicians are not sent with exile parties in Siberia, and politicals who happen to be taken sick on the road are carried forward, regardless of their condition and regardless of the weather, until the party comes to a lazaret, or prison hospital. There are only four such lazarets between Tomsk and Irkútsk, a distance of about a thousand miles, and consequently sick prisoners are sometimes carried in sleighs or telegas, at a snail's pace, for a week or two—if they do not die—before they finally obtain rest, a bed, and a physician. How many days of cold and misery Miss Nikítina endured on the road that winter after she was taken sick, and before she reached Áchinsk and received medical treatment, I do not know; but in the Áchinsk lazaret her brief life ended. It must have been a satisfaction to her, as she lay dying in a foul prison hospital, 3000 miles from her home, to think that she was not undergoing "punishment" for anything that she had done, but was merely being subjected to necessary restraint by a parental Government, in order that she might not sometime be tempted to do something that would have a tendency to raise a presumption that her presence in Kiev was about to become more or less "prejudicial to public tranquillity."

I have not space for a quarter of the evidence that I collected in Siberia to show that administrative exile is not only cruelly unjust, but, in hundreds of cases, is a punishment of barbarous severity. If it attained the objects that it is supposed to attain, there might, from the point of view of a despotic Government, be some excuse if not justification for it; but it does not attain such objects. Regarded even from the side of expediency, it is uselessly and needlessly cruel. In a recent official report to the Minister of the Interior, Major-General Nicolái Baránof, the governor of the province of Archangel, in discussing the subject of administrative exile says:

From the experience of previous years, and from my own personal observation, I have come to the conclusion that administrative exile for political reasons is much more likely to spoil the character of a man than to reform it. The transition from a life of comfort to a life of poverty, from a social life to a life in which there is no society whatever, and from a life of activity to a life of compulsory inaction, produces such ruinous consequences, that, not infrequently, especially of late, we find the political exiles going insane, attempting to commit suicide, and even committing suicide. All this is the direct result of the abnormal conditions under which exile compels an intellectually cultivated person to live. There has not yet been a single case where a man, suspected with good reason of political untrustworthiness and exiled by administrative process, has returned from such banishment reconciled to the Government, convinced of his error, and changed into a useful member of society and a faithful servant of the Throne. On the other hand, it often happens that a man who has been exiled in consequence of a misunderstanding, or an administrative mistake, becomes politically untrustworthy for the first time in the place to which he has been banished—partly by reason of his association there with real enemies of the Government, and partly as a result of personal exasperation. Furthermore, if a man is infected with anti-Government ideas, all the circumstances of exile tend only to increase the infection, to sharpen his faculties, and to change him from a theoretical to a practical—that is, an extremely dangerous—man. If, on the contrary, he has not been guilty of taking part in a revolutionary movement, exile, by force of the same circumstances, develops in his mind the idea of revolution, or, in other words, produces a result directly opposite to that which it was intended to produce. No matter how exile by administrative process may be regulated and restricted, it will always suggest to the mind of the exiled person the idea of uncontrolled official license, and this alone is sufficient to prevent any reformation whatever.

Truer words than these were never written by a high Russian official, and so far as the practical expediency of exile by administrative process is concerned, I should be content to rest the case against it upon this frank report of the governor of Archangel. The subject, however, may be regarded from a point of view other than that of expediency—namely, from the point of view of morals, justice, and humanity. That side of the question I shall reserve for further discussion in later chapters.

CHAPTER FIVE

The Life of Political Exiles

IN THE CITY OF TOMSK, WHERE we spent more time than in any other West Siberian town, we had an opportunity to become well acquainted with a large colony of political exiles and greatly to extend our knowledge of political exile life. We met there, for the first time, men and women who had taken part in the so-called "propaganda" of 1872–75, who had been banished by sentence of a court, and who might fairly be called revolutionists. They did not differ essentially from the administrative exiles in Semipalátinsk, Ulbínsk and Ust Kámenogórsk, except that they had been longer in exile and had had a much wider range of experience. Solomon Chudnófski, for example, a bright and talented publicist, about thirty-five years of age, told me that he was arrested the first time at the age of nineteen, while in the university; and that he had been under police surveillance, in prison, or in exile nearly all his life. He was held four years and three months in solitary confinement before trial, and spent twenty months of that time in a casemate of the Petropávlovsk fortress. For protesting against illegal treatment in that great state-prison, and for insisting pertinaciously upon his right to have pen, ink, and paper, in order that he might address a complaint to the Minister of the Interior, he was tied hand and foot, and was finally put into a strait-jacket. He thereupon refused to take food, and starved himself until the prison surgeon reported that his condition was becoming critical. The warden, Colonel Bogaródski, then yielded, and furnished him with writing materials, but no reply was ever made to the complaint that he drew up. He was finally tried with "the 193," in 1878, upon the charge of importing pernicious books, was found guilty, and was sentenced to five years of penal servitude, with deprivation of all civil rights. In view, however, of the length of time that he had already been held in solitary confinement while awaiting trial—four years and three months—the court recommended to the Tsar that his sentence be commuted to exile in Western Siberia for life.

Most men would have been completely broken down by nearly five years of solitary confinement and seven years of exile; but Mr. Chudnófski's energy and courage were invincible. In spite of the most disheartening obstacles he completed his education, and made a name and career for himself even in Siberia. He is the author of the excellent and carefully prepared history of the development of educational institutions in Siberia, published in the "Official Year Book" of the province of Tomsk for 1855; he has made two scientific expeditions to the Altái under the auspices of the West Siberian Branch of the Imperial Geographical Society; he has been an indefatigable contributor to the Russian periodical press; and his book upon the Siberian province of Yeniséisk took the prize offered by the Krasnoyársk city council for the best work upon that subject. Mr. Chudnófski impressed me as a man who, if he had been born in America, might have had a career of usefulness and distinction, and might have been an honor to the state. He happened to be born in Russia, and was therefore predestined to imprisonment and exile.

Among the most interesting of the newly arrived political exiles in Tomsk was Mr. Constantine Staniukóvich, the editor and proprietor of the Russian magazine *Diélo*, whose history I gave briefly [in the previous chapter]. He was a close and accurate observer of Russian social life, a talented novelist, a writer of successful dramas, and a man of great force, energy, and ability. His wife, who had accompanied him to Siberia, spoke English fluently with the least perceptible accent, and seemed to me to be a woman of more than ordinary culture and refinement. They had one grown daughter, a pretty, intelligent girl seventeen or eighteen years of age, as well as two or three younger children, and the whole family made upon us an extremely pleasant impression. Some of the most delightful evenings that we had in Tomsk were spent in their cozy little parlor, where we sometimes sat until long after midnight listening to duets sung by Miss Staniukóvich and Prince Kropotkin; discussing Russian methods of government and the exile system; or comparing our impressions of London, Paris, Berlin, New York, and San Francisco. Both Mr. and Mrs. Staniukóvich had traveled in the United States, and it seemed not a little strange to find in their house in Siberia visiting-cards of such well-known American officers as Captain James B. Eads and Captain John Rodgers, a photograph of President Lincoln, and Indian bead and birch-bark work in the shape of slippers and toy canoes brought as souvenirs from Niagara Falls. We had not expected to find ourselves linked to political exiles in Siberia by such a multitude of common experiences and memories, nor to be shown in their houses such familiar things as bead-embroidered moccasins and birch-bark watch-pockets made by the Tonawanda Indians. Mr. Staniukóvich was struggling hard, by means of literary work, to support his family in exile; and his wife, who was an accomplished musician, aided him as far as possible by giving music lessons.

I am glad to be able to say that, since my return to the United States, Mr. Staniukóvich has completed his term of exile, has left the empire, and when I last heard of him was in Paris. He continues to write indefatigably for the Russian periodicals, and has recently published a volume of collected sketches entitled *Stories of the Sea*.

Another political exile in whom I became deeply interested at Tomsk was Prince Alexander Kropotkin, brother of the well-known author and socialist who now resides in London.

As his history clearly illustrates certain phases of political exile life I will briefly relate it.

Although banished to Siberia upon the charge of disloyalty Kropotkin was not a nihilist, nor a revolutionist, nor even an extreme radical. His views with regard to social and political questions would have been regarded in America, or even in western Europe, as very moderate, and he had never taken any part in Russian revolutionary agitation. He was, however, a man of impetuous temperament, high standard of honor, and great frankness and directness of speech; and these character-istics were perhaps enough to attract to him the suspicious at-tention of the Russian police.

"I am not a nihilist nor a revolutionist," he once said to me indignantly, "and I never have been. I was exiled simply be-cause I dared to think, and to say what I thought, about the things that happened around me, and because I was the brother of a man whom the Russian Government hated."

Prince Kropotkin was arrested the first time in 1858, while a student in the St. Petersburg University, for having in his possession a copy in English of Emerson's *Self-Reliance* and refusing to say where he obtained it. The book had been lent to him by one of the faculty, Professor Tíkhonrávof, and Kropotkin might perhaps have justified himself and escaped unpleasant consequences by simply stating the fact; but this would not have been in accordance with his high standard of personal honor. He did not think it a crime to read Emerson, but he did regard it as cowardly and dishonorable to shelter himself from the consequences of any action behind the person of an instructor. He preferred to go to prison. When Professor Tíkhonrávof heard of Kropotkin's arrest he went at once to the rector of the university, and admitted that he was the own-er of the incendiary volume, and the young student was there-upon released.

After his graduation from the university Kropotkin went abroad, studied science, particularly astronomy, and upon his return to Russia made a number of important translations of French and English scientific works into his native language. Finally he entered the Government service, and for a time previous to his exile held an important place in the Russian telegraph department. This place, however, he was forced to resign in consequence of a collision with the Minister of the Interior. The latter ordered Kropotkin one day to send to him all the telegrams of a certain private individual that were on file in his office. Kropotkin refused to obey this order upon the ground that such action would be personally dishonorable and degrading. Another less scrupulous officer of the department, however, forwarded the required telegrams and Kropotkin resigned. After this time he lived constantly under the secret supervision of the police. His brother Peter had already become prominent as a revolutionist and socialist; he himself was under suspicion; his record, from the point of view of the Government, was not a good one; he probably injured himself still further by frank but injudicious comments upon public affairs; and in 1876 or 1877 he was arrested and exiled to Eastern Siberia upon the vague but fatal charge of "political untrustworthiness." There were no proofs against him upon which a conviction could be had in a court of justice, and he was therefore banished by administrative process.

His place of exile was a small town called Minusínsk, situated on the Yeniséi River in Eastern Siberia, more than 3000 miles from St. Petersburg, and about 150 miles from the boundary line of Mongolia. Here, with his young wife, who had voluntarily accompanied him into exile, he lived quietly four or five years, devoting himself chiefly to reading and scientific study. There were in Minusínsk at that time no other political exiles, but Kropotkin found there, nevertheless, one congenial companion in the person of a Russian naturalist named Martiánof, with whom he wandered about the country making botanical and geological collections and discussing scientific questions. To Martiánof's enthusiasm and energy and Kropotkin's sympathy and encouragement, Minusínsk is indebted for its really excellent museum, an institution which not only is the pride of all intelligent Siberians, but is becoming known to naturalists and archaeologists in Europe and the United States.

During the long series of tragic events that culminated in the assassination of Alexander II, Siberia filled up rapidly with political exiles, and the little town of Minusínsk had to take its quota. With the arrival of these newcomers began a stricter system of police supervision. As long as Kropotkin was the only political exile in the place, he was allowed a good deal of freedom, and was not harassed by humiliating police regulations; but when the number of politicals increased to twenty, the difficulty of watching them all became greater, and the authorities thought it necessary, as a means of preventing escapes, to require every exile to report himself at stated intervals to the chief of police and sign his name in a book kept for the purpose. To this regulation Kropotkin refused to submit. "I have lived here," he said to the *ispravnik,* "nearly five years and have not yet made the first attempt to escape. If you think that there is any danger of my running away now, you may send a soldier or a police officer to my house every day to watch me; but after being unjustly exiled to Siberia I don't propose to assist the Government in its supervision of me. I will not report at the police office." The *ispravnik* conferred with the governor of the province, who lived in Krasnoyársk, and by the latter's direction told Kropotkin that if he refused to obey the obnoxious regulation he would be banished to some place lying farther to the northward and eastward, where the climate would be more severe and the life less bearable. Kropotkin, however, adhered to his determination, and appealed to General Sheláshnikof, who was at that time the acting governor-general of Eastern Siberia and who had been on terms of personal friendship with Kropotkin before the latter's banishment. General Sheláshnikof replied in a cool, formal note, insisting upon obedience to the regulation, and warning Kropotkin that further contumacy would have for him disastrous consequences. While this appeal was pending, General Anúchin was appointed governor-general of Eastern Siberia, and, as a last re-sort, Kropotkin wrote to his aged mother in St. Petersburg to see Anúchin previous to the latter's departure for his new post and present to him a petition in her son's behalf. When the aged and heart-broken mother appeared with her petition in General Anúchin's reception-room she was treated with in-sulting brutality. Without reading the petition Anúchin threw it violently on the floor, asked her how she dared to come to him with such a petition from a traitor to his country, and de-clared that if her son "had his deserts he would be cleaning the streets in some Siberian city under guard, instead of walk-ing about at liberty."

By this time all of the other political exiles in Minusínsk had submitted to the new regulation and were reporting at the police office, and Kropotkin was notified by the *isprávnik* that if within a stated time he did not follow their example he would be banished to Túrukhánsk, a wretched settlement of twelve or fifteen houses, situated in the province of Yeniséisk, near the coast of the arctic ocean. Kropotkin, however, still adhered to his resolution, and after a terribly trying interview with his wife, to whom he was devotedly attached, he suc-ceeded in extorting from her a promise to return to European Russia with their young child, and let him go to Túrukhánsk alone. What this promise cost them both in misery I could im-agine from the tears which suffused their eyes when they talked to me about it. At the last moment, however, while Mrs. Kropotkin was making preparations to return to European Russia, she happened to see in the *Siberian Gazette* a letter from some correspondent—a political exile, I think—in Túru-khánsk, describing the loneliness, dreariness, and unhealthfulness of the settlement, the arctic severity of the climate, the ab-sence of all medical aid for the sick, and the many miseries of life in such a place. This completely broke down the wife's fortitude. She went to her husband, convulsed with sobs, and told him that she would send her child to European Russia, or leave it with friends in Minusínsk, but go with him to Túrukhánsk she must and should—to let him go there alone was beyond her strength. "After this," said Prince Kropotkin, "there was nothing for me to do but put a pistol to my head, or yield, and I yielded. I went to the police office, and continued to report there as long as I remained in Minusínsk."

I have related this incident in Prince Kropotkin's Siberian life partly because it seems to have first suggested suicide to him as a means of escape from an intolerable position, and partly because it is in many ways an index to his character. He was extremely sensitive, proud, and high-spirited, and often made a fight upon some point which a cooler, more philosophical man would have taken as one of the natural incidents of his situation.

About two years ago Prince Kropotkin was transferred from Minusínsk to Tomsk, a change which brought him a few hundred miles nearer to European Russia, but which in other respects was not perhaps a desirable one. When I saw him in February he was living simply but comfortably in a rather spacious log house, ten minutes' drive from the European Hotel, and was devoting himself to literary pursuits. He had a good working library of two or three hundred volumes, among which I noticed the astronomical works of Professors Newcomb and Holden, Stallo's *Concepts of Science*, of which he expressed a very high opinion, several volumes of *Smithsonian Reports*, and forty or fifty other American books. His favorite study was astronomy, and in this branch of science he would probably have distinguished himself under more favorable circumstances. After his exile, however, he was not only deprived of instruments, but had great difficulty in obtaining books; his private correspondence was under control, and he was more or less constantly disquieted and harassed by police supervision and searches of his house; so that his completed scientific work was limited to a few articles upon astronomical subjects, written for French and German periodicals. He was a fine linguist, and wrote almost equally well in French, German, and Russian. English he read easily but could not speak.

On the last day before my departure from Tomsk he came to my room, bringing a letter which I had promised to carry for him to one of his intimate friends in western Europe. With the keen sense of honor which was one of his distinguishing characteristics, he brought the letter to me open, so that I might assure myself by reading it that it contained nothing which would compromise me in case the Russian police should find it in my possession. I told him that I did not care to read it, that I would run the risk of carrying anything that he would run the risk of writing—his danger in any case would be greater than mine. He thereupon seated himself at my writing-table to address the envelope. We happened at the moment to be talking of his brother, Pierre Kropotkin, and his pen, taking its suggestion from his thoughts, wrote automatically upon the envelope his brother's name instead of the name of the person for whom the letter was intended. He discovered the error almost instantly, and tearing up the envelope and throwing the fragments upon the floor, he addressed another. Late that evening, after I had gone to bed, there came a knock at my door. I opened it cautiously, and was confronted by Prince Kropotkin. He was embarrassed and confused, and apologized for calling at that late hour, but said that he could not sleep without finding and destroying every fragment of the envelope upon which he had inadvertently written the name of his brother. "This may seem to you," he said, "like absurd timidity, but it is necessary. If the police should discover, as they probably will, that I visited you today, they would not only examine the servants as to everything which took place here, but would collect and fit together every scrap of waste paper found in your room. They would thus find out that I had addressed an envelope to my brother, and would jump at the conclusion that I had written him a letter, and had given it to you for delivery. How this would affect you I don't know, but it would be fatal to me. The least I could expect would be the addition of a year to my term of exile, or banishment to some more remote part of Siberia. I am strictly forbidden to communicate with my brother, and have not heard directly from him or been able to write to him in years." I was familiar enough with the conditions of exile life in Siberia to see the force of these statements, and we began at once a search for the fragments of the envelope. Every scrap of paper on the floor was carefully examined, but the pieces that bore the dangerous name, "Pierre A. Kropotkin," could not be found. At last my traveling companion, Mr. Frost, remembered picking up some torn scraps of paper and throwing them into the slop-basin. We then dabbled in the basin for twenty minutes until we found and burned every scrap of that envelope upon which there was the stroke of a pen, and only then could Prince Kropotkin go home and sleep. "Two years hence," he said to me as he bade me good-night, "you may publish this as an illustration of the atmosphere of suspicion and apprehension in which political exiles live. In two years I hope to be beyond the reach of the Russian police." Poor Kropotkin! In less than two years his hope was realized, but not in the way we then anticipated. I had hardly returned to my home in the United States when the *Eastern Review* of St. Petersburg, a newspaper devoted to the interests and the news of Asiatic Russia, made the following brief announcement:

On the 25th of July, about nine o'clock in the evening, Prince A. A. Kropotkin committed suicide in Tomsk by shooting himself with a revolver. He had been in administrative exile about ten years, and his term of banishment would have expired on the 9th of next September. He had begun to make arrangements for returning to Russia, and had already sent his wife and his three children back to his relatives in the province of Kharkóf. He was devotedly attached to them, and soon after their departure he grew lonely and low-spirited, and showed that he felt very deeply his separation from them. To this reason for despondency must also be added anxiety with regard to the means of subsistence. Although, at one time, a rather wealthy landed proprietor, Prince Kropotkin, during his long period of exile in Siberia, had expended almost his whole fortune; so that on the day of his death his entire property did not amount to three hundred rubles. At the age of forty-five, therefore, he was compelled, for the first time, seriously to consider the question how he should live and support his family—a question which was the more difficult to answer for the reason that a scientific man, in Russia, cannot count upon earning a great deal in the field of literature, and Prince Kropotkin was not fitted for anything else. While under the disheartening influence of these considerations he received, moreover, several telegrams from his relatives which he misinterpreted. Whether he committed suicide as a result of sane deliberation, or whether a combination of circumstances superinduced acute mental disorder, none who were near him at the moment of his death can say.

Of course the editor of the *Eastern Review* was not allowed by the censor to say even one last kind word of the innocent man who had been driven to self-destruction by injustice and exile; but I will say—and say it with all my heart—that in Prince Kropotkin's death Russia lost an honest man, a cultivated scholar, a true patriot, and a most gallant gentleman.

To me perhaps the most attractive and sympathetic of the Tomsk exiles was the Russian author Felix Volkhófski, who was banished to Siberia for life in 1878, upon the charge of "belonging to a society that intends, at a more or less remote time in the future, to overthrow the existing form of government." He was about thirty-eight years of age at the time I made his acquaintance, and was a man of cultivated mind, warm heart, and high aspirations. He knew English well, was familiar with American history and literature, and had, I believe, translated into Russian many of the poems of Longfellow. He spoke to me with great admiration, I remember, of Longfellow's "Arsenal at Springfield," and recited it to me aloud. He was one of the most winning and lovable men that it has ever been my good fortune to know; but his life had been a terrible tragedy. His health had been shattered by long imprisonment in the fortress of Petropávlovsk; his hair was prematurely gray, and when his face was in repose there seemed to be an expression of profound melancholy in his dark-brown eyes. I became intimately acquainted with him and very warmly attached to him; and when I bade him good-by for the last time on my return from Eastern Siberia in 1886, he put his arms around me and kissed me, and said, "George Ivánovich, please don't forget us! In bidding you good-by, I feel as if something were going out of my life that would never again come into it."

A little more than a year after my return to the United States, Volkhófski wrote me a profoundly sad and touching letter, in which he informed me of the death of his wife by suicide. He himself had been thrown out of employment by the suspension of the liberal Tomsk newspaper, the *Siberian Gazette;* and his wife, whom I remember as a pale, delicate, sad-faced woman, twenty-five or thirty years of age, had tried to help him support their family of young children by giving private lessons and by taking in sewing. Anxiety and overwork had finally broken down her health; she had become an invalid, and in a morbid state of mind, brought on by unhappiness and disease, she reasoned herself into the belief that she was an incumbrance, rather than a help, to her husband and her children, and that they would ultimately be better off if she were dead. On the 7th of December, 1887, she put an end to her unhappy life by shooting herself through the head with a pistol. Her husband was devotedly attached to her; and her death, under such circumstances and in such a way, was a terrible blow to him. In his letter to me he referred to a copy of James Russell Lowell's poems that I had caused to be sent to him, and said that in reading "After the Burial" he vividly realized for the first time that grief is of no nationality: the lines, although written by a bereaved American, expressed the deepest thoughts and feelings of a bereaved Russian. He sent me with his letter a small, worn, leather match-box, which had been given by Prince Pierre Kropotkin to his exiled brother Alexander; which the latter had left to Volkhófski; and which Volkhófski had in turn presented to his wife a short time before her death. He hoped, he said, that it would have some value to me, on account of its association with the lives of four political offenders, all of whom I had known. One of them was a refugee in London, another was an exile in Tomsk, and two had escaped the jurisdiction of the Russian Government by taking their own lives.

I tried to read Volkhófski's letter aloud to my wife; but as I recalled the high character and lovable personality of the writer, and imagined what this last blow of fate must have been to such a man—in exile, in broken health, and with three helpless children wholly dependent upon him—the written lines vanished in a mist of tears, and with a choking in my throat I put the letter and the little match-box away.

By means of secret prearranged addresses in Russia and in the United States, I succeeded in maintaining a desultory and precarious correspondence with Mr. Volkhófski until 1889. In the spring of that year I received from him two short letters filled with tidings of misfortune, and then—nothing more. The two letters were, in part, as follows:

Tomsk, February 14, 1889

My dear George Ivánovich:

I write you a few lines first to tell you how weary I am of waiting for a letter from you (although I know that you have not written on account of my warning), and second to give you notice that I sent you some time since a manuscript addressed . . . so that if you have not received it you may make inquiries about it.

You have probably heard before this time of the final suppression of the *Siberian Gazette*. It is hard and it is shameful! You need not hesitate any longer to write whatever you like about it for publication. You will not injure the paper because there is no hope of its resurrection. . . .

My youngest daughter is still sick and has grown so thin that it is painful to look at her. She sleeps badly and often I have to be up all night taking care of her. This, together with constant fear for her life, disorders my nerves terribly, and undermines what health I have left. I am greatly disheartened, too, by loneliness, notwithstanding my children and my friends. The affectionate tenderness of a beloved wife is a thing that some natures find it difficult to do without, no matter what else they may have. It is very hard, sometimes, my dear fellow, to live in this world!

Since it became apparent that I should no longer be able to support myself by newspaper work, I have been looking for some

other occupation or place; but, unfortunately, the present governor is expelling political exiles from all public positions, and
even debarring them, to some extent, from private employment,
by showing such hostility to them that private individuals dare not
give them work for fear of getting into trouble. I do not know
how it will all end. I have sent four manuscripts to St. Petersburg,
but none of them has been published.

My dear George Ivánovich, may you be well and happy! I am
impatiently awaiting your photograph and hope that it will have
your autograph on it. With most cordial remembrances to your
wife, I am

Yours,
FELIX

IRKÚTSK, EASTERN SIBERIA, May 7, 1889

MY DEAR GOOD FRIEND:

How long it is since I last received a line from you, and how
much I have needed your letters! They bring to me all the mental
refreshment and all the gladness that life has for me, and at times
I am sorely in need of them. Fate has dealt me another blow. My
youngest daughter Katie died a month or two since of pneumonia.
She had an attack of bronchitis winter before last which developed
into chronic inflammation of the lungs; but in the spring of 1888 I
took her into the country, where she grew better and began to run
about and play. Unfortunately, however, she was exposed there to
whooping-cough, took the infection, and it ended in acute pneumonia and death. She was about three years old—and such a dear
lovable child! But whose child is not dear and lovable? At any
rate—

No! I can't write any more about it! This is the second time
within a few days that I have tried to write you of her—but I cannot—it hurts me too much! As long as I am busy and can talk or
write of other things, it seems as if the wound were healed; but let
my thoughts once go to her, and I feel such grief and pain that I
don't know what to do with myself.

I must explain to you how I happen to be in Irkútsk. It is a very
simple story. Thanks to the recommendation of some of my
Irkútsk friends I was offered here a place that was suited to my
tastes and abilities, and I hastened to migrate. They will always
know my address here at the post-office.[1]

1. When political offenders sentenced merely to "domestication" or
colonization have been ten years in exile, and have behaved during that

All of your Irkútsk friends send you their regards. I could and would write you a great deal more, but I don't want to detain this letter and will therefore postpone the rest until next time. My warmest regards to your wife. Write me!

Affectionately,

FELIX

After the receipt of this letter I wrote Mr. Volkhófski twice, but I heard from him no more. What had happened to him I could only conjecture; but as month after month passed without bringing any news from him, I felt more and more apprehensive that the sorrows and hardships of his life had been too great for his strength and that the next tidings of him would be the news of his death. At last, in November, 1889, when I had almost given up hope, I was astonished and delighted to receive one day a letter addressed in his familiar handwriting, but stamped with a Canadian stamp and postmarked "Vancouver."

"How did he ever get a letter mailed at Vancouver?" I said to myself, and hastily tearing open the envelope I read the first three lines. They were as follows:

"My dear George Ivánovich: At last I am *free!* I am writing this letter to you not from that land of exile, Siberia, but from free America."

If I had suddenly received a letter postmarked "Zanzibar" from a friend whom I believed to be dead and buried in Minnesota, I could hardly have been more astonished or excited. Volkhófski free and in British Columbia! It seemed utterly incredible; and in a maze of bewilderment I stopped reading the letter to look again at the postmark. It was unquestionably "Vancouver," and as I stared at it I came slowly to a realization of the fact that, in some extraordinary and incomprehensible

---

time in a manner satisfactory to the authorities, it is customary to give them more freedom of movement. They are still kept under police surveillance, but are allowed to go anywhere within the limits of certain provinces. After I returned to the United States, Mr. Volkhófski received a "ticket of leave" of this kind.

way, Volkhófski had not only escaped, but had crossed the Pacific and was within a few days' journey of New York. His letter, which was brief and hurried, merely announced his escape from exile by way of the Amúr River, Vladivostok, and Japan, and his intention of coming to me in Washington as soon as he could be sure of finding me there. In the meantime I need not, he said, feel any anxiety about him, because he still had sixty Mexican silver dollars left, and was with a steamer acquaintance who had taken a warm and generous interest in his fortunes.

At the time when I received this letter I was lecturing six nights a week in New York and New England; but I telegraphed and wrote Volkhófski that I would meet him at the Delavan House in Albany on the morning of Sunday, December 8th. I spoke Saturday night in Utica, took the night express for Albany, and reached the Delavan House about two o'clock. Volkhófski had not yet arrived, and as it was uncertain when he would come I went to bed. Early in the morning a bellboy knocked loudly at my door and handed me a slip of paper upon which, in Volkhófski's handwriting, were the words, "My dear fellow, I am here."

If any of the guests of the Delavan House happened to be passing through that corridor on their way to breakfast three minutes later, they must have been surprised to see, at the door of No. 90, a man with disheveled hair and nothing on but his night-shirt locked in the embrace of a traveler who had not had the time to remove his Pacific-coast sombrero and heavy winter overcoat.

Volkhófski was in better health than I had expected to see him, but his face was worn and haggard, and at times there was a peculiar anxious hunted expression in his eyes which showed that he had recently been under great mental and emotional strain. We talked almost without intermission for twelve hours, and he related to me at length the story of his escape. When he wrote me the last time from Siberia in May, 1889, he was living with his little daughter Véra in Irkútsk, where he had found congenial employment, and where he was trying, by means of hard work, to lighten the sense of loneliness and bereavement that he had felt since the death of his wife and his daughter Katie. Hardly had his life begun to seem once more bearable when there came upon him a new misfortune in the shape of an order from the governor-general to leave the city. He had committed no new offense, and there was no reason, so far as he was aware, for this arbitrary and imperative order; but General Ignátief seemed to be of [the] opinion that the presence of a liberal author and journalist, and moreover a "political," in the city of Irkútsk would be "prejudicial to public tranquillity," and Volkhófski was therefore directed to "move on." Leaving his little daughter Véra with acquaintances in Irkútsk, he proceeded to Tróitskosávsk, a small town on the frontier of Mongolia, where one of his friends, a political exile named Charúshin, had for some time been living. The police there, however, had been apprised of his expulsion from Irkútsk, and assuming, of course, that he must be a very dangerous or a very troublesome man, they hastened to inform him that he could not be permitted to take up his residence in Tróitskosávsk. They did not care whither he went, but he must go somewhere beyond the limits of their jurisdiction. Indignant and disheartened, Volkhófski then resolved to abandon temporarily his little daughter Véra, whom he had left in Irkútsk, and make his escape, if possible, to the United States by way of the Pacific Ocean. He had a little money derived from the sale of a small volume of poems which he had published before leaving Tomsk, and if that should fail before he reached his destination, he determined to work as a stevedore, or a common laborer of some sort, until he should earn enough to go on. His objective point was the city of Washington, where he expected to find me. The nearest seaport on the Pacific where he could hope to get on board a foreign steamer was Vladivostok, about 2800 miles away. The distance to be traversed under the eyes of a suspicious and hostile police was immense; but Volkhófski was cautious, prudent, and experienced, and assuming the character of a retired army officer he set out, with "free" horses, for the headwaters of the Amúr River, where he expected to take a steamer. I cannot, of course, go into details of his difficult and perilous journey from Tróitskosávsk to Strétinsk, from Strétinsk down the Amúr by steamer to Khabarófka, and from Khabarófka up the Ússurí and across Lake Khánka to Vladivostok. It was a journey full of adventures and narrow escapes, and nothing but the coolness, courage, and good fortune of the fugitive carried him through in safety. There were four foreign vessels in the port of Vladivostok at that time, and one of them, a coal steamer was flying the flag of Great Britain. Volkhófski went on board, ascertained that the steamer was bound for Japan, and asked the captain if he would take a passenger who had neither passport nor official permission to leave the empire. The captain hesitated at first, but when Volkhófski related his story, said that he was able and willing to pay for his passage, and exhibited my photograph and letters as proofs of his trustworthiness, the captain consented to take him. A hiding-place was soon found for him, and when the Russian officials came on board to clear the vessel, he was nowhere to be seen. A few hours later the steamer was at sea, and the escaping political exile, as he stood on the upper deck and watched the slow fading of the Siberian coast in the west, drew a long deep breath of relief, and turned his face, with reviving hope, toward the land where a personal opinion concerning human affairs is not regarded as "prejudicial to public tranquillity," and where a man who tries to make the world better and happier is not punished for it with seven years of solitary confinement, eleven years of exile, and the loss of more than half his family.

After having paid his steamer fare from Vladivostok to Nagasaki, and from Nagasaki to Yokohama, Volkhófski found himself in the latter place with hardly money enough to get across the Pacific, and not half enough to reach Washington. He made inquiries concerning vessels about to sail for the western coast of America, and found that the English steamer *Batavia* was on the point of clearing for Vancouver, British Columbia. Going at once on board he asked the purser what the fare to Vancouver would be in the steerage. The officer looked at him for a moment, saw that, although a foreigner, he was unmistakably a gentleman, and then replied, bluntly but not unkindly, "You can't go in the steerage—it's jammed full of Chinese emigrants. Nobody ever goes in the steerage except Chinamen; it's no place for you." Volkhófski replied that the case was urgent—that he must get to British Columbia at once—and as he had not money enough to pay even for a second-class passage, there was nothing for him to do but go third class. The purser finally sold him a steerage ticket, but declared, nevertheless, that a white man could not possibly live for three weeks with opium-smoking Chinese coolies, and that he should put him in some other part of the vessel as soon as possible after leaving port.

Until the *Batavia* had actually sailed and was out of the harbor, Volkhófski did not dare to let the passengers, or even the officers, of the steamer know who he really was and whence he had come. The Japanese were in the habit of giving up Siberian refugees to the Russian authorities; and if it should accidentally become known that he was an escaping political exile, he might be arrested, even in Yokohama, and put on board a Russian man-of-war. He believed that he had narrowly escaped detection and capture in Nagasaki, and he did not intend to run any more risks that could be avoided. At last, however, when the *Batavia* was far at sea, and the coast of Japan had sunk beneath the rim of the western horizon, he told his story to the officers of the ship, and afterward admitted to the passengers with whom he became acquainted that he was an escaped political exile from Siberia. The interest and sympathy excited by his narrative deepened as the officers and passengers became better acquainted with him, and long before the *Batavia* reached Vancouver, he had so completely won the hearts of the whole ship's company that they took up a collection for the purpose of providing him with transportation from Vancouver to the city of Washington. To this collection every soul on board contributed, from the captain down to the steward, the cook, and the boy who cleaned the ship's lamps. More than enough money was obtained to defray his expenses across the continent, and when he left the steamer he had not only the sixty Mexican silver dollars about which he wrote me, but a first-class ticket to Washington, and a cordial invitation from one of the passengers—Mr. Allan Huber of Berlin, Ontario—to stay at his house until my whereabouts could be ascertained.

When Volkhófski met me in Albany, he was terribly anxious with regard to the safety of his nine-year-old daughter Véra, whom he had left with friends in the capital of Eastern Siberia. He feared that, as soon as his escape should become known, the Government would seize the little girl, and either use her as a means of compelling him to return or put her into a state asylum, where she would virtually be lost to him forever.

"If I can only get my little girl," he said to me, "I shall feel as if I had strength and spirit enough to begin a new life; but if I lose her, I may as well give up the struggle."

"We'll get your little girl," I replied, "if we have to resort to fraud, violence, false passports, and kidnapping"— and we *did* get her. In June, 1890, Volkhófski went to London, so as to be nearer the field of operations, and six weeks later I received from him a cablegram saying, "Hurrah! my child has arrived."

In a recent letter to a friend in Buffalo, New York, the well-known English novelist, Hesba Stretton, speaks of Volkhófski and his daughter as follows:

Volkhófski, who escaped from Siberia rather more than a year ago, has been lecturing in England all winter. He has a charming little daughter ten years old who was born in exile. She has been staying for a fortnight with my married sister and her two daughters, and they are quite delighted with her; she is so original and affectionate, and she has had so much tragedy in her short life, which she speaks of now and then as if horrors were a natural part of existence to her. She was brought through Siberia and Russia disguised as a boy. We hope to wean her thoughts from these terrible subjects and give her something of the ordinary joys of girlhood. But her destiny must be a sad one, for she will surely throw in her lot with the revolutionists of Russia, and unless the revolution comes soon our little Véra will spend much of her life in prison and in exile. She was showing Annie how the orthodox Russians hold their thumbs and two fingers pressed together to represent the Trinity during their worship, and then she said, "But God doesn't mind how we hold our fingers, does he?" She was moaning in her sleep one night, and when Daisy woke her she said, "I dreamed there were spies in the room, and I pretended to be asleep till they went to sleep, and then I got up and crept to the cot where my baby brother was. I said, 'Hush! don't make a noise, for there are spies in the room,' and I took him up and went to the door watching the spies all the time, and I opened the door and thère were some men hung up, and my father's head lay on the ground and his body was a little way off covered with a white cloth." Think of that for the dream of a child of ten years, and think how countless are the sorrows and wrongs inflicted by the Czar of Russia and his Government! And they say he is a humane, Christian man. Alas! what horrible things are said to be Christian.

Mr. Volkhófski is now editing in London the newspaper *Free Russia*, the organ of the English society known as "The Friends of Russian Freedom."

The extension of our acquaintance in Tomsk, on one side with Government officials, and on the other with political exiles, led now and then to peculiar and embarrassing situations. A day or two before our departure for Irkútsk, while two of the politicals—Messrs. Volkhófski and Chudnófski—were sitting in our room at the European Hotel, a servant suddenly knocked, threw open the door, and announced his Excellency Actual State Councilor Petukhóf, the governor *pro tem.* of the province. My heart, as the Russians say, went into my fingers' ends. I did not know what relations existed between the banished revolutionists and Vice-Governor Petukhóf. We had called several times upon the latter without referring in any way to our acquaintance with this class of criminals; and in all our intercourse with the Tomsk officials we had treated the subject of political exile with studied indifference, in order to avert suspicion and escape troublesome inquiries. To be then surprised by the vice-governor himself while two prominent politicals were sitting in our room and writing at our table was, to say the least, embarrassing. I had just had time to ask Volkhófski and Chudnófski whether or not I should introduce them to the vice-governor, when the latter, in full uniform, entered the room. There was a curious expression of surprise in his good-humored face as he took in at a glance the situation; but the removal of his heavy overcoat and galoshes gave him an opportunity to recover himself, and as he came forward with outstretched hand to greet Mr. Frost and me there was nothing in his manner to indicate the least annoyance or embarrassment. He shook hands cordially with the two political exiles who had been condemned by a court of justice to penal servitude; began at once a conversation in which they could join, and behaved generally with so much tact and courtesy, that in five minutes we were all chatting together as unceremoniously as if we were old acquaintances who had met accidentally at a club. It was, however, a strangely constituted group: an American newspaper man; an American artist; two political exiles who had been punished with solitary confinement, leg-fetters, and the strait-jacket; and, finally, the highest provincial representative of the Government that had so dealt with these exiles—all meeting upon the common footing of personal character, and ignoring, for the time, the peculiar network of interrelations that united them. Whether or not Vice-Governor Petukhóf reported to the Minister of the Interior that we had made the acquaintance of the political criminals in Tomsk, I do not know—probably not. He seemed to me to be a faithful officer of the Crown, but, at the same time, a man of culture, ability, and good sense; and while he doubtless disapproved of the revolutionary movement, he recognized the fact that among the banished revolutionists were men of education, refinement, and high personal character, who might, naturally enough, attract the attention of foreign travelers.

The number of politicals in Tomsk, at the time of our visit, was about thirty, including six or eight women. Some of them were administrative exiles, who had only just arrived from European Russia; some were *poseléntsi*, or forced colonists, who had been banished originally to "the most remote part" of Siberia, but who had finally been allowed to return in broken health to a "less remote part"; while a few were survivors of the famous "193," who had languished for years in the casemates of the Petropávlovsk fortress, and had then been sent to the plains of Western Siberia.

I was struck by the composure with which these exiles would sometimes talk of intolerable injustice and frightful sufferings. The men and women who had been sent to the province of Yakútsk for refusing to take the oath of allegiance to Alexander III, and who had suffered in that arctic wilderness all that human beings can suffer from hunger, cold, sickness, and bereavement, did not seem to be conscious that there was anything very extraordinary in their experience. Now and then some man whose wife had committed suicide in exile would flush a little and clinch his hands as he spoke of her; or some broken-hearted woman whose baby had frozen to death in her arms on the road would sob at intervals as she tried to tell me her story; but, as a rule, both men and women referred to injustice and suffering with perfect composure, as if they were nothing more than the ordinary accidents of life. Mr. Volkhófski showed me one day, I remember, a large collection of photographs of his revolutionary friends. Whenever a face struck me as being noteworthy, on account of its beauty or character, I would ask whose it was.

"That," he would say quietly, "is Miss A——, once a teacher in a peasant school; she died of prison consumption in Kiev three years ago. The man with the full beard is B——, formerly a justice of the peace in N——; he was hanged at St. Petersburg in 1879. The thin-faced girl is Miss C——, one of the so-called propagandists; she went insane in the House of Preliminary Detention while awaiting trial. The pretty young woman with the cross on the sleeve of her dress is Madame D——, a Red Cross nurse in one of the field hospitals during the late Russo-Turkish war; she was sentenced to twenty years of penal servitude and is now at the mines of Kará. The lady opposite her on the same page is Miss E——, formerly a student in the Beztúzhef medical school for women in St. Petersburg; she cut her throat with a piece of broken glass, after two years of solitary confinement in the fortress."

In this way Mr. Volkhófski went through his whole collection of photographs, suggesting or sketching hastily in a few dry, matter-of-fact words the terrible tragedies in which the originals of the portraits had been actors. He did not show the least emotional excitement, and from his manner it might have been supposed that it was the commonest thing in the world for one's friends to be hanged, sent to the mines, driven insane by solitary confinement, or tortured into cutting their throats with broken glass. His composure, however, was not insensibility, or lack of sympathy. It was rather the natural result of long familiarity with such tragedies. One may become accustomed in time even to the sights and sounds of a field hospital, and the Russian revolutionists have become so accustomed to injustice and misery that they can speak without emotional excitement of things that made my face flush and my heart beat fast with indignation or pity.

"Twice in my life," said a well-known Russian liberal to me, "I have fully realized what it means to be a free citizen. The first time was when I returned to Russia from the United States in 187——, and noticed at the frontier the difference between the attitude taken by the gendarmes toward me and their attitude toward Englishmen who entered the empire with me. The second time was just now, when I saw the effect produced upon you by the story that Mr. B—— was relating to you. That story seemed to you—as I could plainly see from the expression of your face—something awful and almost incredible. To me it was no more surprising or extraordinary than an account of the running-over of a man in the street. As I watched the play of expression in your face—as I was forced to look at the facts, for a moment, from your point of view—I felt again, to the very bottom of my soul, the difference between a free citizen and a citizen of Russia."

In Tomsk we began to feel for the first time the nervous strain caused by the sight of irremediable human misery. Our journey through southwestern Siberia and the Altái had been off the great exile route; the politicals whose acquaintance we had made in Semipalátinsk, Ulbínsk, and Ust Kámenogórsk were fairly well treated and did not seem to be suffering; and it was not until we reached Tomsk that we were brought face to face with the tragedies of exile life. From that time, however, until we recrossed the Siberian frontier on our way back to St. Petersburg, we were subjected to a nervous and emotional strain that was sometimes harder to bear than cold, hunger, or fatigue. One cannot witness unmoved such suffering as we saw in the hospital of the Tomsk forwarding prison, nor can one listen without the deepest emotion to such stories as we heard from political exiles in Tomsk, Krasnoyársk, Irkútsk, and the Trans-Baikál. One pale, sad, delicate woman, who had been banished to Eastern Siberia, and who had there gone down into the valley of the shadow of death, undertook, one night, I remember, to relate to me her experience. I could see that it was agony for her to live over in narration the sufferings and bereavements of her tragic past, and I would gladly have spared her the self-imposed torture; but she was so determined that the world should know through me what Russians endure before they become terrorists, that she nerved herself to bear it, and between fits of half-controlled sobbing, during which I could only pace the floor, she told me the story of her life. It was the saddest story I had ever heard. After such an interview as this with a heart-broken woman—and I had many such—I could neither sleep nor sit still; and to the nervous strain of such experiences, quite as much as to hardship and privation, was attributable the final breaking down of my health and strength in the Trans-Baikál.

Before I left the city of Tomsk for Eastern Siberia, most of my long-cherished opinions with regard to nihilists and the working of the exile system had been completely overthrown. I could not, by any process of readjustment or modification, make my preconceived ideas fit the facts as I found them. In a letter written from Tomsk to the President of the Century Company on the 26th of August, 1885, I indicated the change that had taken place in my views as follows:

The exile system is much worse than I supposed. Mr. ——'s examination of prisons and study of the exile system were extremely superficial. I cannot understand how, if he really went through the Tiumén and Tomsk forwarding prisons, he could have failed to see that their condition and the condition of their wretched inmates were in many respects shocking. Nobody here has tried to conceal it from me. The acting governor of this province said to me very frankly yesterday that the condition of the Tomsk prison is awful, but that he cannot help it. . . . What I have previously written and said about the treatment of the political exiles seems to be substantially true and accurate—at least so far as Western Siberia is concerned—but my preconceived ideas as to their character have been rudely shaken. The Russian liberals and revolutionists whom I have met here are by no means half-educated enthusiasts, crazy fanatics, or men whose mental processes it is difficult to understand. On the contrary, they are simple, natural, perfectly comprehensible, and often singularly interesting and attractive. One sees at once that they are educated, reasonable, self-controlled gentlemen, not different in any essential respect from one's self. When I write up this country for *The Century*, I shall have to take back some of the things that I have said. The exile system is worse than I believed it to be, and worse than I have described it. It isn't pleasant, of course, to have to admit that one has written upon a subject without fully understanding it; but even that is better than trying, for the sake of consistency, to maintain a position after one sees that it is utterly untenable.

CHAPTER SIX

Deportation by "Étape"

I<small>N</small> TOMSK, AND DURING OUR journey from that city to Irkútsk, we had for the first time a satisfactory opportunity to study the life of Siberian exiles on the road. Marching parties of convicts three or four hundred strong leave Tomsk for Irkútsk weekly throughout the whole year, and make the journey of 1040 miles in about three months. *Étapes*, or exile station-houses, stand along the road at intervals of from twenty-five to forty miles; and at every *étape* there is a "convoy command" consisting of a commissioned officer known as the "*nachálnik* of the convoy," two or three under-officers, and about forty soldiers. As the distance from one *étape* to another is too great to be walked in a single day by prisoners in leg-fetters, buildings known as *polu-étapes*, or "half-*étapes*," have been constructed midway between the true *étapes* for the shelter of the convicts at night. These half-way houses are generally smaller than the regular *étapes*, as well as somewhat different from the latter in architectural plan, and they have no "convoy commands." Marching parties are expected to make about 500 versts, or 330 miles, a month, with twenty-four hours of rest every third day. If a party leaves Tomsk Monday morning, it reaches a *polu-étape* Monday night, arrives at the first regular *étape* Tuesday night, and rests in the latter all day Wednesday. Thursday morning it resumes its journey with another convoy, Thursday night it spends in the second *polu-étape*, Friday night it reaches the second regular *étape*, and Saturday it again rests and changes convoy. In this way the party proceeds slowly for months, resting one day out of every three, and changing convoys at every other station. Each prisoner receives five cents a day in money for his subsistence, and buys food for himself from peasants along the road who make a business of furnishing it. The dress of the exiles in summer consists of a shirt and a pair of trousers of coarse gray linen; square foot-wrappers of the same material in lieu of stockings; low shoes or slippers called *katí;* leather ankle-guards to prevent the leg-fetters from chafing; a visorless Glengarry cap; and a long gray overcoat. The dress of female convicts is the same, except that a petticoat takes the place of the trousers. Women and children who voluntarily accompany relatives to Siberia are permitted to wear their own clothing, and to carry severally as much baggage as can be put into a two-bushel bag. No distinction is made between common convicts and political convicts, except that the latter, if they are nobles or belong to one of the privileged classes, receive seven and a half cents a day for their subsistence instead of five, and are carried in *telégas* instead of being forced to walk.[1]

Up to the year 1883 there was no separation of the sexes in marching parties; but since that time an attempt has been made to forward unmarried male prisoners apart from "family parties," and to include in the latter all children and unmarried women. This reform has lessened somewhat the demoralization resulting from the promiscuous association of men, women, and children for months in overcrowded *étapes;* but the state of affairs is still very bad, since even "family parties" contain large numbers of depraved men and boys.

1. At one time politicals were sent to Siberia separately in post vehicles under guard of gendarmes, and were carried to their destinations almost as quickly as if they had been private travelers. That practice, however, has been abandoned on account of its inconvenience and expense, and all politicals are now forwarded with common criminal parties. The result of the change is to prolong by many months the miseries of *étape* life, and to increase enormously the chances of sickness and death.

Three or four days before we left Tomsk for Irkútsk, Mr. Frost and I, by invitation of Captain Gudím, the *nachálnik* of the Tomsk convoy command, drove to the forwarding prison at 7 A.M. to see the departure of a marching party. The morning was cool, but a clear sky gave promise of a warm, sunshiny day. As we drew up before the prison we saw that the party had not yet made its appearance; and, presuming that Captain Gudím was busy, we did not send for him, but sat in our *dróshky* watching the scenes at the gate. On each side of the lead-colored portal was a long wooden bench, upon which half-a-dozen soldiers, in dark green uniforms, were sitting in lazy attitudes, waiting for the party to come out, and amusing themselves meanwhile by exchanging coarse witticisms with three or four female provision-venders, squatted near them on the ground. An occasional high-pitched jingle of chains could be heard from within the inclosure, and now and then half of the double gate was thrown open to admit a couple of fettered convicts carrying water in a large wooden bucket slung between them on a shoulder-pole. Every person who entered the prison yard was hastily searched from head to foot by one of the two sentries at the gate, in order to prevent the smuggling in of prohibited articles, and especially of vodka.

About eight o'clock *telégas* for the transportation of the weak and infirm began to gather in the street in front of the prison; a shabby under-officer who had been lounging with the soldiers on one of the benches rose, yawned, and went discontentedly into the prison courtyard; the soldiers put on their blanket-rolls and picked up their Berdan rifles; and a louder and more continuous jingling of chains from the other side of the palisade announced that the convict party was assembling. At last the prison blacksmith came out, bringing a small portable forge, a lap anvil, a hammer or two, and an armful of chains and leg-fetters, which he threw carelessly on the ground beside him; the soldiers shouldered their guns and took positions in a semicircle so as to form a cordon; an under-officer with the muster-roll of the party in his hand and another with a leather bag of copper coins slung over his shoulder stationed themselves near the gate; and at the word "Ready!" the convicts, in single file, began to make their appearance. The officer with the muster-roll checked off the prisoners as they answered to their names; the blacksmith, with the aid of a soldier, examined their leg-fetters to see that the rivets were fast and that the bands could not be slipped over the heel; and, finally, the second under-officer gave to every man ten cents in copper coin for two days' subsistence between *étapes*. When all of the *kátorzhniki*, or hard-labor convicts, had come out of the prison yard, they arranged themselves in two parallel lines so that they could be conveniently counted, and removed their caps so that the under-officer could see that their heads had been half shaved as required by law. They were then dismissed, and the *poseléntsi*, or penal colonists, went through the same routine—the soldiers of the convoy stepping backward and extending the limits of their cordon as the number of prisoners outside the palisade gradually increased.

At length the whole party, numbering 350 or 400, was assembled in the street. Every prisoner had a gray linen bag in which were stored his scanty personal effects; many of them were provided with copper kettles which dangled from the leather belts that supported their leg-fetter chains; and one convict was carrying to the mines in his arms a small brown dog.

When the whole party had again been counted, and while the gray bags were being put into *telégas*, I availed myself of what seemed to be a favorable opportunity to talk with the prisoners. In a moment, to my great surprise, I was addressed by one of them in good English.

"Who are you?" I inquired in astonishment.

"I am a vagabond," he said quietly and seriously.

"What is your name?"

"Ivan Dontremember," he replied; and then glancing around, and seeing that none of the convoy officers were near, he added in a low tone, "My real name is John Anderson, and I am from Riga."

"How do you happen to know English?" I asked.

"I am of English descent; and, besides that, I was once a sailor, and have been in English ports."

At this point the approach of Captain Gudím put a stop to our colloquy. The number of *brodyágs*, or "vagabonds," in this party was very large, and nearly all of them were runaway convicts of the "Dontremember" family, who had been recaptured in Western Siberia, or had surrendered themselves during the previous winter in order to escape starvation.

"I have no doubt," said Captain Gudím to me, "that there are *brodyágs* in this very party who have escaped and been sent back to the mines half a dozen times."

"Boys!" he shouted suddenly, "how many of you are now going to the mines for the sixth time?"

"There are lots of them," replied several voices; and finally one gray-bearded convict in leg-fetters came forward and admitted that he had made four escapes from the mines, and that he was going into penal servitude for the fifth time. In other words, this man had traversed eight times on foot the distance of nearly 2000 miles between Tomsk and the mines of Kará.

"I know *brodyágs*," said Captain Gudím, "who have been over this road sixteen times in leg-fetters, and who have come back sixteen times across the steppes and through the woods. God only knows how they live through it!"

When one considers that crossing Eastern Siberia thirty-two times on foot is about equivalent to walking twice the circumference of the globe at the equator, one can appreciate the indomitable resolution of these men, and the strength of the influence that draws them toward home and freedom. In the year 1884, 1360 such *brodyágs* were recaptured in Western Siberia and sent back to the mines of the Trans-Baikál, and hundreds more perished from cold and starvation in the forests. M. I. Orfánof, a Russian officer who served many years in Eastern Siberia, says that he once found 200 "Ivan Dontremembers" in a single prison—the prison of Kaidálova, between Chíta and Nérchinsk.

Some of the *brodyágs* with whom I talked were men of intelligence and education. One of them, who was greatly interested in our photographic apparatus, and who seemed to know all about "dry plates," "drop shutters," and "Dallmeyer lenses," asked me how convicts were treated in the United States, and whether they could, by extra work, earn a little money, so as not to leave prison penniless. I replied that in most American penitentiaries they could.

"It is not so," he said, "with us. Naked we go to the mines, and naked we come out of them; and we are flogged while there."

"Oh, no!" said Captain Gudím good-naturedly, "they don't flog at the mines now."

"Yes, they do, your Nobility," replied the *brodyág* firmly but respectfully. "If you are sick or weak, and can't finish your stint, you are given twenty blows with the cat."

I should have been glad to get further information from the *brodyág* with regard to his life at the mines, but just at this moment Captain Gudím asked me if I would not like to see the loading of the sick and infirm, and the conversation was interrupted.

The *telégas* intended for prisoners physically unable to walk were small one-horse carts, without springs of any kind, and with only one seat, in front, for the driver and the guard. They looked to me like the halves of longitudinally bisected hogsheads mounted upon four low wheels, with their concave sides up-permost. More wretchedly uncomfortable vehicles to ride in were never devised. A small quantity of green grass had been put into each one to break the jolting a little, and upon this grass, in every cart, were to sit four sick or disabled convicts.

"All prisoners who have certificates from the doctor, step out!" shouted Captain Gudím, and twenty-five or thirty "in-capables"—some old and infirm, some pale and emaciated from sickness—separated themselves from the main body of convicts in the road. An under-officer collected and examined their certificates, and as fast as their cases were approved they climbed in the *teléga*. One man, although apparently sick, was evidently a malingerer, since, as he took his place in a partly filled *teléga*, he was greeted with a storm of groans and hoots from the whole convict party.

The number of prisoners who, when they leave Tomsk, are unable to walk is sometimes very large. In the year 1884, 658 *telégas* were loaded there with exiles of this class, and if every *teléga* held four persons the aggregate number of "incapables" must have exceeded 2500. Such a state of things, of course, is the natural result of the overcrowding of the Tomsk forwarding prison.

When the sick and infirm had all taken the places assigned them in the invalid carts, Captain Gudím took off his cap, crossed himself and bowed in the direction of the prison church, and then, turning to the convicts, cried, "Well, boys! Go ahead! A safe journey to you!"

"Party—to the right! Party—march!" shouted one of the under-officers, and with a clinking of chains which sounded like the jingling of innumerable bunches of keys the gray throng, hemmed in by a cordon of soldiers, began its long journey of 1800 miles to the mines of the Trans-Baikál. The marching convicts, who took the lead, were closely followed by the *telégas* with the sick and the infirm; next came three or four carts loaded with gray linen bags; and, finally, in a *tárántas* behind the rear guard of soldiers rode Captain Gudím, the *nachálnik* of the convoy. The column moved at the rate of about two miles an hour; and long before noon it was enveloped in a suffocating cloud of dust raised by the shuffling, fetter-incumbered feet of the prisoners. In warm, dry weather, when there is no wind, dust is a source of great misery to marching parties—particularly to the sick, the women, and the children. There is no possible way of escaping it, and when a prisoner is suffering from one of the diseases of the respiratory organs that are so common in *étape* life it is simply torture to sit in a cramped position for six or eight hours in an open *teléga*, breathing the dust raised by the feet of 350 men marching in close column just ahead. I have traced the progress of an invisible exile party more than a mile away by the cloud of dust that hung over it in the air.

Five or six miles from Tomsk the party passed a *chasóvnaya*, or roadside shrine, consisting of an open pavilion, in which hung a ghastly wooden effigy of the crucified Christ. Here, as upon our departure from Tomsk, I noticed that two-thirds of the convicts removed their caps, crossed themselves devoutly, and muttered brief supplications. A Russian peasant may be a highway robber or a murderer, but he continues, nevertheless, to cross himself and say his prayers.

The first halt of the party for rest was made about ten miles from Tomsk, at the entrance to a small village. Here, on a patch of greensward by the roadside, had assembled ten or twelve girls and old women with baskets of provisions, bottles of milk, and jugs of *kvas* for sale to the prisoners. At first sight of these preparations for their refreshment, the experienced *brodyágs*, who marched at the head of the column, raised a joyous shout of *Privál! Privál!*—the exiles' name for the noonday halt. The welcome cry was passed along the line until it reached the last wagon of "incapables," and the whole party perceptibly quickened its pace. A walk of ten miles does not much tire a healthy and unincumbered man; but to convicts who have been in prison without exercise for months, and who are hampered by five-pound leg-fetters united by chains that clash constantly between the legs, it is a trying experience. In less than a minute after the command to halt was given, almost every man in the party was either sitting on the ground or lying upon it at full length. After a short rest, the prisoners began buying food from the provision venders, in the shape of black rye-bread, fish-pies, hard-boiled eggs, milk, and *kvas*, and in half an hour they were all sitting on the ground, singly or in groups, eating their lunch.

When our convicts, after their toilsome march of twenty-nine versts from Tomsk, reached at last the red-roofed *polu-étape* of Semilúzhnaya, they were marshaled in rows in front of the palisade and again carefully counted by the under-officers in order to make sure that none had escaped, and then the wooden gate of the courtyard was thrown wide open. With a wild, mad rush and a furious clashing of chains, more than three hundred men made a sudden break for the narrow gateway, struggled, fought, and crowded through it, and then burst into the *kámeras,* in order to secure, by preoccupation, places on the sleeping-platforms. Every man knew that if he did not succeed in preëmpting a section of the *nári* he would have to lie on the dirty floor, in one of the cold corridors, or out-of-doors; and many prisoners who did not care particularly where they slept sought to secure good places in order to sell them afterward for a few kopeks to less fortunate but more fastidious comrades.

At last the tumult subsided, and the convicts began their preparations for supper. Hot water was furnished by the soldiers of the convoy at an average price of about a cent a teakettleful; soup was obtained by a few from the soldiers' kitchen; and the tired exiles, sitting on the sleeping-platforms or on the floor, ate the black bread, the fish-pies, or the cold boiled meat that they had purchased from the provision venders. The evening meal is sometimes an exceedingly scanty one, on account of the failure of the peasant women to bring to the *étape* for sale an adequate supply of food. They are not obliged to furnish subsistence to convicts on the road, and the exile administration attempts no regulation of the commissariat beyond furnishing the prisoners with money for rations, and allowing the peasants or the soldiers of the convoy to act as purveyors. In times of scarcity it is impossible to buy, with the money given to each exile for his subsistence, enough food to satisfy hunger. In one district of Eastern Siberia, where there had been a partial failure of the crops, the exiles could scarcely buy, with five cents a day, a pound and a half of black rye bread. The *étape* officers complained bitterly to me of the indifference of the Government to the sufferings of the prisoners, and declared that it was unjust and cruel to give men only a pound and a half of black bread, and at the same time force them to march twenty miles a day in leg-fetters, and in bitterly cold weather.

After supper the roll of the party was called in the courtyard; a sentry was stationed at each corner of the quadrangular stockade, and another at the gate; a cheap tallow-candle was lighted in each *kámera; paráshas*, or large uncovered wooden tubs for excrement, were placed in the cells and corridors; and the prisoners were locked up for the night. More than half the party lay on the dirty floors without blankets or pillows, and the atmosphere of the rooms in the course of the night became foul and polluted to an extent that can be imagined only by one who has been present at the opening of the doors in the morning. How human beings, under such conditions, live to reach the mines of Kará, I do not know. It was my intention to ask a friendly *étape* officer to allow me to spend one night with the convicts in an *étape kámera;* but after breathing the air of one of those cells when the doors were reopened in the morning, I decided not to make the experiment.

The second day's march of the convict party that left Tomsk on the 24th of August differed little from the first. A hasty and rather scanty breakfast in the *kámeras* was followed by the assembling of the convicts, the morning roll-call, and the departure; the day's journey was again broken by the *privál*, or halt for lunch; and early in the afternoon the party reached the first regular *étape*, where it was to change convoys and stop one day for rest.

Our convict party spent Tuesday night in the first regular *étape* at Khaldéyeva, under almost precisely the same conditions that prevailed the previous night in the *polu-étape* of Semilúzhnaya. Half the prisoners slept on the floor, under the *nári*, and in the corridors, breathing all night an atmosphere poisoned by carbonic acid and exhalations from uncovered *paráshas*. Wednesday was a day of rest; and the exiles lounged about all day in the prison courtyard, or studied the "record of current events," on the walls of the *étapes*. The sleeping-platforms and the walls of every Siberian *étape* bear countless inscriptions, left there by the exiles of one party for the information or instruction of their comrades in the next. Among such inscriptions are messages and greetings to friends; hints and suggestions for *brodyágs* who meditate escape; names of exiles who have died, broken jail, or been recaptured; and items of news, of all sorts, from the mines and the forwarding prisons. For the convicts, therefore, the *étape* walls are equivalent to so many pages of a daily newspaper, containing an exile directory, open letters, obituary notices, a puzzle department of *brodyág* ciphers, and a personal intelligence column of the highest interest to all "travelers on Government account." One of the first things that an experienced convict does, after his arrival at an *étape*, is to search the walls for news; and his fortunes not infrequently turn upon the direction or the warning contained in a message that he finds there from a comrade who has preceded him. Mr. Gálkine Wrásskoy, chief of the prison administration, has come at last to appreciate the significance and importance of these mural inscriptions, and has recently ordered *étape* officers to see that they are carefully erased. I doubt, however, whether the order will secure the desired results. The prison authorities are constantly outwitted by convicts, and the latter will soon learn to write their messages in places where an *étape* officer would never think of looking for them, but where an experienced convict will discover them at once.

Soon after leaving Tomsk, usually at the first regular *étape*, every exile party organizes itself into an *artél*, or "union," elects a chief or head man known as the *stárosta*, and lays the foundation of an *artél* fund by levying an assessment upon each of its members, and by selling at auction to the highest bidder the privilege of keeping an exile sutler's store or *maidán*, where the prisoners can openly buy tea, sugar, or white bread, and where they can secretly obtain tobacco, playing-cards, and intoxicating liquor. The organization of the party into an *artél* has for its primary object concerted and combined action against the common enemy—the Government. A single convict, regarded as an individual, has neither rights nor means of self-defense. He is completely at the mercy, not only of the higher authorities in the forwarding prisons and the provincial towns, but of every petty officer in the convoy command that escorts him from *étape* to *étape;* and the only way in which he can acquire even a limited power of self-protection is by associating himself with his fellow-convicts in an *artél,* or union. This *artél,* as an organized body, exercises all of its functions in secret, and strives to attain its ends, first, by enforcing solidarity and joint action on the part of all its members, and, secondly, by deceiving, outwitting, or bribing the officers and soldiers with whom it has to deal. It concerts plans of escape; it contrives means of obtaining forbidden articles, such as playing-cards and tobacco; it hires *telégas,* or sleighs, from the peasants along the road, and sells or grants to its members the privilege of riding in them for short distances when exhausted; it bribes executioners to flog lightly, it pays soldiers for smuggling intoxicating liquor into the forwarding prisons and *étapes;* and, finally, it sanctions and enforces all contracts and agreements entered into by its convict members. It is, in short, the body politic of the criminal world; and it fills, in the life of the exile, the same place that the *mir,* or commune, fills in the life of the free peasant. Within the limits of its prison environment the power of the *artél* over its members is absolute. It has its own unwritten laws, its own standards of honor and duty, and its own penal code. Its laws recognize only two crimes—disobedience and disloyalty—and its penal code provides for only one punishment—death. The exile may lie, he may rob, he may murder if he will, provided his action does not affect injuriously the interests of the *artél* to which he belongs; but if he disobeys that organization, or betrays its secrets to the prison authorities—even under the compulsion of the lash—he may count himself as dead already. Siberia is not large enough to furnish a safe hiding-place for the exile who has been unfaithful to his *artél*. More than once, in the large convict prisons, I saw criminals who had been condemned to death as traitors by this merciless Siberian *Vehmgerichte*, who, therefore, dared not associate with their fellow-prisoners, and who were living, by permission of the prison authorities, in the strictest solitary confinement. Over the head of every one of these men hung an invisible sword of Damocles, and sooner or later, in one place or another, it was sure to fall. The records of Russian prisons are full of cases in which the sentence of death pronounced by an *artél* has been executed years afterward, and in a place far removed from the scene of the offense. In one recent case the traitor was choked to death one night, at sea, while on his way in a convict steamer to the island of Saghalín, and in another the informer was found one morning with his throat cut in a Caucasian *étape*.

The prison officials throughout Siberia have long been aware of the existence of this secret criminal organization, but they have never been able to suppress it, and they now give to it a certain sort of recognition—putting up with its inevitable evils and making the most of its merits. A convoy officer, for example, wishes to be able to report to his superior at the end of the year that not a single exile has escaped while in his charge. He summons the *stárosta*, or chief of the *artél*, and says to him, "Call the boys together and tell them, from me, that if the *artél* will agree not to allow any escapes from the party on my beat, I will look the other way when they take off their leg-fetters."[2] The *stárosta* replies, "I hear, sir," and goes back into the *kámera* to lay this proposition before the *artél*. The *artél* accepts it, and every chained convict begins pounding at the ankle-bands of his leg-fetters. The convoy officer, of course, has himself committed a penal offense in entering into this sort

2. The ankle-bands of Russian leg-fetters fit so loosely that when they have been pounded with a stone into the form of an ellipse they can generally be slipped off over the heel. Of course this cannot be done, however, without the connivance of the convoy officers and the soldiers of the guard.

of an agreement, but he knows that the *artél* will never betray him, and he is relieved at once from all anxiety with regard to escapes. If, after the negotiation of such a treaty, an exile should attempt to get away from the party within the limits of that officer's jurisdiction, he would have to answer for it to the *artél*, and sooner or later he would pay dearly—perhaps with his life—for thus breaking faith and dishonoring the organization of which he was a member. The late Colonel Zagárin, inspector of exile transportation for Eastern Siberia, told me that he himself had often made a substantial contribution to the fund of an exile *artél* merely in order to secure from the latter a promise that no attempts to escape should be made within the limits of his jurisdiction. Such promises, he said, were always faithfully observed by the *artél* in its corporate capacity, and were rarely disregarded even by individuals. If, however, an inexperienced "first-timer," tempted by a favorable opportunity, should try to escape, in defiance of the *artél's* prohibition, the veterans of the party, namely, the *brodyágs*, would always undertake either to recapture the fugitive, or to bring in some other runaway convict as a substitute, and thus save the honor of the *artél*. He could not remember a single case, he said, in which the *artél* had broken faith. It must not be supposed, however, that the prison commune, in such dealings with the authorities, is actuated by any high or honorable motives. In keeping its promise, in enforcing solidarity, and in punishing disloyalty and disobedience with death, it is merely protecting its own existence and securing what a majority of its members believe to be the greatest good of the greatest number. It has no sentimental regard for truthfulness or faithfulness in the abstract. It simply knows that, at certain times and in certain circumstances, honesty is the best policy, and then it enforces honesty under penalty of death. If, however, circumstances so change as to render dishonesty the best policy, then the *artél* sanctions and compels the practice of deception, fraud, untruthfulness, and treachery, under the same tremendous penalty.

One of the most important functions of the exile *artél* is the enforcement of agreements entered into by its members, and particularly agreements to exchange names and identities. Every exile party is made up of two great classes, namely: A, criminals sentenced to hard labor with imprisonment; and B, criminals sentenced merely to forced colonization without imprisonment. Every convict in class "A" strives to escape the hard labor and the imprisonment by exchanging his name and identity for the name and identity of some convict in class "B." It would seem, at first thought, as if the difficulties in the way of such a transaction would be virtually insuperable. It is not only strictly forbidden by law, but it is a transaction in which one of the parties, apparently, gets all the benefit. Why should convoy officers allow such exchanges of names, and why should the colonist be willing to go to the mines in the place of the hard-labor convict, even if permitted to do so? The difficulties are only apparent, and the questions are easily answered. The convicts in every marching party that leaves Tomsk for Eastern Siberia number about 400, and they change convoy every third day. It is utterly impossible for a convoy officer to so familiarize himself, in three days, with the faces of 400 convicts, that he can tell one from another. If Ivan Pávlof answers to the name of Mikháiel Ivánof at the roll-call of the party, he virtually becomes Mikháiel Ivánof. The convoy officer does not know either of them by sight, and even if he called the roll himself, and looked attentively at every man, he would not notice the substitution. So far as the authorities are concerned, therefore, names and identities can be exchanged without the least difficulty or danger. The willingness of the colonist to exchange names with the hard-labor convict and go into penal servitude in the latter's stead may be explained almost as easily.

In every exile party there are a few reckless, improvident, hard-drinking peasants who have been condemned to forced colonization. When one of these poor wretches has spent all his money, and perhaps has gambled away all of his clothing and mortgaged his food-allowance for weeks in advance, he gets into such a condition that for five or ten rubles and a bottle of vodka he will sell his very soul. The hard-labor convict, who is generally a bold, enterprising, experienced recidivist, and a man, moreover, who has won and saved some money on the road, then approaches the hungry, thirsty, half-naked, and wholly destitute colonist, and says to him, "If you will exchange names with me and go in my place to the mines, I'll give you my warm overcoat, five rubles in money, and a bottle of vodka. You won't have to stay at the mines long. After I have had time to reach your place of colonization and run away, you can tell the *nachálnik* at the mines who you really are, and say that you have been sent there by mistake. He will make inquiries, and as soon as he finds out that you are not me, he will send you back to your place of colonization; and then we'll both be all right."

The persuasive eloquence of the hard-labor convict, backed by five rubles, a warm coat, and a bottle of vodka, is generally too much for the resolution of the unfortunate colonist. He consents to the proposed exchange of names and identities, and the *artél* is at once convened to note, sanction, and mentally record the transaction. At the next and at every subsequent roll-call of the party, the hard-labor convict answers to the name of the colonist, and the colonist must answer to the name of the hard-labor convict. The more dangerous criminal, who, perhaps, should serve out a life sentence at the mines for murder, is turned loose in some East-Siberian village from which he immediately makes his escape, while the petty thief, drunkard, or wife-beater goes into penal servitude at the mines of Nérchinsk or Kará.

Although the exchanging of names has been practiced by convicts in Siberia from time immemorial, and although it is manifestly unjust, prejudicial to the interests of the state and detrimental in the highest degree to the welfare of the Siberian people, all suggestions made by experienced *étape* officers with regard to methods of stopping it have been disregarded. Ten years ago Colonel Zagárin, the inspector of exile transportation for Eastern Siberia, made a report upon the subject to Governor-General Anúchin in which he recommended that hard-labor convicts, as a class, be made distinguishable from forced colonists, as a class, by means of a different shaving of the head. Both classes now have their heads half shaven on the same side. Colonel Zagárin suggested that the heads of all hard-labor convicts be shaved on the right side and of all forced colonists on the left. The exchanging of names and identities between the two classes would then become impossible, for the reason that every *étape* officer and every soldier of the convoy could see at a glance to which class any particular criminal belonged. The forced colonist Ivan Pávlof might answer, as before, to the name of the hard-labor convict Mikháiel Ivánof at roll-call, but it would be perfectly useless to do so, because the cut of his hair would at once betray him.

"What did the governor-general say to your suggestion?" I inquired, when Colonel Zagárin finished telling me about this report.

"Nothing," he replied. "It was never acted upon. Anúchin referred, even in his report to the Gossudár, to the bad results of this practice of changing names, but he never tried to stop it in the way that I suggested."

"What preposterous stupidity!" I exclaimed. "The method is simplicity itself, it would cost nothing, and it would make the exchanging of names absolutely impossible. What conceivable reason could Anúchin have for not adopting it?"

"I don't know any reason," replied Colonel Zagárin, "except that he didn't happen to think of it himself. Our high officials don't take suggestions very kindly—especially from their subordinates."

Since my return from Siberia an attempt has been made to secure certainty of identification in criminal parties by means of small photographs of the convicts attached to their *statéini spíski*, but I do not know how it has resulted.

Deportation by *étape* in Siberia is attended by miseries and humiliations of which a European or an American reader can form only a faint conception. I had many opportunities, during our journey from Tomsk to Irkútsk, to see convicts on the march in sunshine and in rain; to inspect the wretched *étapes* in which they were herded like cattle at night; to visit the lazarets where they sometimes lie sick for weeks without skilled medical attention or proper care; and to talk with intelligent officers of the prison department who had been familiar for years with every feature of the exile system. The result of my investigation was a deliberate conviction that the suffering involved in the present method of transporting criminals to Siberia is not paralleled by anything of the kind that now exists in the civilized world outside of the Russian Empire. Some of this suffering is due, of course, to negligence, indifference, or official corruption; but a very large part of it is the necessary result of a bad and cruel system, and it can be removed only by the complete abolition of the system itself, and by the substitution for it of imprisonment for life, or for a term of years, in European Russia. Only a moment's reflection is needed to satisfy anyone that, even under the most favorable circumstances, six or eight thousand men, women, and children cannot march two thousand miles across such a country as Eastern Siberia without suffering terrible hardships. The physical exposure alone is enough to break down the health and strength of all except the most hardy, and when to such inevitable exposure are added insufficient clothing, bad food, the polluted air of overcrowded *étapes,* and the almost complete absence of medical care and attention, one is surprised, not that so many die, but that so many get through alive.

The exile parties that leave Tomsk in July and August are overtaken by the frosts and the cold rains of autumn long before they reach Irkútsk. They have not yet been supplied with winter clothing, and most of them have no better protection from rain, sleet, or cold wind than that afforded by a coarse linen shirt, a pair of linen drawers, and a gray frieze overcoat. Imagine such a party marching in a cold, northeast storm along the road over which we passed between Áchinsk and Krasnoyársk. Every individual is wet to the skin by the drenching rain, and the nursing women, the small children, and the sick lie quivering on water-soaked straw in small, rude *telégas*, without even a pretense of shelter from the storm. The mud, in places, is almost knee-deep, and the wagons wallow through it at the rate of about two miles an hour. The bodies of the marching convicts, kept warm by the exertion of walking in heavy leg-fetters, steam a little in the raw, chilly air, but a large number of the men have lost or removed their shoes, and are wading through the freezing mud with bare feet. The Government, influenced, I presume, by considerations of economy, furnishes its exiles in summer and fall with low shoes or slippers called *kati*, instead of with boots. These *kati* are made by contract and by the thousand, of the cheapest materials, and by the Government itself are expected to last only six weeks. As a matter of fact they frequently do not last one week.

A high officer of the exile administration told me that it was a common thing to see exiles leave Tomsk or Krasnoyársk with new *kati* and come into the second *étape* barefooted—their shoes having gone to pieces in less than two days. Even when the *kati* hold out for their nominal period of service, they are not fitted to the feet of the wearer; they cannot be secured, because they have no laces; they are so low that they fill with mire and water and are constantly sticking fast or coming off in mud-holes; and on such a road as that between Áchinsk and Krasnoyársk scores of convicts either remove their shoes and hang them around their necks, or throw them away altogether, and walk for days at a time with bare feet, through mud whose temperature is little above the freezing-point.

As the party, wet, tired, and hungry, approaches one of the little log villages that lie along its route, the *stárosta*, or chief of the *artél*, asks the convoy officer to allow them to sing the "begging song" as they pass through the settlement. The desired permission is granted; certain prisoners are designated to receive the expected alms; the convicts all remove their gray caps; and entering the village with a slow, dragging step, as if they hardly had strength enough to crawl along, they begin their mournful appeal for pity.

I shall never forget the emotions roused in me by this song when I heard it for the first time. We were sitting, one cold, raw autumnal day, in a dirty post-station on the great Siberian road, waiting for horses. Suddenly my attention was attracted by a peculiar, low-pitched, quavering sound which came to us from a distance, and which, although made apparently by human voices, did not resemble anything that I had ever before heard. It was not singing, nor chanting, nor wailing for the dead, but a strange blending of all three. It suggested vaguely the confused and commingled sobs, moans, and entreaties of human beings who were being subjected to torture, but whose sufferings were not acute enough to seek expression in shrieks or high-pitched cries. As the sound came nearer we went out into the street in front of the station-house and saw approaching a chained party of about a hundred bare-headed convicts, who, surrounded by a cordon of soldiers, were marching slowly through the settlement, singing the "exiles' begging song." No attempt was made by the singers to pitch their voices in harmony, or to pronounce the words in unison; there were no pauses or rests at the ends of the lines; and I could not make out any distinctly marked rhythm. The singers seemed to be constantly breaking in upon one another with slightly modulated variations of the same slow, melancholy air, and the effect produced was that of a rude fugue, or of a funeral chant, so arranged as to be sung like a round or catch by a hundred male voices, each independent of the others in time and melody, but all following a certain scheme of vocalization, and taking up by turns the same dreary, wailing theme. The words were as follows:

> Have pity on us, O our fathers!
> Don't forget the unwilling travelers,
> Don't forget the long-imprisoned.

Feed us, O our fathers—help us!
Feed and help the poor and needy!
Have compassion, O our fathers!
Have compassion, O our mothers!
For the sake of Christ, have mercy
On the prisoners—the shut-up ones!
Behind walls of stone and gratings,
Behind oaken doors and padlocks,
Behind bars and locks of iron,
We are held in close confinement.
We have parted from our fathers,
From our mothers;
We from all our kin have parted,
We are prisoners;
Pity us, O our fathers!

If you can imagine these words, half sung, half chanted, slowly, in broken time and on a low key, by a hundred voices, to an accompaniment made by the jingling and clashing of chains, you will have a faint idea of the *milosérdnaya*, or "exiles' begging song." Rude, artless, and inharmonious as the appeal for pity was, I had never in my life heard anything so mournful and depressing. It seemed to be the half-articulate expression of all the grief, the misery, and the despair that had been felt by generations of human beings in the *étapes*, the forwarding prisons, and the mines.

As the party marched slowly along the muddy street between the lines of gray log houses, children and peasant women appeared at the doors with their hands full of bread, meat, eggs, or other articles of food, which they put into the caps or bags of the three or four shaven-headed convicts who acted as alms-collectors. The jingling of chains and the wailing voices of the exiles grew gradually fainter and fainter as the party passed up the street, and when the sounds finally died away in the distance, and we turned to reënter the post-station, I felt a strong sense of dejection, as if the day had suddenly grown colder, darker, and more dreary, and the cares and sorrows of life more burdensome and oppressive.

At the first halt that a party makes after passing through a village, the food that has been collected is distributed and eaten, and the convicts, somewhat refreshed, resume their march. Late in the evening they arrive, wet and weary, at an *étape*, where, after supper and the roll-call, they are locked up in the close, unventilated *kámeras* for the night. Most of them are in a shiver—or, as they sometimes call it, a "gypsy sweat"—from cold and from long exposure to rain; but they have neither dry clothing to put on nor blankets with which to cover themselves, and must lie down upon the hard plank *nári*, or upon the floor, and seek warmth in close contact with one another. Some of them have, perhaps, a change of clothing in their gray linen bags, but both bags and clothing have been exposed for eight or ten hours to a pouring rain, and are completely soaked through. If the Government really cared anything about the comfort or health of exiles on the road, it would furnish convoy officers with tarpaulins or sheets of oilcloth to put over and protect the exiles' baggage in rainy weather. This would add a mere trifle to the cost of exile transportation, and it would make all the difference between life and death to hundreds of weak or half-sick human beings, who come into an *étape* soaked to the skin after a march of twenty miles in a cold rain, and who have no dry clothing to put on. The very money spent for the burial of the poor wretches who die from croup, pleurisy, or pneumonia, as a result of sleeping in wet clothes on the road, would buy a substantial tarpaulin for every exile baggage-wagon in Siberia— and yet the tarpaulins are not bought. If it be asked why not, I can only say, because the officials who care have not the power, and the officials who have the power do not care. I went through Siberia with the words "Why so?" and "Why not?" upon my lips, and this, in effect, was the answer that I everywhere received.

"I have recommended again and again," said a high officer of the exile administration to me, "that the convicts be taken to their destinations in summer and in wagons, instead of being obliged to walk throughout the whole year. I have shown conclusively, by exact figures and carefully prepared estimates, that the transportation of exiles from Áchinsk to Irkútsk in wagons, and in summer, would not only be infinitely more merciful and humane than the present method of forwarding them on foot the year around, but would actually cost fourteen rubles less per man, on account of the saving in time, food, and winter clothing."

"Why, then, is it not done?" I inquired.

His only reply was a significant shrug of the shoulders.

"I have repeatedly protested," said another exile officer, "against the acceptance, from dishonest contractors, of articles of exile clothing that did not correspond with the specification or the samples; but I have accomplished nothing. Shoes so worthless that they fall to pieces in two days are accepted in place of the good shoes that ought to be furnished, and the exiles go barefooted. All that I can do is to lay before my superiors the facts of the case."

While in the city of Irkútsk, I called one day upon Mr. Petróf, the acting-governor of the province, and found in his office Colonel Zagárin, the inspector of exile transportation for Eastern Siberia. The latter had brought to the governor some *kati*, or exile shoes, that had just been accepted by the provincial administration, and was exhibiting them side by side with the original samples that had been furnished as models to the contractor. The accepted shoes did not resemble the models, they were perfectly worthless, and might have been made, I think, by the thousand, for ten or fifteen cents a pair. Colonel Zagárin was protesting against the acceptance of such shoes, and was asking for an investigation. The fraud was so manifest and so glaring, and the results of it would be so calamitous to thousands of poor wretches who would wear these *kati* for a day or two and then be forced to walk barefooted over icy ground or through freezing mud, that I thought something would certainly be done about it. Upon my return from the mines of the Trans-Baikál five months later, I asked Colonel Zagárin what had been the result of the protest that he had made to the governor in my presence. He replied, "It had no result."

"And were those shoes issued to marching exile parties?"

"They were."

I asked no more questions.

I could furnish innumerable illustrations of the way in which the life of convicts on the road is made almost intolerable by official indifference or fraud; but it is perhaps unnecessary to do so. The results of that life are shown by the records of the hospitals and lazarets, and by the extraordinarily high rate of mortality in exile parties. Hundreds of prisoners, of both sexes and all ages, fall sick on the road, and after being carried for a week, or perhaps two weeks, in jolting *telégas*, are finally left to recover or to die in one of the *étape* lazarets between Áchinsk and Irkútsk. It seems barbarous, and of course it is barbarous, to carry forward in a springless *teléga*, regardless of weather, an unfortunate man or woman who has been taken sick with pneumonia or typhus fever on the road; but, under existing circumstances, there is nothing else for a convoy officer to do. He and his soldiers must go on with the exile party, and he cannot leave the sick for five days in a deserted *étape* wholly without attendance. He is forced, therefore, to carry them along until they either die or reach one of the widely separated lazarets, where they can be left and cared for.

Many times on the great Siberian road, when I had been jolted until my pulse had become imperceptible at the wrist from weakness, sleeplessness, and incessant shocks to the spinal cord and the brain, and when it seemed to me that I could endure no more, I maintained my grip by thinking of the hundreds of exiled men and women who, sick unto death, had been carried over this same road in open *telégas;* who had endured this same jolting while their heads ached and throbbed with the quick pulses of fever; who had lain for many hours at a time on water-soaked straw in a pitiless storm while suffering from pneumonia, and who had nothing to sustain them except the faint hope of reaching at last some fever-infected lazaret. If men can bear all this, I thought, we ought not to complain of our trivial hardships, nor break down under a little unusual fatigue.

It is not surprising that exiles sometimes endeavor to escape from a life so full of miseries as this by making a break for liberty between *étapes*. The more experienced *brodyágs*, or recidivists, generally try to get away by exchanging names and identities with some forced colonist who is soon to reach his destination; but now and then two or three daring or desperate convicts attempt to escape "with a hurrah"—that is, by a bold dash through the line of soldiers. They are instantly fired upon, and one or more of them is usually brought to the ground. The soldiers have a saying that "a bullet will find a runaway," and a slug from a Berdan rifle is always the first messenger sent after a fugitive who tries to escape "with a hurrah." Now and then, when the party happens to be passing through a dense forest, the flying convicts get under cover so quickly that the soldiers can only fire into the bushes at random, and in such cases the runaways make good their escape. As soon as they reach a hiding-place they free themselves from their leg-fetters by pounding the circular bands into long ellipses with a stone and slipping them over their heels, and then join some detachment of the great army of *brodyágs* which is constantly marching westward through the woods in the direction of the Urals.

The life of exiles on the road, which I have tried to roughly sketch, continues, with little to break its monotony, for many months. In sunshine and in storm, through dust and through mud, the convicts march slowly but steadily eastward, crossing the great Siberian rivers on pendulum ferry-boats; toiling up the sides of forest-clad mountains in drenching rains, wading through mire in swampy valleys; sleeping every night in the heavy mephitic atmosphere of overcrowded *étapes*, and drawing nearer, day by day, to the dreaded mines of the Trans-Baikál.

CHAPTER SEVEN

A Visit to a Lamasery

O<small>N A BAD, ROUGH ROAD AN EAST</small> Siberian Teléga will simply jolt a man's soul out in less than twenty-four hours. Before we had traveled sixty miles in the Trans-Baikál I was so exhausted that I could hardly sit upright; my head and spine ached so violently, and had become so sensitive to shock, that every jolt was as painful as a blow from a club; I had tried to save my head by supporting my body on my bent arms until my arms no longer had any strength; and when we reached the post-station of Ílinskaya, at half-past ten o'clock Saturday night, I felt worse than at any time since crossing the Urals. After drinking tea and eating a little bread, which was all that we could get, we immediately went to bed, Frost lying on the floor near the oven, while I took a wooden bench beside the window. After a long struggle with parasitic vermin, I finally sank into a doze. I was almost immediately awakened by the arrival of an under-officer traveling on a Government *padarózhnaya*. Candles were lighted; the officer paced back and forth in our room, talking loudly with the station-master about the condition of the roads; and sleep, of course, was out of the question. In half an hour he went on with fresh horses, the lights were again put out, and we composed ourselves for slumber. In twenty minutes the post arrived from Irkútsk. The transferring of twelve *teléga*-loads of mailbags from one set of vehicles to another, and the changing of about thirty horses, caused a general hubbub which lasted another hour. Every time the door was opened there was a rush of cold air into the overheated room, and we alternated between a state of fever and a state of chill. About half-past one o'clock in the morning the post finally got away, with much shouting and jangling of bells, the lights were put out, and the station again quieted down. We had hardly closed our eyes when the door was thrown wide open, and somebody stalked in shouting lustily in the dark for the station-master. This party of travelers proved to be a man, his wife, and a small baby with the croup. The woman improvised a bed for the infant on two chairs, and then she and her husband proceeded to drink tea. The hissing of the *samovár*, the rattling of dishes, the loud conversation, and the croupy coughing of the child kept us awake until about four o'clock, when this party also went on and the lights were once more extinguished. All the bedbugs in the house had by this time ascertained my situation, and in order to escape them I went and lay down on the floor beside Frost. In the brief interval of quiet that followed I almost succeeded in getting to sleep, but at half-past four there was another rush of cold air from the door, and in came two corpulent merchants from the lower Amúr on their way to Irkútsk. They ordered the *samovár*, drank tea, smoked cigarettes, and discussed methods of gold-mining until half-past five, when, as there were no horses, they began to consider the question of taking a nap. They had just decided that they would lie down for a while when the jangling of horse-bells in the courtyard announced another arrival, and in came a white-bearded old man with a shotgun. Where he was going I don't know; but when he ordered the *samovár* and began an animated conversation with the two merchants about gristmills I said to Frost, with a groan, "It's no use. I haven't had a wink of sleep, I've been tormented by bedbugs, I've taken cold from the incessant opening of that confounded door and have a sharp pain through one lung, and I am going to get up and drink tea." It was then broad daylight. The white-bearded old man with the shotgun invited us to take tea with him. We talked about the newly discovered Mongolian gold placer known as the "Chinese California," which was then attracting the attention of the Siberian public, and under the stimulating influence of social intercourse and hot tea I began to feel a little less miserable and dejected.

About half-past ten o'clock we finally obtained horses, put our baggage into another rough, shallow *teléga*, and resumed our journey. The night had been cold, and a white frost lay on the grass just outside the village; but as the sun rose higher and higher the air lost its chill, and at noon we were riding without our overcoats. About ten versts from Ílinskaya the road turned more to the southward and ran up the left bank of the Selengá River. The bold bluff on the right was a solid mass of canary-colored birches, with here and there a dull-red poplar; the higher and more remote mountains on the left, although not softened by foliage, were

> . . . bathed in the tenderest purple of distance,
> And tinted and shadowed by pencils of air;

while in the foreground, between the bluff and the mountains, lay the broad, tranquil river, like the Highland lake, reflecting in its clear depths the clumps of colored trees on its banks and the soft rounded outlines of its wooded islands. The valley of the Selengá between Ílinskaya and Vérkhni Údinsk seemed to me to be warmer and more fertile than any part of the Trans-Baikál that we had yet seen. The air was filled all the afternoon with a sweet autumnal fragrance like that of ripe pippins; the hillsides were still sprinkled with flowers, among which I noticed asters, forget-me-nots, and the beautiful lemon-yellow alpine poppy; the low meadows adjoining the river were dotted with haystacks and were neatly fenced; and the log houses and barns of the Buriát farmers, scattered here and there throughout the valley, gave to the landscape a familiar and homelike aspect.

If we had felt well, and had had a comfortable vehicle, we should have enjoyed this part of our journey very much; but as the result of sleeplessness, insufficient food, and constant jolting, we had little capacity left for the enjoyment of anything. We passed the town of Vérkhni Údinsk at a distance of two or three miles and reached Múkhinskoe, the next station on the Kiákhta road, about seven o'clock in the evening. Mr. Frost seemed to be comparatively fresh and strong; but I was feeling very badly, with a pain through one lung, a violent headache, great prostration, and a pulse so weak as to be hardly perceptible at the wrist. I did not feel able to endure another jolt nor to ride another yard; and although we had made only thirty-three miles that day we decided to stop for the night. Since landing in the Trans-Baikál we had had nothing to eat except bread, but at Múkhinskoe the station-master's wife gave us a good supper of meat, potatoes, and eggs. This, together with a few hours of troubled sleep which the fleas and bedbugs permitted us to get near morning, so revived our strength that on Monday we rode seventy miles, and just before midnight reached the village of Selengínsk, near which was situated the lamasery of Goose Lake.

On the rough plank floor of the cold and dirty post-station house in Selengínsk we passed another wretched night. I was by this time in such a state of physical exhaustion that in spite of bedbugs and of the noise made by the arrival and departure of travelers I lost consciousness in a sort of stupor for two or three hours. When I awoke, however, at daybreak I found one eye closed and my face generally so disfigured by bedbug bites that I was ashamed to call upon the authorities or even to show myself in the street. Cold applications finally reduced the inflammation, and about ten o'clock I set out in search of the Buriát chief of police, Khainúief Munkú, who had been recommended to us as a good Russian and Buriát interpreter, and a man well acquainted with the lamasery that we desired to visit. I found Khainúief at the office of the district *isprávnik*, where he was apparently getting his orders for the day from the *isprávnik*'s secretary. He proved to be a tall, athletic, heavily built Buriát, about sixty years of age, with a round head, close-

ly cut iron-gray hair, a thick bristly mustache, small, half-
closed Mongol eyes, and a strong, swarthy, hard-featured, and
rather brutal face. He was dressed in a long, loose Buriát gown
of some coarse grayish material, girt about the waist with a
sash, and turned back and faced at the wrists with silk. His
head was partly covered with a queer Mongol felt hat, shaped
like a deep pie-dish, and worn with a sort of devil-may-care
tilt to one side.

I introduced myself to the *ispravnik*'s secretary, exhibited
my open letters, and stated my business. "This is Khainúief
Munkú," said the secretary, indicating the Buriát officer; "he
can go to the lamasery with you if he likes."

As I looked more closely at the hard-featured, bullet-headed
chief of police, it became apparent to me that he had been
drinking; but he had, nevertheless, the full possession of his
naturally bright faculties, and the severe judicial gravity of his
demeanor as he coolly defrauded me out of six or eight rubles
in making the necessary arrangements for horses excited my
sincere admiration. For his services as interpreter and for the
use of three horses I paid him seventeen rubles, which was
more than the amount of his monthly salary. The money, however, was well invested, since he furnished us that day with
much more than seventeen rubles' worth of entertainment.

About an hour after my return to the post-station, Khainúief,
in a peculiar clumsy gig called a *sidéika*, drove into the courtyard. He was transfigured and glorified almost beyond recognition. He had on a long, loose, ultramarine-blue silk gown
with circular watered figures in it, girt about the waist with a
scarlet sash and a light-blue silken scarf, and falling thence to
his heels over coarse cowhide boots. A dishpan-shaped hat of
bright red felt was secured to his large round head by means
of a colored string tied under his chin, and from this red hat
dangled two long narrow streamers of sky-blue silk ribbon.
He had taken six or eight more drinks, and was evidently in
the best of spirits. The judicial gravity of his demeanor had
given place to a grotesque middle-age friskiness, and he looked

like an intoxicated Tatar prize-fighter masquerading in the gala dress of some color-loving peasant girl. I had never seen such an extraordinary chief of police in my life, and could not help wondering what sort of a reception would be given by his Serene Highness the Grand Lama to such an interpreter.

In a few moments the ragged young Buriát whom Khainúief had engaged to take us to the lamasery made his appearance with three shaggy Buriát horses and a rickety old *pavóska* not half big enough to hold us. I asked Khainúief if we should carry provisions with us, and he replied that we need not; that we should be fed at the lamasery. "But," he added, with a grin and a leer of assumed cunning, "if you have any insanity drops don't fail to take them along; insanity drops are always useful."

When we had put into the *pavóska* our blankets, sheepskin overcoats, the bread-bag, and my largest liquor-flask, Frost and I took seats at the rear of the vehicle with our legs stretched out on the bottom, and Khainúief, who weighed at least two hundred pounds, sat on our feet. Not one of us was comfortable; but Frost and I had ceased to expect comfort in an East Siberian vehicle, while Khainúief had been so cheered and inebriated by the events of the morning, and was in such an *exalté* mental condition, that mere physical discomfort had no influence upon him whatever. He talked incessantly; but noticing after a time that we were disposed to listen rather than to reply, and imagining that our silence must be due to the overawing effect of his power and glory, he said to me with friendly and reassuring condescension, "You needn't remember that I am the chief of police; you can treat me and talk to me just as if I were a private individual."

I thanked him for his generous attempt to put us at our ease in his august presence, and he rattled on with all sorts of nonsense to show us how gracefully he could drop the mantle of a dread and mighty chief of police and condescend to men of low degree.

About five versts from the town we stopped for a moment to change positions, and Khainúief suggested that this would be a good time to try the "insanity drops." I gave him my flask, and after he had poured a little of the raw vodka into the palm of his hand and thrown it to the four cardinal points of the compass as a libation to his gods, he drank two cupfuls, wiped his wet, bristly mustache on the tail of his ultramarine-blue silk gown, and remarked with cool impudence, "Prostáya kabách-naya!" ("Common gin-mill stuff!") I could not remember the Russian equivalent for the English proverb about looking a gift-horse in the mouth, but I suggested to Khainúief that it was not necessary to poison himself with a second cupful after he had discovered that it was nothing but "common gin-mill stuff." I noticed that poor as the stuff might be he did not waste any more of it on his north-south-east-and-west gods. The raw, fiery spirit had less effect upon him than I anticipated, but it noticeably increased the range of his self-assertion and self-manifestation. He nearly frightened the life out of our wretched driver by the fierceness with which he shouted "Yábo! Yábo!" ("Faster! faster!"), and when the poor driver could not make his horses go any faster, Khainúief sprang upon him, apparently in a towering rage, seized him by the throat, shook him, choked him, and then, leaving him half dead from fright, turned to us with a bland, self-satisfied smile on his hard, weather-beaten old face, as if to say, "That's the way I do it! You see what terror I inspire!" He looked very hard at every Buriát we passed, as if he suspected him of being a thief, shouted in a commanding, tyrannical voice at most of them, greeted the Chinese with a loud "How!" to show his familiarity with foreign languages and customs, and finally, meeting a picturesquely dressed and rather pretty Buriát woman riding into town astride on horseback, he made her dismount and tie her horse to a tree in order that he might kiss her. The woman seemed to be half embarrassed and half amused by this remarkable performance; but Khainúief, re-moving his red dishpan hat with its long blue streamers, kissed her with "ornamental earnestness" and with a grotesque imita-tion of stately courtesy, and then, allowing her to climb back into her saddle without the least assistance, he turned to us with a comical air of triumph and smiling self-conceit which seemed to say, "There, what do you think of that? That's the kind of man I am! *You* can't make a pretty woman get off her horse just to kiss you." He seemed to think that we were regarding all his actions and achievements with envious admiration, and as he became more and more elated with a consciousness of appearing to advantage, his calls for "insanity drops" became more and more frequent. I began to fear at last that before we should reach the lamasery he would render himself absolutely incapable of any service requiring judgment and tact, and that as soon as the Grand Lama should discover his condition he would order him to be ducked in the lake. But I little knew the Selengínsk chief of police.

The road that we followed from Selengínsk to the lamasery ran in a northwesterly direction up a barren, stony valley between two ranges of low brownish hills, and the scenery along it seemed to me to be monotonous and uninteresting. I did not notice anything worthy of attention until we reached the crest of a high divide about twenty versts from Selengínsk and looked down into the valley of Goose Lake. There, between us and a range of dark blue mountains in the northwest, lay a narrow sheet of tranquil water, bounded on the left by a grassy steppe, and extending to the right as far as a projecting shoulder of the ridge would allow us to trace it. The shores of this lake were low and bare, the grass of the valley had turned yellow from frost or drought, there were no trees to be seen except on the higher slopes of the distant mountains, and the whole region had an appearance of sterility and desolation that suggested one of the steppes of the upper Írtish. On the other side of the lake, and near its western extremity, we could just make out from our distant point of view a large white building surrounded by a good-sized Buriát village of scattered log houses. It was the lamasery of Gusínnoi Ózera.

At sight of the sacred building, Khainúief, who was partly intoxicated at ten o'clock in the morning, and who had been taking "insanity drops" at short intervals ever since, became perceptibly more sober and serious; and when, half an hour later, we forded a deep stream near the western end of the lake, he alighted from the *pavóska* and asked us to wait while he took a cold bath. In about five minutes he reappeared perfectly sober, and resuming the severe judicial gravity of demeanor that characterized him as a Russian official, he proceeded to warn us that it would be necessary to treat the Grand Lama with profound respect. He seemed to be afraid that we, as Christians and foreigners, would look upon Khambá Lamá as a mere idolatrous barbarian, and would fail to treat him with proper deference and courtesy. I told him that we were accustomed to meet ecclesiastical authorities of the highest rank, and that we knew perfectly well how to behave toward them. Feeling reassured on this point, Khainúief proceeded to consider the probable attitude of the Grand Lama toward us, and the statements that should be made to that high dignitary concerning us.

"How are you magnified?" he asked me suddenly, after a short reflective pause. He might as well have asked me, "How are you electrified?" or "How are you galvanized?" so far as the conveyance of any definite idea to my mind was concerned. I made no reply.

"What are you called in addition to your name?" he repeated, varying the form of his question. "What is your rank?"

"We have no rank in our country," said Mr. Frost; "we are simply private American citizens."

"Then you are not nobles?"

"No."

"You have no titles?"

"Not a title."

"You are not in the service of your Government?"

"No."

"Then for what purpose are you traveling in Siberia?"

"Merely for our own amusement."

"Then you must be rich?"

"No; we are not rich."

Khainúief was disappointed. He could not get any glory out of introducing to the Grand Lama two insignificant foreigners who had neither rank, title, nor position, who were confessedly poor, and who were not even traveling in the service of their Government.

"Well," he said, after a few moments' consideration, "when the Grand Lama asks you who you are and what your business is in Siberia, you may say to him whatever you like; but I shall translate that you are high *chinóvniks*—deputies, if not ambassadors—sent out by the Government of the great American—what did you say it was, republic?—of the great American republic, to make a survey of Siberia and report upon it; and that it is not impossible that your Government may conclude to buy the country from our Góssudár."

"All right," I said laughing, "I don't care how you translate what I say to the Grand Lama; only don't expect me to help you out if you get into trouble."

Khainúief's face assumed again for a moment the expression of drunken cunning, self-conceit, and "friskiness" that it had worn earlier in the day, and it was evident that the mischievous-schoolboy half of the man looked forward with delight to the prospect of being able to play off two insignificant foreign travelers upon the Grand Lama for "high *chinóvniks*" and deputies, if not ambassadors, of the great American republic."

As we drove into the little village of brown log houses that surrounded the lamasery, Khainúief became preternaturally grave, removed his blue-streamered red hat, and assumed an air of subdued, almost apprehensive, reverence. One might have supposed this behavior to be an expression of his profound respect for the sacred character of the place; but in reality it was nothing more than a necessary prelude to the little comedy that he purposed to play. He desired to show even the monks whom we passed in the street that he, the great Selengínsk chief of police, did not presume to smile, to speak, or to wear his hat in the majestic presence of the two Lord High Commissioners from the great American republic.

We drove directly to the house of the Grand Lama, in front of which we were met and received by four or five shaven-headed Buddhist acolytes in long brown gowns girt about the waist with dark sashes. Khainúief, still bareheaded, sprang out of the *pavóska*, assisted me to alight with the most exaggerated manifestations of respect, and supported me up the steps as carefully and reverently as if an accidental stumble on my part would be little short of a great national calamity. Every motion that he made seemed to say to the Buriát monks and acolytes, "This man with the bedbug-bitten face, rumpled shirt, and short-tailed jacket doesn't look very imposing, but he's a high *chinóvnik* in disguise. You see how I have to behave toward him? It would be as much as my life is worth to put on my hat until he deigns to order it."

The house of the Grand Lama was a plain but rather large one-story log building, the main part of which was divided in halves by a central hall. We were shown into an icy-cold reception-room, furnished with an India-shawl-pattern carpet of Siberian manufacture, a low couch covered with blue rep-silk, and a few heavy Russian tables and chairs. On the walls hung roller pictures of various holy temples in Mongolia and Tibet, life-size portraits by native artists of eminent Buddhist lamas and saints, coarse colored lithographs of Alexander II and Alexander III, and a small card photograph of the Emperor William of Germany.

Khainúief presently came in and seated himself quietly on a chair near the door like a recently corrected schoolboy. There was not a trace nor a suggestion in his demeanor of the half-intoxicated, frisky, self-conceited Tatar prize-fighter who had made the Buriát woman get off her horse to kiss him. His eyes looked heavy and dull and showed the effects of the "insanity drops," but his manner and his self-control were perfect. He did not venture to address a word to us unless he was spoken to, and even then his voice was low and deferential.

Once in a while, when none of the brown-gowned acolytes were in the room, his assumed mask of reverential seriousness would suddenly break up into a grin of cunning and drollery, and making a significant gesture with his hand to his mouth he would wink at me, as if to say, "I'm only pretending to be stupid. I wish I had some insanity drops."

All the acolytes and servants in the place spoke, when they spoke at all, in low whispers, as if there were a dead body in the house, or as if the Grand Lama were asleep and it would be a terrible thing if he should be accidentally awakened. The room into which we were at first shown was so damp and cellar-like that we were soon in a shiver. Noticing that we were cold, Khainúief respectfully suggested that we go into the room on the other side of the hall, which had a southern exposure and had been warmed a little by the sun. This was a plainer, barer apartment, with unpainted woodwork and furniture; but it was much more cheerful and comfortable than the regular reception-room.

We waited for the Grand Lama at least half an hour. At the expiration of that time Khainúief, who had been making a reconnaissance, came rushing back, saying, "He's coming!" In a moment the door opened, and as we rose hastily to our feet the Grand Lama entered. He wore a striking and gorgeous costume, consisting of a superb long gown of orange silk shot with gold thread, bordered with purple velvet, and turned back and faced at the wrists with ultramarine-blue satin so as to make wide cuffs. Over this beautiful orange gown was thrown a splendid red silk scarf a yard wide and five yards long, hanging in soft folds from the left shoulder and gathered up about the waist. On his head he wore a high, pointed, brimless hat of orange felt, the extended sides of which fell down over his shoulders like the ends of a Russian *bashlík*, and were lined with heavy gold-thread embroidery. From a cord about his waist hung a large, flat, violet-velvet bag, which had a curiously wrought bronze stopper and which looked like a cloth bottle. Every part of the costume was made of the finest material, and the general effect of the orange gown and hat, the dark-blue facings, the red scarf, and the violet bag was extremely brilliant and striking. The wearer of this rich ecclesiastical dress was a Buriát about sixty years of age, of middle height and erect figure, with a beardless, somewhat wrinkled, but strong and kindly face. He represented the northern Mongol rather than the Chinese type, and seemed to be a man of some education and knowledge of the world. He greeted us easily and without embarrassment, and when we had all taken seats he listened with an impassive countenance to the ingenious but highly colored story into which Khainúief translated my modest account of ourselves, our plans, and our object in coming to the lamasery. Whether he believed it all or not I have no means of knowing; but from the subsequent course of events, and from statements made to me in Selengínsk after our return from Kiákhta, I am inclined to believe that Khainúief's diplomacy—not to give it a harsher name—was crowned with success. The bright-witted interpreter certainly played his part to perfection, and he even had the cool assurance to make me say to the Grand Lama that Governor Petróf in Irkútsk had particularly recommended him (Khainúief) to me as a valuable and trustworthy man, and that it was at the request of the governor that he came with us to the lamasery. The modest, deprecatory way in which he twisted into this form my innocent statement that Governor Petróf had sent a telegram about us to the authorities in the Trans-Baikál should have entitled the wily chief of police of Selengínsk to a high place among the great histrionic artists.

After we had drunk tea, which was served from a *samovár* in Russian style, I asked Khambá Lamá whether we should be permitted to inspect the temple. He replied that as soon as he had heard—through Khainúief of course—that such distinguished guests had come to call upon him he had given orders for a short thanksgiving service in the temple in order that we might see it. He regretted that he could not participate in this service himself, on account of recent illness; but Khainúief would go with us and see that we were provided with seats. We then saluted each other with profound bows, the Grand Lama withdrew to his own apartment, and Khainúief, Mr. Frost, and I set out for the temple.

An East Siberian lamasery is always, strictly speaking, a monastic establishment. It is situated in some lonely place, as far away as possible from any village or settlement, and consists generally of a temple, or place of worship, and from 50 to 150 log houses for the accommodation of the lamas, students, and acolytes, and for the temporary shelter of pilgrims, who come to the lamasery in great numbers on certain festival occasions. At the time of our visit three-fourths of the houses in the Goose Lake lamasery seemed to be empty. The *datsán*, or temple proper, stood in the middle of a large grassy inclosure formed by a high board fence. In plan it was nearly square, while in front elevation it resembled somewhat a three-story pyramid. It seemed to be made of brick covered with white stucco, and there was a great deal of minute ornamentation in red and black along the cornices and over the portico.

Upon entering this building from the portico on the first floor we found ourselves in a spacious but rather dimly lighted hall, the dimensions of which I estimated at 80 feet by 65. Large round columns draped with scarlet cloth supported the ceiling; the walls were almost entirely hidden by pictures of holy places, portraits of saints, and bright festooned draperies; while colored banners, streamers, and beautiful oriental lanterns hung everywhere in great profusion. The temple was so crowded with peculiar details that one could not reduce his observations to anything like order, nor remember half of the things that the eye noted; but the general effect of the whole was very striking, even to a person familiar with the interiors of Greek and Roman Catholic cathedrals. The impression made upon my mind by the decorations was that of great richness and beauty, both in color and in form. Across the end of the temple opposite the door ran a richly carved lattice-work screen, or partition, in front of which, equidistant one from another, were three large chairs or thrones. These thrones were covered with old-gold silk, were piled high with yellow cushions, and were intended for the Grand Lama, the Sheretúi, or chief lama of the *datsán,* and his assistant. The throne of the Grand Lama was vacant, but the other two were occupied when we entered the temple. In front of these thrones, in two parallel lines, face to face, sat seventeen lamas with crossed legs on long, high divans covered with cushions and yellow felt. Opposite each one, in the aisle formed by the divans, stood a small red table on which lay two or three musical instruments. The lamas were all dressed alike in orange silk gowns, red silk scarfs, and yellow helmet-shaped hats faced with red. On each side of the door as we entered was an enormous drum—almost as large as a hogshead—and the two lamas nearest us were provided with iron trumpets at least eight feet long and ten inches in diameter at the larger end. Both drums and trumpets were supported on wooden frames. Chairs were placed for us in the central aisle between the two lines of lamas, and we took our seats.

The scene at the beginning of the service was far more strange and impressive than I had expected it to be. The partial gloom of the temple, the high yellow thrones of the presiding dignitaries, the richness and profusion of the decorations, the colossal drums, the gigantic trumpets, the somber crowd of students and acolytes in black gowns at one end of the room, and the two brilliant lines of orange and crimson lamas at the other made up a picture the strange barbaric splendor of which surpassed anything of the kind that I have ever witnessed. For a moment after we took our seats there was a perfect stillness. Then the Sheretúi shook a little globular rattle, and in response to the signal there burst forth a tremendous musical uproar, made by the clashing of cymbals, the deep-toned boom of the immense drums, the jangling of bells, the moaning of conch-shells, the tooting of horns, the liquid tinkle of triangles, and the hoarse bellowing of the great iron trumpets. It was not melody, it was not music; it was simply a tremendous instrumental uproar. It continued for about a minute, and then, as it suddenly ceased, the seventeen lamas began a peculiar, wild, rapid chant, in a deep, low monotone. The voices were exactly in accord, the time was perfect, and the end of every line or stanza was marked by the clashing of cymbals and the booming of the colossal drums. This chanting continued for three or four minutes, and then it was interrupted by another orchestral charivari which would have leveled the walls of Jericho without any supernatural intervention. I had never heard such an infernal tumult of sound. Chanting, interrupted at intervals by the helter-skelter playing of twenty or thirty different instruments, made up the "thanksgiving" temple service, which lasted about fifteen minutes. It was interesting, but it was quite long enough.

Mr. Frost and I then walked around the temple, accompanied by the Sheretúi and Khainúief. Behind the lattice-work screen there were three colossal idols in the conventional sitting posture of the Buddhists, and in front of each of them were lighted tapers of butter, porcelain bowls of rice, wheat, and millet, artificial paper flowers, fragrant burning pastils, and bronze bowls of consecrated water. Against the walls, all around this part of the temple, were bookcases with glass doors in which were thousands of the small figures known to the Christian world as "idols" and called by the Buriáts *burkháns*. I could not ascertain the reason for keeping so great a number of these figures in the lamasery, nor could I ascertain what purpose they served. They presented an almost infinite variety of types and faces; many of them were obviously symbolical, and all seemed to be representative in some way either of canonized mortals or of supernatural spirits, powers, or agencies. According to the information furnished me by Khainúief, these *burkháns*, or idols, occupy in the lamaistic system of religious belief the same place that images or pictures of saints fill in the Russian system. From the appearance, however, of many of the idols in the lamasery collection, I concluded that a *burkhán* might represent an evil as well as a beneficent spiritual power. The word *burkhán* has long been used all over Mongolia in the general sense of a sacred or supernatural being. Dr. Erman believes that "the Mongolian *burkhán* is identical with the Indian Buddha." The *burkháns* in the lamasery of Goose Lake were crowded together on the shelves of the cases as closely as possible, and apparently no attempt had been made to arrange them in any kind of order. They varied in height from two inches to a foot, and were made generally of brass, bronze, or stone. In one corner of the *kumírnia*, or idol-room, stood a prayer-wheel, consisting of a large cylinder mounted on a vertical axis and supposed to be filled with written prayers or devotional formulas. I did not see it used, but in the Ónonski lamasery, which we visited a few weeks later, we found an enormous prayer-wheel which had a building to itself and which was in constant use.

From the idol-room we went into the upper stories of the temple, where there were more *burkháns* as well as a large collection of curious Mongolian and Tibetan books. If we had not been told that the objects last named were books, we never should have recognized them. They were rectangular sheets of thin Chinese paper twelve or fourteen inches in length by about four in width, pressed together between two thin strips of wood or pasteboard, and bound round with flat silken cords or strips of bright-colored cloth. They looked a little like large, well-filled bill-files tied with ribbons or crimson braid. The leaves were printed only on one side, and the characters were arranged in vertical columns. In a few of the volumes that I examined an attempt apparently had been made to illuminate, with red and yellow ink or paint, the initial characters and the beginnings of chapters, but the work had been coarsely and clumsily done.

From the principal temple of the lamasery we were taken to a chapel or smaller building in the same inclosure to see the great image of Máidera, one of the most highly venerated *burkháns* in the lamaistic pantheon. It proved to be a colossal human figure in a sitting posture, skilfully carved out of wood and richly overlaid with colors and gold. I estimated its height at thirty-five feet. It stood in the center of a rather narrow but high-domed chapel, hung round with banners, streamers, and lanterns, and really was a very imposing object. Tapers and incense were burning upon an altar covered with silken drapery which stood directly in front of the great idol, and upon the same altar were offerings in the shape of flowers made out of hardened butter or wax, and a large number of bronze or porcelain bowls filled with millet, rice, wheat, oil, honey, or consecrated water. Some of these bowls were open so that their contents could be seen, while others were covered with napkins of red, blue, or yellow silk. Here, as in the great temple, the partial gloom was lighted up by the brilliant coloring of the decorations and draperies, and by the splendid orange and crimson dresses of the attendant lamas.

From the chapel of Máidera we were conducted to a third building in another part of the same inclosure, where we found ourselves in the presence of the sacred white elephant. I had always associated the white elephant with Siam, and was not a little surprised to find a very good imitation of that animal in an East Siberian lamasery. The elephant of Goose Lake had been skilfully carved by some Buriát or Mongol lama out of hard wood, and had then been painted white, equipped with suitable trappings, and mounted on four low wheels. The sculptured elephant was somewhat smaller than the living animal, and his tusks had been set at an angle that would have surprised a naturalist; but in view of the fact that the native artist probably never had seen an elephant, the resemblance of the copy to the original was fairly close. The white elephant is harnessed to a large four-wheel wagon, on which stands a beautiful and delicately carved shrine, made in imitation of a two-story temple. On the occasion of the great annual festival of the lamaists in July a small image of one of the high gods is put into this shrine, and then the elephant and the wagon are drawn in triumphal procession around the lamasery to the music of drums, trumpets, conch-shells, cymbals, and gongs, and with an escort of perhaps three hundred brilliantly costumed lamas.

While we were examining the white elephant, Khainúief came to me and said that Khambá Lamá, in view of the fact that we were the first foreigners who had ever visited the lamasery, had ordered an exhibition to be given for us of the sacred "dance of the *burkháns*." I strongly suspected that we were indebted for all these favors to Khainúief's unrivaled skill as a translator of truth into fiction; but if we had been introduced to the Grand Lama as "deputies, if not ambassadors, from the great American republic," it was in no sense our fault, and there was no reason why we should not accept the courtesies offered us.

When we returned to the great temple we found that everything was in readiness for the dance. It was to take place out of doors on the grass in front of the *datsán*, where seats had already been prepared for the musicians and for the Sheretúi and his assistant. The big drums and the eight-foot iron trumpets were brought out, the presiding lamas seated themselves cross-legged on piles of flat yellow cushions in their chairs, and we took the positions assigned to us. At the sounding of a small rattle twelve or fifteen of the strangest, wildest-looking figures I had ever seen rushed out into the open space in front of the temple, and to the crashing, booming accompaniment of cymbals and big iron trumpets began a slow, rhythmical, leaping dance. Four or five of the dancers had on enormous black helmet masks representing grinning Mongolian demons, and from their heads radiated slender rods to which were affixed small colored flags. Two figures had human skulls or death's-heads on their shoulders, one man's body had the head and antlers of a *marál*, or Siberian stag, and another was surmounted by the head and horns of a bull. Three or four dancers, who represented good spirits and defenders of the faith, and who were without masks, wore on their heads broad-brimmed hats with a heart-shaped superstructure of gold open-work, and were armed with naked daggers. It seemed to be their province

THE GRAND LAMA

DANCE OF THE "BURKÁNS"

to drive the black-masked demons and the skull-headed figures out of the field. The dresses worn by all the dancers were of extraordinary richness and beauty, and were so complicated and full of detail that two or three pages would be needed for a complete and accurate description of a single one of them. The materials of the costumes were crimson, scarlet, blue, and orange silk, old-gold brocade, violet velvet, satin of various colors, bright-colored cords, tassels, and fringes, wheel-shaped silver brooches supporting festooned strings of white beads, and gold and silver ornaments in infinite variety, which shone and flashed in the sunlight as the figures pirouetted and leaped hither and thither, keeping time to the measured clashing of cymbals and booming of the great drums. The performance lasted about fifteen minutes, and the last figures to retire were the *burkháns* with the golden lattice-work hats and the naked daggers. It seemed to me evident that this sacred "dance of the *burkháns*" was a species of religious pantomime or mystery play; but I could not get through Khainúief any intelligible explanation of its significance.

When we returned to the house of the Grand Lama we found ready a very good and well-cooked dinner, with fruit cordial and madeira to cheer the "ambassadors," and plenty of vodka to inebriate Khainúief. After dinner I had a long talk with the Grand Lama about my native country, geography, and the shape of the earth. It seemed very strange to find anywhere on the globe, in the nineteenth century, an educated man and high ecclesiastical dignitary who had never even heard of America, and who did not feel at all sure that the world is round. The Grand Lama was such a man.

"You have been in many countries," he said to me through the interpreter, "and have talked with the wise men of the West; what is your opinion with regard to the shape of the earth?"

"I think," I replied, "that it is shaped like a great ball."

"I have heard so before," said the Grand Lama, looking

thoughtfully away into vacancy. "The Russian officers whom I have met have told me that the world is round. Such a belief is contrary to the teachings of our old Tibetan books, but I have observed that the Russian wise men predict eclipses accurately; and if they can tell beforehand when the sun and the moon are to be darkened, they probably know something about the shape of the earth. Why do you think that the earth is round?"

"I have many reasons for thinking so," I answered; "but perhaps the best and strongest reason is that I have been around it."

This statement seemed to give the Grand Lama a sort of mental shock.

"How have you been around it?" he inquired. "What do you mean by 'around it?' How do you know that you have been around it?"

"I turned my back upon my home," I replied, "and traveled many months in the course taken by the sun. I crossed wide continents and great oceans. Every night the sun set before my face and every morning it rose behind my back. The earth always seemed flat, but I could not find anywhere an end nor an edge; and at last, when I had traveled more than thirty thousand versts, I found myself again in my own country and returned to my home from a direction exactly opposite to that which I had taken in leaving it. If the world was flat, do you think I could have done this?"

"It is very strange," said the Grand Lama, after a thoughtful pause of a moment. "Where is your country? How far is it beyond St. Petersburg?"

"My country is farther from St. Petersburg than St. Petersburg is from here," I replied. "It lies nearly under our feet; and if we could go directly through the earth, that would be the shortest way to reach it."

"Are your countrymen walking around there heads downward under our feet?" asked the Grand Lama with evident interest and surprise, but without any perceptible change in his habitually impassive face.

"Yes," I replied; "and to them we seem to be sitting heads downward here."

The Grand Lama then asked me to describe minutely the route that we had followed in coming from America to Siberia, and to name the countries through which we had passed. He knew that Germany adjoined Russia on the west, he had heard of British India and of England—probably through Tibet— and he had a vague idea of the extent and situation of the Pacific Ocean; but of the Atlantic and of the continent that lies between the two great oceans he knew nothing.

After a long talk, in the course of which we discussed the sphericity of the earth from every possible point of view, the Grand Lama seemed to be partly or wholly convinced of the truth of that doctrine, and said, with a sigh, "It is not in accordance with the teachings of our books; but the Russians must be right."

It is a somewhat remarkable fact that Dr. Erman, one of the few foreigners who had seen the lamasery of Goose Lake previous to our visit, had an almost precisely similar conversation concerning the shape of the earth with the man who was then (in 1828) Grand Lama. Almost sixty years elapsed between Dr. Erman's visit and ours, but the doctrine of the sphericity of the earth continued throughout that period to trouble ecclesiastical minds in this remote East Siberian lamasery; and it is not improbable that sixty years hence some traveler from the western world may be asked by some future Grand Lama to give his reasons for believing the world to be a sphere.

About five o'clock in the afternoon, after exchanging photographs with the Grand Lama, thanking him for his courtesy and hospitality, and bidding him a regretful good-by, we were lifted carefully into our old *pavóska* by the anxious, respectful, and bare-headed Khainúief in the presence of a crowd of black-robed acolytes and students, and began our journey back to Selengínsk.

CHAPTER EIGHT

The Convict Mines of Kará

The MINES OF KARÁ ARE DISTANT from Chíta, the capital of the Trans-Baikál, about 300 miles; but for more than 200 miles the traveler in approaching them follows a fairly good post-road, which runs at first through the valley of the Ingodá and then along the northern or left bank of the Shílka River, one of the principal tributaries of the Amúr. At a small town called Strétinsk, where the Shílka first becomes navigable, this post-road abruptly ends, and beyond that point communication with the Kará penal settlements is maintained by boats in summer and by sledges drawn over the ice in winter. For two or three weeks in autumn, while the ice is forming, and for a somewhat shorter period in the spring, after the river breaks up, the Kará mines are virtually isolated from all the rest of the world, and can be reached only by a difficult and dangerous bridle path, which runs for a distance of seventy or eighty miles, parallel with the river, across a series of steep and generally forest-clad mountain ridges. We hoped to reach Strétinsk in time to descend the Shílka to the Kará River in a boat; and when we left Chíta, on Saturday, October 24th, there seemed to be every probability that we should succeed in so doing. The weather, however, turned suddenly colder; snow fell to a depth of an inch and a half or two inches; and Wednesday morning, when we alighted from our *teléga* on the northern bank of the Shílka opposite Strétinsk, winter had set in with great severity. The mercury in our ther-

mometer indicated zero (Fahr.); our fur coats and the bodies
of our horses were white with frost; and the broad, rapid current of the Shílka was so choked with masses of heavy ice as
to be almost, if not quite, impassable. A large open skiff was
making a perilous attempt to cross from Strétinsk to our side
of the river, and a dozen or more peasants, who stood shivering
around a small campfire on the beach, were waiting for it,
with the hope that it would come safely to land and that the
ferrymen might be persuaded to make a return trip with passengers. After watching for a quarter of an hour the struggles
of this boat with the ice, Mr. Frost and I decided that it would
be hazardous to attempt, in an open skiff, the passage of a rapid
and ice-choked river half a mile wide, even if the boatman
were willing to take us; and we therefore sought shelter in the
small log house of a young Russian peasant named Záblikof,
who good-humoredly consented to give us a night's lodging
provided we had no objection to sleeping on the floor with the
members of his family. We were too much exhausted and too
nearly frozen to object to anything; and as for sleeping on the
floor, we had become so accustomed to it that we should have
felt out of place if we had tried to sleep anywhere else. We
therefore had our baggage transported to Záblikof's house, and
in half an hour were comfortably drinking tea in the first
decently clean room we had seen since leaving Nérchinsk.

We devoted most of the remainder of the day to a discussion
of our situation and of the possibility of reaching the Kará
mines at that season of the year by an overland journey across
the mountains.

Descending the river in a boat was manifestly impracticable
on account of the great quantity of running ice; we could not
waste two or three weeks in inaction, and the horseback ride
to the mines over the mountains seemed to be the only feasible
alternative. There were, on our side of the river, a few horses
that Záblikof thought might be hired; but they belonged to a
merchant who lived in Strétinsk, and in order to get permission
to use them, as well as to obtain the necessary saddles and

equipments and secure the services of a guide, it would be necessary to cross the Shílka to the town. This, in the existing condition of the river, was a somewhat perilous undertaking; but Záblikof offered to accompany me with two or three of his men, and early Thursday morning we carried his light, open skiff down to the beach for the purpose of making the attempt. The weather had moderated a little, but it was still very cold; the river had become an almost continuous field of swiftly moving ice, intersected by narrow lanes of black open water; and a belt of fixed ice extended from the shore a distance of forty or fifty yards, becoming thinner and thinner as it approached the water's edge. Out over this treacherous surface we cautiously pushed our skiff, holding ourselves in readiness to spring into it quickly all together at the instant when the ice should give way under our feet. Four or five yards from the black, eddying current the ice yielded, we felt a sudden sinking sensation, and then, with a great confused crash, we went into the water, Záblikof shouting excitedly, "Now! Into the boat!" The skiff gave a deep roll, first to one side and then to the other, as we all sprang into it; but fortunately it did not capsize, and in another moment we were whirled away and swept rapidly down-stream amid huge grinding ice-tables, which we fended off, as well as we could, with oars and boathooks. As soon as the first excitement of the launch was over, two of the men settled down to steady rowing, while Záblikof, boat-hook in hand, stood in the bow as pilot, and guided our frail craft through the narrow lanes of water between the swiftly running ice-floes. We were carried down-stream about half a mile before we could reach the opposite shore, and when we did reach it the making of a landing on the thin, treacherous edge of the fast ice proved to be more a difficult and dangerous task then even the launching of the skiff. Three or four times while we were clinging with boathooks to the crumbling edge of the ice-foot I thought we should certainly be crushed or capsized by the huge white fields and tables that came grinding down upon us from above; but we finally broke our way into the stationary ice-belt far enough to get shelter. Záblikof sprang out upon a hummock and made fast a line, and after being immersed in the freezing water up to my hips as the result of an awkward jump, I gained a footing upon ice that was firm enough to sustain my weight. The weather was so cold that getting wet was a serious matter; and leaving Záblikof and the men to pull out the boat, I started at a brisk run for the town and took refuge in the first shop I could find. After drying and warming myself I sent a telegram to Mr. Wurts, the Secretary of the United States Legation in St. Petersburg, to apprise him of our whereabouts; found the owner of the horses and made a bargain with him for transportation to the first peasant village down the river in the direction of the mines; hired an old guide named Nikífer; procured the necessary saddles and equipments, and late in the afternoon made, without accident, the perilous return trip across the river to Záblikof's house.

As early as possible on Friday we saddled our horses and set out for the mines, taking with us nothing except our blanket rolls and notebooks, a bag of provisions, the camera, and about a dozen dry plates. The weather had again moderated and our thermometer indicated a temperature of eighteen degrees above zero; but the sky was dark and threatening, a light snow was falling, and as we rode up on the summit of the first high ridge and looked ahead into the wild, lonely mountainous region that we were to traverse, I felt a momentary sinking of the heart. I was still weak from my sickness in Tróitskosávsk, winter had set in, and I feared that my slender stock of reserve strength would not carry me through a ride of eighty miles on horseback over such a trail as this was represented to be. Moreover, our winter equipment was scanty and not at all adapted to such a journey. Presuming that we should be able to descend the Shílka in a boat, we had not provided ourselves with fur sleeping-bags; our sheepskin overcoats were not long enough to protect our knees; we had not been able to obtain fur hoods; and our felt boots were so large and heavy that they would not go into our stirrups, and we were forced either to ride without them or to dispense with the support that the stirrups might afford. Fortunately the trail that we followed was at first fairly good, the weather was not very cold, and we succeeded in making a distance of twenty miles without a great deal of suffering. We stopped for the night in the small log village called Lómi, on the bank of the Shílka, slept on the floor of a peasant's house, in the same room with two adults and five children, and Saturday morning, after a breakfast of tea, black bread, and cold fish-pie, resumed our journey, with fresh horses and a new guide. The weather had cleared off cold during the night, and our thermometer, when we climbed into our saddles, indicated a temperature of eight degrees below zero. The bodies of the horses were white and shaggy with frost, icicles hung from their nostrils, and they seemed as impatient to get away as we were. With our departure from Lómi began the really difficult part of our journey. The trail ran in a tortuous course across a wilderness of rugged mountains, sometimes making long detours to the northward to avoid deep or precipitous ravines; sometimes climbing in zigzags the steep sides of huge transverse ridges; and occasionally coming out upon narrow shelf-like cornices of rock, high above the dark, ice-laden waters of the Shílka, where a slip or stumble of our horses would unquestionably put an end to our Siberian investigations. That we did not meet with any accident in the course of this ride to Kará seems to me a remarkable evidence of good luck. Our horses were unshod, and the trail in many places was covered with ice formed by the overflow and freezing of water from mountain springs, and then hidden by a thin sheet of snow, so that it was impossible to determine from the most careful inspection of a steep and dangerous descent whether or not it would afford secure foothold for our horses. Throughout Saturday and Sunday we walked most of the time; partly because we were too nearly frozen to sit in the saddle, and partly because we dared not take the risks of the slippery trail. Three days of riding, walking, and climbing over rugged mountains, in a temperature that ranged from zero to ten degrees below, finally exhausted my last reserve of strength; and when we reached the peasant village of Shílkina at a late hour Sunday night, a weak and thready pulse, running at the rate of 120, warned me that I was near the extreme limit of my endurance. Fortunately the worst part of our journey was over. Ust Kará, the most southerly of the Kará penal settlements, was distant from Shílkina only ten or twelve miles; the trail between the two places presented no unusual difficulties; and about noon on Monday we dismounted from our tired horses in the large village at the mouth of the Kará River, hobbled with stiffened and benumbed legs into the house of a peasant known to our guide, and threw ourselves down to rest.

The mines of Kará, which are the private property of his Imperial Majesty the Tsar, and are worked for his benefit, consist of a series of open gold placers, situated at irregular intervals along a small rapid stream called the Kará River, which rises on the watershed of the Yáblonoi mountains, runs in a southeasterly direction for a distance of forty or fifty miles, and finally empties into the Shílka between Strétinsk and the mouth of the Argún. The name "Kará," derived from a Tatar adjective meaning "black," was originally used merely to designate this stream; but it is now applied more comprehensively to the whole chain of prisons, mines, and convict settlements that lie scattered through the Kará valley. These prisons, mines, and convict settlements, taking them in serial order from south to north, are known separately and distinctively as Ust Kará or Kará mouth, the Lower Prison, the Political Prison, the Lower Diggings, Middle Kará, Upper Kará, and the Upper or Amúrski Prison. The administration of the whole penal establishment centers in the Lower Diggings, where the governor of the common-criminal prisons resides, and where there is a convict settlement of two or three hundred inhabitants and a company or two of soldiers in barracks. It seemed to me best to make this place our headquarters; partly because it was the residence of the governor, without whose consent we could do nothing, and partly because it was distant only about a mile from the political prison in which we were especially interested. We therefore left our horses and our guide at Ust Kará with orders to wait for us, and after dining and resting for an hour or two, set out in a *teléga* for the Lower Diggings. The road ran up the left bank of the Kará River through a shallow valley averaging about half a mile in width, bounded by low hills that were covered with a scanty second growth of young larches and pines, and whitened by a light fall of snow. The floor of the valley was formed by huge shapeless mounds of gravel and sand, long ago turned over and washed in the search for gold, and it suggested a worked-out placer in the most dreary and desolate part of the Black Hills.

We reached the settlement at the Lower Diggings just before dark. It proved to be a spacious but straggling Siberian village of low whitewashed cabins, long unpainted log barracks, officers' tin-roofed residences, with wattle-inclosed yards, and a black, gloomy, weather-beaten log prison of the usual East Siberian type. The buildings belonging to the Government were set with some show of regularity in wide open spaces or along a few very broad streets; and they gave to the central part of the village a formal and official air that was strangely at variance with the disorderly arrangement of the unpainted shanties and dilapidated driftwood cabins of the ticket-of-leave convicts which were huddled together, here and there, on the outskirts of the settlement or along the road that led to Ust Kará. On one side of an open square, around which stood the prison and the barracks, forty or fifty convicts in long gray overcoats with yellow diamonds on their backs were at work upon a new log building, surrounded by a cordon of Cossacks in sheepskin *shúbas*, felt boots, and muff-shaped fur caps, who stood motionless at their posts, leaning upon their Berdan rifles and watching the prisoners. At a little distance was burning a campfire, over which was hanging a tea-kettle, and around which were standing or crouching a dozen more Cossacks, whose careless attitudes and stacked rifles showed that they were temporarily off duty. In the waning light of the cold, gloomy autumnal afternoon, the dreary snowy square, the gray group of convicts working listlessly as if hopeless or exhausted, and the cordon of Cossacks leaning upon their bayoneted rifles made up a picture that for some reason exerted upon me a chilling and depressing influence. It was our first glimpse of convict life at the mines.

We drove at once to the house of the governor of the prisons, for the purpose of inquiring where we could find shelter for the night. Major Pótulof, a tall, fine-looking, soldierly man about fifty years of age, received us cordially, and said that he had been apprised of our coming by a telegram from the acting governor in Chíta; but he did not really expect us, because he knew the Shílka was no longer navigable, and he did not believe foreign travelers would undertake, at that season of the year, the difficult and dangerous journey across the mountains. He expressed great pleasure, however, at seeing us, and invited us at once to accept the hospitalities of his house. I told him that we did not intend to quarter ourselves upon him, but merely wished to inquire where we could find shelter for the night. He laughed pleasantly, and replied that there were no hotels or boarding-houses in Kará except those provided by the Government for burglars, counterfeiters, and murderers; and that he expected us, of course, to accept his hospitality and make ourselves at home in his house. This was not at all in accordance with our wishes or plans. We had hoped to find some place of abode where we should not be constantly under official surveillance; and I did not see how we were secretly to make the acquaintance of the political convicts if we consented to become the guests of the governor of the prisons. As there did not, however, seem to be any alternative, we accepted Major Pótulof's invitation, and in ten minutes were comfortably quartered in a large, well-furnished house, where our eyes were gladdened by the sight of such unfamiliar luxuries as long mirrors, big soft rugs, easy-chairs, and a piano.

The Kará prisons and penal settlements at the time of our visit contained, approximately, 1800 hard-labor convicts. Of this number about one-half were actually in close confinement, while the remainder were living in barracks, or in little cabins of their own, outside the prison walls.

The penal term of a Russian convict at the mines is divided into two periods or stages. During the first of these periods he is officially regarded as "on probation," and is held in prison under strict guard. If his conduct is such as to merit the approval of the prison authorities, he is released from confinement at the end of his probationary term and is enrolled in a sort of ticket-of-leave organization known as the "free command." He is still a hard-labor convict; he receives his daily ration from the prison, and he cannot step outside the limits of the penal settlement without a permit; but he is allowed to live with other "reforming" criminals in convict barracks, or with his family in a separate house of his own; he can do extra work for himself in his leisure hours, if he feels so disposed, and he enjoys a certain amount of freedom. At the end of this second or "reforming" period he is sent as a "forced colonist" to some part of Eastern Siberia for the remainder of his life.

The prisons connected with the Kará penal establishment at the time of our visit were seven in number, and were scattered along the Kará River for a distance of about twenty miles. The slow but steady movement of the working convict force up-stream in the search for gold had left the Lower Diggings and Ust Kará prisons so far behind that their inmates could no longer walk in leg-fetters to and from the placers, and a large number of them were therefore living in enforced idleness. The direct supervision of the common-criminal prisons was intrusted to *smatrítels*, or wardens, who reported to Major Pótulof; and the prison buildings were guarded by detachments of Cossacks from the Kará battalion, which numbered about one thousand men. The two political prisons—one at the Lower Diggings for men, and the other at Ust Kará for women—were not under the control of Major Pótulof, but were managed by a gendarme officer named Captain Nikólin, who had been sent out from St. Petersburg for this particular duty, and who was at the head of a carefully selected prison guard of 140 gendarmes. The political prisons had also their free command, which at the time of our visit consisted of twelve or fifteen men and women, who had finished their terms of probation and were living in little huts or cabins of their own on the outskirts of the Lower Diggings. All of these facts were known to us long before we reached the mines, and we shaped our course in accordance with them.

The objects that we had in view at Kará were, first, to go through the common-criminal prisons and see the criminals actually at work in the mines; secondly, to make the acquaintance of the political convicts of the free command; and, thirdly, to visit the political prison and see how the condemned revolutionists lived, even if we were not permitted to talk with them. That we should succeed in attaining the first of these objects I felt confident, of the second I was not at all sure, and of the third I had little hope; but I determined to try hard for all. What instructions Major Pótulof had received with regard to us I did not know; but he treated us with great cordiality, asked no awkward questions, and when, on the day after our arrival, I asked permission to visit the prisons and mines, he granted it without the least apparent surprise or hesitation, ordered out his horses and *dróshky*, and said that it would give him great pleasure to accompany us.

It is not my purpose to describe minutely all of the prisons in Kará that we were permitted to inspect, but I will sketch hastily the two that seemed to me to be typical, respectively, of the worst class and of the best.

The Ust Kará prison, which, in point of sanitary condition and overcrowding, is perhaps the worst place of confinement in the whole Kará valley, is situated on low, marshy ground in the outskirts of the penal settlement of the same name, near the junction of the Kará River with the Shílka. It was built nearly half a century ago, when the Government first began to work the Kará gold placers with convict labor. As one approaches it from the south it looks like a long, low horse-car stable made of squared but unpainted logs, which are now black, weather-beaten, and decaying from age. Taken in connection with its inclosed yard it makes a nearly perfect square of about one hundred feet, two sides of which are formed by the prison buildings and two sides by a stockade about twenty-five feet in height, made of closely set logs, sharpened at the top like colossal lead pencils. As we approached the courtyard gate, an armed Cossack, who stood in the black-barred sentry-box beside it, presented arms to Major Pótulof and shouted, "Stárshe!" —the usual call for the officer of the day. A Cossack corporal ran to the entrance with a bunch of keys in his hand, unlocked the huge padlock that secured the small door in the larger wooden gate, and admitted us to the prison courtyard. As we entered, three or four convicts, with half-shaven heads, ran hastily across the yard to take their places in their cells for inspection. We ascended two or three steps incrusted with an indescribable coating of filth and ice an inch and a half thick, and entered, through a heavy plank door, a long, low, and very dark corridor, whose broken and decaying floor felt wet and slippery to the feet, and whose atmosphere, although warm, was very damp, and saturated with the strong peculiar odor that is characteristic of Siberian prisons. A person who has once inhaled that odor can never forget it; and yet it is so unlike any other bad smell in the world that I hardly know with what to compare it. I can ask you to imagine cellar air, every atom of which has been half a dozen times through human lungs and is heavy with carbonic acid; to imagine that air still further vitiated by foul, pungent, slightly ammoniacal exhalations from long unwashed human bodies; to imagine that it has a suggestion of damp, decaying wood and more than a suggestion of human excrement—and still you will have no adequate idea of it. To unaccustomed senses it seems so saturated with foulness and disease as to be almost insupportable. As we entered the corridor, slipped upon the wet, filthy floor, and caught the first breath of this air, Major Pótulof turned to me with a scowl of disgust, and exclaimed, "Atvratítelni tiurmá!" ["It is a repulsive prison!"].

The Cossack corporal who preceded us threw open the heavy wooden door of the first *kámera* and shouted, "Smírno!" the customary warning of the guard to the prisoners when an officer is about to enter the cell. We stepped across the threshold into a room about 24 feet long, 22 feet wide, and 8 feet high, which contained 29 convicts. The air here was so much worse than the air in the corridor that it made me faint and sick. The room was lighted by two nearly square, heavily grated windows with double sashes, that could not be raised or opened, and there was not the least apparent provision anywhere for ventilation. Even the brick oven, by which the cell was warmed, drew its air from the corridor. The walls of the *kámera* were of squared logs and had once been whitewashed; but they had become dark and grimy from lapse of time, and were blotched in hundreds of places with dull red blood-stains where the convicts had crushed bedbugs; the floor was made of heavy planks, and, although it had recently been swept, it was incrusted with dry, hard-trodden filth. Out from the walls on three sides of the room projected low, sloping wooden platforms about six feet wide, upon which the convicts slept, side by side, in closely packed rows, with their heads to the walls and their feet extended toward the middle of the cell. They had neither pillows nor blankets, and were compelled to lie down upon these sleeping-benches at night without removing their clothing, and without other covering than their coarse gray overcoats. The cell contained no furniture of any kind except these sleeping-platforms, the brick oven, and a large wooden tub. When the door was locked for the night each one of these 29 prisoners would have, for 8 or 10 hours' consumption, about as much air as would be contained in a packing-box 5 feet square and 5 feet high. If there was any way in which a single cubic foot of fresh air could get into that cell after the doors had been closed for the night I failed to discover it.

We remained in the first *kámera* only two or three minutes.

I think I was the first to get out into the corridor, and I still vividly remember the sense of relief with which I drew a long breath of that corridor air. Heavy and vitiated as it had seemed to me when I first entered the prison, it was so much better than the atmosphere of the overcrowded cell that it gave me an impression of freshness and comparative purity. We then went through hastily, one after another, the seven *kámeras* that composed the prison. They all resembled the first one except that they varied slightly in dimensions, in shape, or in the number of prisoners that they contained. The results of breathing such air for long periods of time may be seen in the Kará prison hospital, where the prevalent diseases are scurvy, typhus and typhoid fevers, anaemia, and consumption. No one whom we met in Kará attempted to disguise the fact that most of these cases of disease are the direct result of the life that the convicts are forced to live in the dirty and overcrowded *kámeras*. The prison surgeon admitted this to me frankly, and said: "We have more or less scurvy here all the year round. You have been through the prisons, and must know what their sanitary condition is. Of course such uncleanliness and overcrowding result in disease. We have 140 patients in the hospital now; frequently in spring we have 250."

Most of these cases come from a prison population of less than one thousand; and the hospital records do not, by any means, represent the aggregate of sickness in the Kará penal settlements. Many convicts of the free command lie ill in their own little huts or cabins, and even in the prison *kámeras* there are scores of sick whose cases are not regarded as serious enough to necessitate their removal to a hospital that is perhaps overcrowded already. A convict in the early stages of scurvy may therefore lie in a prison *kámera* for a week or two, poisoning with his foul, diseased breath the air that must be breathed by men who are still comparatively well.

After visiting all the *kámeras* in the men's prison, we came out at last into the pure, cold, delicious air, crossed the courtyard, went through another gate in the stockade, and entered the women's prison—a similar but smaller log building, which contained two large cells opening into each other. These rooms were well warmed and lighted, were higher than the cells in the men's prison, and had more than twice as much air space per capita; but their sanitary condition was little, if any, better. The air in them had perhaps been less vitiated by repeated respiration, but it was so saturated with foul odors from a neglected water-closet that one's senses could barely tolerate it. The floor was uneven and decayed, and in places the rotten planks had either settled or given way entirely, leaving dark holes under which there was a vacant space between the floor and the swampy ground. Into these holes the women were evidently in the habit of throwing slops and garbage. I went and stood for a moment over one of them, but I could see nothing in the darkness beneath; and the damp air, laden with the effluvium of decaying organic matter that was rising from it, seemed to me so suggestive of typhoid fever and diphtheria that I did not venture to take a second breath in that vicinity. The *kámeras* in the women's prison had no furniture of any kind except the plank sleeping-platforms, which, of course, were entirely destitute of bedding. I did not see in either room a single pillow or blanket. In these two cells were imprisoned forty-eight girls and women, six or seven of whom were carrying in their arms pallid, sickly looking babies.

At every step in our walk through the two prisons Major Pótulof was besieged by unfortunate convicts who had complaints to make or petitions to present. One man had changed names with a comrade on the road while intoxicated, and had thus become a hard-labor convict when he should have been merely a forced colonist, and he wanted his case investigated. Another insisted that he had long since served out his full prison term and should be enrolled in the free command. Three more declared that they had been two months in prison and were still ignorant of the nature of the charges made against them. Many of the convicts addressed themselves eagerly to me, under the impression, apparently, that I must be an inspector sent to Kará to investigate the prison management. In order to save Major Pótulof from embarrassment and the complainants from possible punishment, I hastened to assure them that we had no power to redress grievances or to grant relief; that we were merely travelers visiting Kará out of curiosity. The complaints and the manifestly bad condition of the prisons seemed to irritate Major Pótulof, and he grew more and more silent, moody, and morose as we went through the *kámeras*. He did not attempt to explain, defend, or excuse anything, nor did he then, nor at any subsequent time, ask me what impression the Ust Kará prisons made upon me. He knew very well what impression they *must* make.

In another stockaded yard, adjoining the one through which we had passed, stood the political prison for women; but Major Pótulof could not take us into it without the permission of the gendarme commandant, Captain Nikólin. From all that I subsequently learned with regard to this place of punishment, I have little doubt that, while it is cleaner and less overcrowded than the common-criminal prisons, it does not rank much above the latter in comfort or in sanitary condition.

Early Tuesday afternoon we visited the Middle Kará prison, which was perhaps the best one we inspected at the mines. It was distant from the Lower Diggings about three miles, and was reached by a road that ran up the right bank of the Kará River through a desolate, snowy valley, dotted here and there with the dilapidated huts and cabins of the free command. More wretched and cheerless places of abode than these can hardly be imagined. Readers who remember the so-called "shanties on the rocks" in the upper part of New York City can form, perhaps, some faint idea of their appearance. The best of them could hardly bear comparison with the poorest of the Irish laborers' houses that stand, here and there, along our railroads, while the worst of them were mere dog-kennels of driftwood and planks, in which it was almost incredible that human beings could exist throughout a Siberian winter.

The ostensible object of organizing a free command in connection with the Kará prisons was to encourage reformation among the convicts by holding out to them, as a reward for good behavior, the hope of obtaining release from confinement and an opportunity to better their condition. It does not seem to me, however, that this object has been attained. The free command is a demoralizing rather than a reforming agency; it promotes rather than discourages drunkenness and licentiousness; it does not guarantee, even to criminals who are actually reforming, any permanent amelioration of condition; and every decade it is the means of turning loose upon the Siberian population three or four thousand common criminals of the worst class. The custom of allowing the wives and children of convicts to accompany them to Siberia, and to live—sometimes alone and unprotected—in the free command, results necessarily in great demoralization. Such wives and children are supported—or at least aided to exist—by the Government, with the hope that they will ultimately exert a beneficial domestic influence over their criminal husbands and fathers; but the results rarely justify official anticipations. The women and girls in a great majority of cases go to the bad in the penal settlements, even if they have come uncorrupted through two or three hundred overcrowded *étapes* and forwarding prisons. There is little inducement, moreover, for a convict in the free command to reform and establish himself with his family in a comfortable house of his own, because he knows that in a comparatively short time he will be sent away to some other part of Siberia as a "forced colonist," and will lose all the material results of his industry and self-denial. He generally tries, therefore, to get through his term in the free command with as little labor and as much vicious enjoyment as possible. Hundreds, if not thousands, of convicts look forward with eagerness to enrolment in the free command merely on account of the opportunities that it affords for escape. Every summer, when the weather becomes warm enough to make life out of doors endurable, the free command begins to overflow into the forests; and for two or three months a narrow but almost continuous

stream of escaping convicts runs from the Kará penal settlements in the direction of Lake Baikál. The signal for this annual movement is given by the cuckoo, whose notes, when first
heard in the valley of the Kará, announce the beginning of the
warm season. The cry of the bird is taken as an evidence that
an escaped convict can once more live in the forests; and to
run away, in convict slang, is to "go to General Kukúshka for
orders." (Kukúshka is the Russian name for the cuckoo.) More
than 200 men leave the Kará free command every year to join
the army of "General Kukúshka"; and in Siberia, as a whole,
the number of runaway exiles and convicts who take the field in
response to the summons of this popular officer exceeds 30,000.
Most of the Kará convicts who "go to General Kukúshka for
orders" in the early summer come back to the mines under new
names and in leg-fetters the next winter; but they have had their
outing, and have breathed for three whole months the fresh, free
air of the woods, the mountains, and the steppes. With many
convicts the love of wandering through the trackless forests
and over the great plains of Eastern Siberia becomes a positive
mania. They do not expect to escape altogether; they know
that they must live for months the life of hunted fugitives, sub-
sisting upon berries and roots, sleeping on the cold and often
water-soaked ground, enduring hardships and miseries innumerable, and facing death at almost every step. But, in spite of all
this, they cannot hear in early summer the first soft notes of
the cuckoo without feeling an intense, passionate longing for
the adventures and excitements that attend the life of a *brodyág*
(a vagrant or tramp).

"I had once a convict servant," said a prison official at Kará
to me, "who was one of these irreclaimable vagrants, and who
ran away periodically for the mere pleasure of living a no-
madic life. He always suffered terrible hardships; he had no
hope of escaping from Siberia; and he was invariably brought
back in leg-fetters, sooner or later, and severely punished; but
nothing could break him of the practice. Finally, after he had
become old and gray-headed, he came to me one morning in

early summer—he was then living in the free command—and said to me 'Bárin, I wish you would please have me locked up.' 'Locked up!' said I. 'What for? What have you been doing?' 'I have not been doing anything,' he replied, 'but you know I am a *brodyág*. I have run away many times, and if I am not locked up I shall run away again. I am old and gray-headed now, I can't stand life in the woods as I could once, and I don't want to run away; but if I hear General Kukúshka calling me I must go. Please do me the favor to lock me up, your High Nobility, so that I *can't* go.' I did lock him up," continued the officer, "and kept him in prison most of the summer. When he was released the fever of unrest had left him, and he was as quiet, contented, and docile as ever."

There seems to me something pathetic in this inability of the worn, broken old convict to hear the cry of the cuckoo without yielding to the enticement of the wild, free, adventurous life with which that cry had become associated. He knew that he was feeble and broken; he knew that he could no longer tramp through the forests, swim rapid rivers, subsist upon roots, and sleep on the ground, as he once had done; but when the cuckoo called he felt again the impulses of his youth, he lived again in imagination the life of independence and freedom that he had known only in the pathless woods, and he was dimly conscious that if not prevented by force he "must go." As Ulysses had himself bound in order that he might not yield to the voices of the sirens, so the poor old convict had himself committed to prison in order that he might not hear and obey the cry of the cuckoo, which was so intimately associated with all that he had ever known of happiness and freedom.

It may seem to the reader strange that convicts are able to escape from penal settlements garrisoned and guarded by a force of a thousand Cossacks, but when one knows all the circumstances this ceases to be a matter for surprise. The houses of the ticket-of-leave convicts in the free command are not watched; there is no cordon of soldiers around the penal settlements; and it is comparatively an easy matter for a convict who is not under personal restraint to put into a gray bag a small quantity of food saved from his daily ration, tie a kettle to his belt, take an ax in his hand, and steal away at night into the trackless forest. It is a well-known fact, moreover, that many prison officials wink at escapes because they are able to turn them to pecuniary account. This they do by failing to report the runaways as "absent," by continuing to draw for weeks or months the clothing and the rations to which such runaways would be entitled if present, and by selling to the local representatives of Jewish speculators the food and garments thus acquired. Not infrequently these speculators have contracts to furnish prison supplies, and they fill them by reselling to the Government at a high price the very same flour and clothing that have just been stolen from it by its own officials. To an unscrupulous prison warden every dead or runaway convict is a source of steady revenue so long as his death or flight can be concealed and his name carried on the prison rolls. Under such circumstances, energetic measures to prevent the escape of criminals or to secure their recapture could hardly be expected.

The prison of Middle Kará, which is situated in the penal settlement of the same name, is a one-story log building of medium size, placed in such a way that one of its longer sides stands flush with the line of the street, while the other is inclosed by a high stockade so as to form a nearly square yard. It did not seem to me to differ much in appearance or plan from the prison at Ust Kará; but it was in better sanitary condition than the latter, and was evidently of more recent construction. As most of the prisoners that belonged there were at work in the upper gold placer when we arrived, I could not determine by inspection whether or not the building would be overcrowded at night. Major Pótulof told me, in reply to a question, that the number of criminals confined in it was 107. At the time of our visit, however, its *kámeras* contained only a few men, who had been excused from hard labor on account of temporary disability, or who had been assigned to domestic work, such as sweeping or cooking. The atmosphere of the *kámeras* was heavy and lifeless, but it seemed to be infinitely better than the air in the Ust Kará prison, and I could breathe it without much repugnance. By fastening against the walls over the sleeping-platforms large fresh boughs of hemlock and pine, an attempt had apparently been made to disguise the peculiar odor that is characteristic of Siberian prisons. Between these boughs in some of the *kámeras* I noticed, tacked against the logs, rectangular cards about twenty inches long by twelve inches wide, bearing in large printed letters verses from the New Testament. The only ones that I can now remember were: "Him that cometh to me I will in no wise cast out," and "Come unto me, all ye that labor and are heavy laden, and I will give you rest." Whence these scriptural cards came I do not know, but there seemed to me to be a strange and almost ghastly incongruity between the dark, grimy prison walls and the festal decorations of aromatic evergreens—between the rough plank sleeping-benches infested with vermin and the promise of rest for the weary and heavy-laden. How great a boon even bodily rest would be to the hard-labor convicts was shown in the pitiful attempts they had made to secure it by spreading down on the hard sleeping-benches thin patchwork mattresses improvised out of rags, cast-off foot-wrappers, and pieces cut from the skirts of their gray overcoats. Not one of these mattresses contained less than twenty scraps and remnants of old cloth, while in some of them there must have been a hundred. They all looked like dirty "crazy-quilts" made out of paper-rags in a poorhouse, and they could hardly have made any appreciable difference in the hardness of the plank sleeping-platforms. A man might as well seek to obtain a comfortable night's rest on a front door-step by interposing between it and his tired body a ragged and dirty bath-towel. There can be no reasonable excuse, it seems to me, for the failure of the Russian Government to provide at least beds and pillows of straw for its hard-labor convicts. Civilized human beings put straw even into the kennels of their dogs; but the Russian Government forces men to work for ten or twelve hours a day in its East Siberian mines; compels them after this exhausting toil to lie down on a bare plank; and then, to console them in their misery, tacks up on the grimy wall over their heads the command and the promise of Christ, "Come unto me, all ye that labor and are heavy laden, and I will give you rest." Mr. Frost and I made a careful examination of ten prisons in the province of the Trans-Baikál, and in none of them—with the single exception of the new central prison in Vérkhni Údinsk—did we find a bed, a pillow, or a blanket. Everywhere the prisoners lay down at night in their gray overcoats on bare planks, and almost everywhere they were tortured by vermin, and were compelled to breathe the same air over and over again until it seemed to me that there could not be oxygen enough left in it to support combustion in the flame of a farthing rush-light.

After we had finished our inspection of the cells in the Middle Kará prison, we made an examination of the kitchen. Hard-labor convicts at Kará receive a daily ration consisting of three pounds of black rye-bread; about four ounces of meat, including the bone; a small quantity of barley, which is generally put into the water in which the meat is boiled for the purpose of making soup, and a little brick tea. Occasionally they have potatoes or a few leaves of cabbage; but such luxuries are bought with money made by extra work, or saved by petty "economies" in other ways. This ration seemed to me ample in quantity, but lacking in variety and very deficient in vegetables. The bread, which I tasted, was perhaps as good as that eaten by Russian peasants generally; but it was very moist and sticky, and pieces taken from the center of the loaf could be rolled back into dough in one's hands. The meat, which I saw weighed out to the convicts after it had been boiled and cut up into pieces about as large as dice, did not have an inviting appearance, and suggested to my mind small refuse scraps intended for use as soap-grease. The daily meals of the convicts were arranged as follows: in the morning, after the roll-call or "verification," breakfast, consisting of brick tea and black rye-bread, was served to the prisoners in their cells. The working parties then set out on foot for the gold placers, carrying with them bread and tea for lunch. This midday meal was eaten in the open air beside a campfire, regardless of weather, and sometimes in fierce winter storms. Late in the afternoon the convicts returned on foot to their cells and ate on their sleeping-platforms the first hearty and nourishing meal of the day, consisting of hot soup, meat, bread, and perhaps a little more brick tea. After the evening verification they were locked up for the night, and lay down to sleep in closely packed rows on the *nári*, or sleeping-benches, without removing their clothing, and without making any preparations for the night beyond bringing in the *paráshas*, or excrement buckets, spreading down their thin patchwork crazy-quilts, and rolling up some of their spare clothing to put under their heads. The clothing furnished to a hard-labor convict at Kará consists—or should, by law, consist—of one coarse linen shirt and one pair of linen trousers every six months; one cap, one pair of thick trousers, and one gray overcoat every year; a *pólushúba*, or outer coat of sheepskin, every two years; one pair of *bródni*, or loose leather boots, every three and a half months in winter; and one pair of *kati*, or low shoes, every twenty-two days in summer. The quality of the food and clothing furnished by the Government may be inferred from the fact that the cost of maintaining a hard-labor convict at the mines is about $50 a year, or a little less than fourteen cents a day.

After having examined the Middle Kará prison as carefully as time and circumstances would permit, we proceeded up the valley to a point just beyond the penal settlement of Upper Kará, and, leaving our vehicles there, walked down toward the river to the mines.

The auriferous sand in the valley of the Kará lies buried under a stratum of clay, gravel, or stones, varying in thickness from ten to twenty feet. The hard labor of the convicts consists in the breaking up and removal of this overlying stratum and the transportation of the "pay gravel," or gold-bearing sand, to the "machine," where it is agitated with water in a sort of huge iron hopper and then allowed to run out with the water into a series of shallow inclined troughs, or flumes, where the "black sand" and the particles of gold fall to the bottom and are stopped by low transverse cleats.

The day was cold and dark, a light powdery snow was falling, and a more dreary picture than that presented by the mine can hardly be imagined. Thirty or forty convicts, surrounded by a cordon of Cossacks, were at work in a sort of deep gravel pit, the bottom of which was evidently at one time the bed of the stream. Some of them were loosening with pointed crowbars the hardpacked clay and gravel, some were shoveling it upon small hand-barrows, while others were carrying it away and dumping it at a distance of 150 or 200 yards. The machine was not in operation, and the labor in progress was nothing more than the preliminary "stripping," or laying bare of the gold-bearing stratum. The convicts, most of whom were in leg-fetters, worked slowly and listlessly, as if they were tired out and longed for the night; the silence was broken only by the steady clinking of crowbars, a quick, sharp order now and then from one of the overseers, or the jingling of chains as the convicts walked to and fro in couples carrying hand-barrows. There was little or no conversation except that around a small campfire a few yards away, where half a dozen soldiers were crouching on the snowy ground watching a refractory tea-kettle, and trying to warm their benumbed hands over a sullen, fitful blaze. We watched the progress of the work for ten or fifteen minutes, and then, chilled and depressed by the weather and the scene, returned to our vehicle and drove back to the Lower Diggings.

The hours of labor in the Kará mines are from 7 A.M. to 5 P.M. in winter, and from 5 A.M. to 7 P.M. in summer. A considerable part of this time, however, is spent by the convicts in going back and forth between the *razréis*, or "cutting," and the prisons where they spend their nights. The amount of gold extracted from the placers annually is eleven *puds*, or about four hundred pounds, all of which goes into the private purse of his Majesty the Tsar. The actual yield of the mines is probably a little more than this, since many of the convicts of the free command surreptitiously wash out gold for themselves and sell it to dealers in that commodity, who smuggle it across the Chinese frontier. To have "golden wheat," as the convicts call it, in one's possession at all in Siberia is a penal offense; but the profits of secret trade in it are so great that many small speculators run the risk of buying it from the convicts, while the latter argue that "the gold is God's," and that they have a perfect right to mine it for themselves if they can do so without too much danger of detection and punishment. The cost of maintaining the Kará penal establishment was estimated by Major Pótulof at 500,000 rubles, or about $250,000 a year. What proportion of this expense is borne by the Tsar, who takes the proceeds of the convicts' labor, I could not ascertain. He receives from all his gold-mines in Eastern Siberia—the "cabinet mines," as they are called—about 3600 pounds of pure gold per annum.

CHAPTER NINE

The History of the Kará Political Prison

A<small>LMOST THE LAST WORK THAT</small>
Colonel Kononóvich [Major Pótulof's predecessor] accomplished at the mines of Kará was the erection of the new political prison near the Lower Diggings. In general type it differs
little from the common-criminal prisons, but it is larger, better
lighted, and more spacious than the latter, and is, in all respects,
a more comfortable place of abode. It contains four *kámeras*,
exclusive of the hospital, or lazaret, and in each of them there
are three windows, a large table, a brick oven, and sleeping-
platform accommodations for about twenty-five men. There
are no beds, except in the lazaret, and all the bedclothing
that the prisoners have was purchased with their own money.
Originally the palisade did not entirely inclose the building,
and the prisoners could look out of their front windows across
the Kará valley; but Governor-General Anúchin, on the occasion of one of his rare visits to the mines, disapproved of this
arrangement, remarked cynically that "a prison is not a palace," and ordered that the stockade of high, closely set logs
be so extended as to cut off the view from the windows, and
completely shut the building in. It is hard to see in this order
anything but a deliberate intention on the part of a cruel
official to make the life of the political convicts as miserable
and intolerable as possible. Every common-criminal prison in
Kará, without exception, has windows that overlook the settlement or the valley; and every burglar and murderer in the

whole penal establishment can see from his cell something of the outside world. The political convicts, however, in the opinion of the governor-general, had no right to live in a "palace" from which they could see the green trees, the glimmer of the sunshine on the water, and the tender purple of the distant hills at sunset or at dawn. They must be shut up in a tight box; the fresh invigorating breeze from the mountains must be prevented from entering their grated windows; and the sight of a human being not clothed in a turnkey's uniform must never gladden their weary, homesick eyes. I have wished many times that his Excellency Governor-General Anúchin might be shut up for one year in the political prison at the mines of Kará; that he might look out for 365 days upon the weather-beaten logs of a high stockade; that he might lie for 365 nights on a bare sleeping-platform infested with vermin; and that he might breathe, night and day, for fifty-two consecutive weeks, the air of a close *kámera*, saturated with the poisonous stench of an uncovered excrement-bucket. *Then* he might say to himself, with a more vivid realization of its meaning, "A prison is not a palace."

When Colonel Kononóvich, in 1881, resigned his position as governor of the Kará penal establishment, his place was taken by Major Pótulof, who had previously been connected in some official capacity with the prison administration of the Nérchinsk silver mines. Shortly after Pótulof assumed command, all of the male political convicts, who then numbered about one hundred, were transferred to the new political prison erected by Colonel Kononóvich at the Lower Diggings, where they were divided into gangs of twenty-five men each and shut up in four large *kámeras*. Their life, as described in letters surreptitiously written by some of them to their friends, was hard and hopeless, but not absolutely intolerable. They were allowed to exercise every day in the courtyard, they were permitted to receive small sums of money from their friends, they had in the prison a fairly good library consisting of books purchased by them or sent to them from European Russia, and they could amuse themselves occasionally by working with carpenter's or blacksmith's tools in a small shop situated in one corner of the courtyard. On the other hand, they were living under very bad sanitary conditions; some of them were kept night and day in handcuffs and leg-fetters; two or three of them were chained to wheelbarrows; those who still had possession of their mental faculties were forced to listen constantly to the babbling or the raving of their insane comrades; they were no longer allowed to diversify their monotonous existence by work in the gold placers; they were deprived of the privilege of enrolment in the free command at the expiration of their terms of probation; they were forbidden to communicate with their relatives; and their whole world was bounded by the high serrated wall of the prison stockade. That their life was a terribly hard one seems to have been admitted, even by the most indifferent of Siberian officials.

It is a fact worthy, perhaps, of remark that the life of the political convicts at Kará which Governor-General Anúchin describes as "unbearable," was made unbearable by the direct and deliberate action of the Government itself. Anúchin caused to be erected in front of the prison windows the high stockade that hid from the prisoners the whole outside world and turned their place of confinement into a huge coverless box; while the Minister of the Interior, apparently without the least provocation, abolished the free command, and ordered the "complete isolation" which resulted in the suicide and insanity that the governor-general seems to deplore. The condition of the state criminals was not "unbearable" under the administration of Colonel Kononóvich. It became unbearable as a consequence of the orders that forced the latter's resignation.

It was hardly to be expected that young and energetic men would quietly submit to a state of things that was officially recognized as "unbearable," and that was gradually driving the weaker among them to suicide or insanity. In April, 1882, less than a year after Colonel Kononóvich's resignation, and less than a month after the delivery of Governor-General Anúchin's report to the Tsar, a few of the boldest and bravest of the state criminals at Kará made an attempt to escape by digging a tunnel under the prison wall. The excavation, which was made under the floor in one of the *kámeras*, was not discovered; but owing to the marshy nature of the ground upon which the building stood, the hole quickly filled with water, and work in it was abandoned. It then occurred to some of the prisoners that they might escape by concealing themselves during the day in the small shop in one corner of the courtyard where they were allowed to work, and then scaling the stockade from its roof at night. The most serious difficulty in the way was the evening "verification." After supper every night the prisoners in all the cells were counted, and the men concealed in the workshop would be missed before it grew dark enough to render the scaling of the stockade reasonably safe. This difficulty the prisoners hoped to overcome by making dummies to take the places of the missing men in the *kámeras*. It was not customary to waken prisoners who happened to be asleep at the time of the evening verification. The officer on duty merely included them in the count without disturbing them, and as he did not enter the dimly lighted cell, but made his count from the door, he was not likely to notice the difference between the figure of a dummy and the figure of a real man lying asleep on the platform with his face to the wall. If the proposed stratagem should succeed, the men who escaped were to make their way down the valley of the Amúr River to the Pacific Ocean, and there endeavor to get on board of some American whaling or trading vessel. In the meantime their comrades in the prison were to supply their places with dummies at every verification, in order to conceal their escape as long as possible, and give them time enough to reach the coast before the inevitable hue and cry should be raised. Late one afternoon in April, when all necessary preparations had been made, two political convicts named Muíshkin and Khrúshchef concealed themselves in a large box in the prison workshop, and just before the time for the evening verification their places were taken by two skilfully constructed dummies in convict dress which were laid on the sleeping-platform in the cell that they had occupied. The substitution was not noticed by the officer who made the evening count, and at a late hour of the night Muíshkin and Khrúshchef crept out of the box in the workshop, climbed up on the roof, scaled the stockade without attracting the attention of the sentry, and stole away into the forest. A few days later two more men escaped in the same way, and at the end of two weeks the prison authorities were counting every night and morning no less than six dummies, while the six prisoners represented by these lay figures were far on their way toward the coast of the Pacific. Sometime in the course of the third week after the departure of Muíshkin and Khrúshchef two more dummies were laid on the sleeping-platforms in the prison *kámeras*, and a forth couple escaped. In getting away from the stockade, however, one of them unfortunately fell into a ditch or a pool of water, and the splash attracted the attention of the nearest sentry, who promptly fired his rifle and raised an alarm. In ten minutes the whole prison was in commotion. A careful count was made of the prisoners in all the *kámeras*, and it was found that eight men were missing. A few days before this time a visit of inspection had been made to the prison by Mr. Gálkine Wrásskoy, chief of the Russian prison administration, and General Ilyashévich, governor of the Trans-Baikál, and when the escape was discovered these high officials were on their way from Kará to Chíta. In response to a summons from Major Pótulof they hurried back to the Lower Diggings and personally superintended the organization of a thorough and widely extended search for the missing men. Telegrams were dispatched to all the seaport towns along the coast of the Pacific, as well as to all points on the Amúr that could be reached by telegraph; descriptions and photographs of the fugitives were mailed to police officials throughout Eastern Siberia; orders were issued to arrest all suspicious or unknown persons; and searching parties of natives, stimulated by the promise of reward, scoured the forests in all parts of the Trans-Baikál. It was impossible, of course, for men who were unfamiliar with the country, who had neither guides, maps, nor compasses, and who were enfeebled by long imprisonment, to elude, for any great length of time, so persistent and far-reaching a pursuit. Although two of them, Muíshkin and Khrúshchef, made a journey of more than a thousand miles, and actually reached the seaport town of Vladivostok, every one of the fugitives was ultimately recaptured and brought back to Kará in handcuffs and leg-fetters.

In the meantime the prison authorities at Kará were making preparations to "give the political convicts a lesson" and "reduce the prison to order." This they purposed to do by depriving the prisoners of all the privileges that they had previously enjoyed; by taking away from them books, money, underclothing, bedclothing, and every other thing not furnished by the Government to common criminals of the penal-servitude class; by distributing them in small parties among the common-convict prisons at Ust Kará, Middle Kará, and Upper Kará; and by subjecting them to what are known to Russian prisoners as "dungeon conditions."[1] Anticipating, or pretending to anticipate, insubordination or resistance to these measures on the part of the politicals, Ilyashévich and Gálkine Wrásskoy concentrated at the Lower Diggings six *sótnias* of Cossacks, and after ten days of inaction, intended, apparently, to throw the prisoners off their guard, ordered a sudden descent upon the prison in the night. This unprovoked attack of an armed force upon sleeping and defenseless prisoners is known in the history of the Kará political prison as "the pogrom of May 11." Three or four hundred Cossacks with bayoneted rifles marched noise-

1. A prisoner living under "dungeon conditions" is deprived of money, books, writing-materials, underclothing, bedclothing, tobacco, and all other luxuries; he is not allowed to walk for exercise in the courtyard nor to have any communication with the outside world; and he must live exclusively upon black rye-bread and water, with now and then a little of the soup, or broth thickened with barley, which is known to the political convicts as *balánda*.

lessly into the courtyard under direction of Lieutenant-Colonel Rúdenko, filled the prison corridor, and then, throwing open suddenly and simultaneously the doors of all the *kámeras,* rushed in upon the bewildered politicals, dragged them from their sleeping-platforms, and proceeded with great roughness and brutality to search them, deprive them of their personal property, strip them of their clothing, and hale them out into the courtyard. All the remonstrances and protests of the sufferers were answered with insults; and when some of the more impetuous of them, indignant at the unprovoked brutality of the assault, armed themselves with boards torn up from the sleeping-platforms and made an attempt to defend themselves, they were knocked down and mercilessly beaten by the Cossacks with the butt-ends of their guns. It is not necessary to go minutely into the details of this scene of cruelty and violence. I do not wish to make it out any worse than it really was, and for my purpose it is sufficient to say that before noon on the 11th of May, 1882, the bruised and bleeding political convicts, robbed of all their personal possessions and stripped of the boots and underclothing that they had bought with their own money and that they had previously been permitted to wear, set out in three parties, on foot and without breakfast, for the common-criminal prisons of Ust, Middle, and Upper Kará. They were guarded by convoys of from fifty to one hundred Cossacks, who had express instructions from Governor Ilyashévich not to spare the butt-ends of their guns. The party destined for Ust Kará, in which there was one man chained to a wheelbarrow, asked permission to stop and rest on the road, as they had had nothing to eat or drink that day and were marching a distance of fifteen versts (about ten miles). The soldiers of the convoy, however, refused to allow them to stop, and pricked them on with their bayonets. Thereupon the prisoners who were not handcuffed attacked the Cossacks with stones. An unequal contest followed, in the course of which the men who resisted were knocked down and beaten again with the butt-ends of guns, and all who were not already manacled had

their hands tied securely behind their backs. Late in the afternoon, bruised, tired, hungry, and thirsty, they reached Ust
Kará, and after being again carefully searched were shut up
by twos in the dark and dirty "secret" cells of the common-
criminal prison, where they threw their weary bodies down
on the cold, damp floors and congratulated themselves that the
day was over.[2] The parties sent respectively to the Amúrski
prison and the prison in Middle Kará had an experience similar
to that of the Ust Kará party, except that they were not beaten
by their guards. Before dark the hundred or more state criminals who had occupied the *kámeras* of the political prison were
distributed in small parties among the common-criminal prisons
of Ust Kará, the Lower Diggings, Middle Kará, and Upper
Kará; the long-term convicts were in both handcuffs and leg-

2. "Secret" cells in Siberian prisons are those intended for the solitary confinement of persons accused of murder or other capital crimes.
They were not generally shown us in our visits to prisons, but I was
permitted by Colonel Makófski to inspect the "secret" cells in the
prison at Irkútsk. These had neither beds nor sleeping-platforms, and
contained no furniture of any kind except a *parásha,* or excrement
bucket. The prisoners confined in them were forced to sleep without
pillows or bedclothing on the cold cement or stone floor, and during
the day had either to sit on this floor or to stand. I saw men who had
not yet been tried occupying such cells as these in the Irkútsk prison.
If I had power to summon as witnesses the subordinate officials of the
House of Preliminary Detention in St. Petersburg, I could prove, in a
Russian court, that even in that show-prison of the Empire there were
kártsers, or disciplinary cells, where there was not so much as a *parásha,* and where the floors were covered with excrement. Of course, Mr.
Gálkine Wrásskoy and Mr. Kokóftsef, the heads of the Russian prison
administration, were not aware of this fact; but, nevertheless, it is a
fact, unless both political prisoners and the prison officials themselves
severally and independently lied to me. The political offender Diches-
kúlo was put into such a cell as this after the riot in the House of Preliminary Detention that followed the flogging of Bogoliúbof. I did not
see the "secret" cells in the Kará prisons, but there is no reason to
suppose that they were in any better condition than the *kámeras* that
I did see and that I have described. I do not mean to have the reader
draw the sweeping and mistaken conclusion that all cells, or even all
"secret" cells, in Russian prisons are of this kind, nor that the higher
prison officials are in all cases responsible for such a state of affairs. All
that I aim to do is to make plain the conditions under which educated
and delicately nurtured political offenders in Russian prisons are *sometimes* compelled to live.

fetters, and all were living under "dungeon conditions." In this manner Governor Ilyashévich and Mr. Gálkine Wrásskoy put down the "insurrection" that a hundred or more sleeping prisoners presumably would have raised when they awoke, taught the "insurgents" a valuable and much-needed "lesson," and showed the Minister of the Interior how vigorously and successfully his subordinates could deal with a sudden and threatening emergency—and with sleeping men! The political prison had been "reduced to order," but it was the "order" that once "reigned in Warsaw."

For two months the political convicts lived under "dungeon conditions" in the cells of the common-criminal prisons, seeing little of one another and knowing nothing of what was happening in the outside world. Bad air, bad and insufficient food, and the complete lack of exercise soon began injuriously to affect their health; scurvy broke out among them, and in less than a month several, including Tíkhonof and Zhukófski, were at the point of death, and many more were so weak that they could not rise to their feet when ordered to stand up for verification. During all of this time the prison authorities had in their possession money belonging to these wretched convicts; but they would not allow the latter to use it, nor to direct its expenditure for the underclothing, bedding, and nourishing food of which the sick especially were in such urgent need. It was not until scurvy threatened to become epidemic that Major Khaltúrin, a cruel gendarme officer from Irkútsk who had succeeded Major Pótulof in the command of the political prison, consented to allow the prisoners to have bedding.

In the women's prison at Ust Kará the state of affairs was little better. The women, of course, had had nothing whatever to do with the escape, nor with the artificially created "insurrection," but they had, nevertheless, to take their share of the consequences. The new commandant, Major Khaltúrin, believed in strict discipline with no favors; and he regarded the permission that had tacitly been given the women to wear their own dress instead of the prison costume as an unnecessary concession to a foolish and sentimental weakness. He therefore ordered that their own clothing be taken away from them, and that they be required to put on the convict garb. Some of the women were sick and unable to change their dress, others did not believe that the order would really be enforced, and they refused to obey it, and finally the overseer of the prison resorted to violence. The scene that ensued produced such an effect upon Madam Léschern that she attempted to commit suicide.

Outside the political prison at the Lower Diggings were living a number of women who had voluntarily come to the mines in order to be near their husbands. Previous to the escape and the pogrom these women had been allowed to have interviews with their imprisoned husbands once or twice a week, and had received from the latter small sums of money, with the help of which they contrived to exist. After the prison had been "reduced to order" and the political convicts had been subjected to "dungeon conditions," interviews between husbands and wives were no longer permitted; and as the prisoners' money was all held in the possession of the authorities, the unfortunate women and children were soon reduced almost to starvation. Véra Rogatchóf, wife of Lieutenant Dmítri Rogatchóf, a young artillery officer then in penal servitude, was brought to such a state of destitution and despair that she finally shot herself.

On the 6th of July, 1882, eight of the political convicts, who were regarded by the Government for some reason as particularly dangerous, were sent back in chains from Kará to St. Petersburg to be immured for life in the "stone bags" of the castle of Schlusselburg. A few days later—about the middle of July—all the rest of the state criminals were brought back to the political prison at the Lower Diggings, where they were put into new and much smaller cells that had been made by erecting partitions in the original *kámeras* in such a manner as to divide each of them into thirds. The effect of this change was to crowd every group of seven or eight men into a cell that was so nearly filled by the sleeping-platform as to leave no room for locomotion. Two men could not stand side by side in the narrow space between the edge of the platform and the wall, and the occupants of the cell were therefore compelled to sit or lie all day on the plank *nári* without occupation for either minds or bodies. To add to their misery, *paráshas* were set in their small cells, and the air at times became so offensive and polluted that, to use the expression of one of them in a letter to me, "it was simply maddening." No other reply was made to their petitions and remonstrances than a threat from Khaltúrin that if they did not keep quiet they would be flogged. With a view to intimidating them Khaltúrin even sent a surgeon to make a physical examination of one political, for the avowed purpose of ascertaining whether his state of health was such that he could be flogged without endangering his life. This was the last straw. The wretched state criminals, deprived of exercise, living under "dungeon conditions," poisoned by air laden with the stench of excrement-buckets, and finally threatened with the whip when they complained, could endure no more. They resolved to make that last desperate protest against cruelty which is known in Russian prisons as a *golodófka*, or "hunger-strike." They sent a notification to Major Khaltúrin that their life had finally become unendurable, that they preferred death to such an existence, and that they should refuse to take food until they either perished or forced the Government to treat them with more humanity. No attention was paid to their notification, but from that moment not a mouthful of the food that was set into their cells was touched. As day after day passed, the stillness of death gradually settled down upon the prison. The starving convicts, too weak and apathetic even to talk to one another, lay in rows, like dead men, upon the plank sleeping-platforms, and the only sounds to be heard in the building were the footsteps of the sentries, and now and then the incoherent mutterings of the insane. On the fifth day of the *golodófka* Major Khaltúrin, convinced that the hunger-strike was serious, came to the prison and asked the convicts to state definitely upon what terms they would discontinue their protest. They replied that the conditions of their life were unbearable, and that they should continue their self-starvation until the excrement-buckets were taken out of their cells, until they were permitted to have books and to exercise daily in the open air, until they were allowed to direct the expenditure of their money for better food and better clothing than were furnished by the Government, and until he (Khaltúrin) gave them a solemn assurance that none of them should be flogged. The commandant told them that the talk about flogging was nonsense; that there had never been any serious intention of resorting to the whip, and that, if they would end their strike, he would see what could be done to improve the material conditions of their life. Not being able to get any positive assurances that their demands would be complied with, the prisoners continued the *golodófka*. On the tenth day the state of affairs had become alarming. All of the starving men were in the last stages of physical prostration, and some of them seemed to be near their death. Count Dmítri Tolstoï, the Minister of the Interior, who had been apprised of the situation, telegraphed the commandant to keep a *skórbnoi list*, or "hospital sheet," setting forth the symptoms and condition of the strikers, and to inform him promptly of any marked change.[3] Every day thereafter a *feld-*

3. I have never been able to understand why a government that is capable when irritated of treating prisoners in this way should hesitate a moment about letting them die, and thus getting rid of them. However, I believe it is a fact that in every case where political hunger-strikers have had courage and nerve enough to starve themselves to the point of death the authorities have manifested anxiety and have ultimately yielded. It is one of many similar inconsistencies in Russian penal administration. The Government seems to be sensitive to some things and brutally insensible to others. It prides itself upon its humanity in expunging the death penalty from its civil code, and yet it inflicts death constantly by sentences of courts-martial in civil cases. It has abolished the *knut*, but it flogs with the *plet*, which, according to the testimony of Russian officers, can be made to cause death in a hundred blows. It shrinks from allowing political convicts to die of self-starvation and yet it puts them to a slow death in the "stone bags" of the castle of Schlusselburg. To the practical American intelligence it

sher or hospital-steward went through the cells taking the pulse and the temperature of the starving men. On the thirteenth day of the *golodófka* Major Khaltúrin sent word to the wives of all the political convicts living at the Lower Diggings that they might have an interview with their husbands—the first in more than two months—if they would try to persuade them to begin taking food. They gladly assented, of course, to this condition, and were admitted to the prison. At the same time Khaltúrin went himself to the starving men and assured them, on his honor, that if they would end the hunger-strike he would do everything in his power to satisfy their demands. The entreaties of the wretched, heart-broken women, and the promises of the commandant finally broke down the resolution of the politicals, and on the thirteenth day the first hunger-strike in the history of the Kará political prison came to an end.

While these events were taking place, a young married woman about twenty-four years of age, named Maria Kutitónskaya, who had been condemned to penal servitude on account of her revolutionary activity in Odessa, finished her prison term in Kará, and was sent as a forced colonist to a small village called Akshá, situated in the southern part of the Trans-Baikál, on the frontier of Mongolia. She had been an eye-witness of the brutalities that attended the "reduction of the political prison to order" by Rúdenko and Pótulof; she had seen the "lesson" given to the political convicts with the butt-ends of guns; she herself had felt the shame and misery that impelled Madam Léschern and Mrs. Rogatchóf to attempt self-destruction; she was acquainted with the causes and history of the long and desperate hunger-strike that had just ended; and, stirred to the very depths of her soul by a feeling of intense indignation, she determined, as a last resort and at the cost of

would seem to be safer, as well as more humane, to order political convicts out into the prison courtyard and have them shot, than to kill them slowly under "dungeon conditions." Society would not be half so much shocked and exasperated by summary executions as it now is by suicides, hunger-strikes, and similar evidences of intolerable misery among the political convicts in prison and at the mines.

her own life, to assassinate General Ilyashévich, the governor of the Trans-Baikál, and thus call the attention of the world to the cruelties practiced by his authority, and in part under his direction, at the mines of Kará. She was at this time pregnant, and was aware of her condition; she knew that it would be impossible to escape after committing the crime that she contemplated; she knew that she was about to sacrifice her own life, and probably the life also of her unborn child; but so intense were the emotions aroused by all she had seen and known at Kará, that she was ready to commit murder, and to die for it, upon the chance that the deed and its investigation would give publicity to the wrongs and outrages that she and her companions had suffered. As soon as she could get together money enough for her traveling expenses after her arrival at Akshá, she bought a small, cheap revolver from a common-criminal colonist, ran away from her place of banishment, and, hiring horses from the peasants in the villages through which she passed, made her way toward Chíta, which was the governor's place of residence. As it was not customary for young and attractive women to travel entirely alone in that part of the world, she was regarded with a good deal of interest and curiosity by the peasants, and just before she reached her destination she was arrested by a village official upon suspicion. She persuaded this man to take her to Chíta and turn her over to the *isprávnik*, with whom she was personally acquainted. To the *isprávnik* she admitted frankly that she had run away from her place of exile, but said that in so doing she had not intended to escape, but merely to get an interview with the governor. After some conversation the *isprávnik* went with her to the governor's house, and, leaving her in a reception room, went to apprise Ilyashévich of her presence and her desire for an interview.

"Have you searched her?" inquired the governor suspiciously.

"No," replied the *isprávnik;* "I didn't think of it."

"Never mind," said Ilyashévich. "What can a woman do?"

And with these words he entered the reception room where Madam Kutitónskaya, with a cocked revolver hidden under a handkerchief in her right hand, was awaiting him. As he advanced to greet her she raised the revolver, and saying, "This is for the 11th of May," shot him through the lungs. The wound was not mortal, but he fell to the floor and was carried to a couch by some of the servants, while the *ispravnik* seized and disarmed Madam Kutitónskaya, caused her to be bound, and sent her under strong guard to the Chíta prison. Her life there was a life of terrible loneliness and misery. She was put into a cold, dirty, "secret" cell, which the district architect of the Trans-Baikál described to me as "hardly long enough to lie down in or high enough to stand up in." Her own dress and underclothing were taken away from her, and in place of them she was given an old prison suit that had already been worn by a common convict and was full of vermin. She lived under strict "dungeon conditions," and for three months lay without bedclothing on the bare floor. When, as a result of such hardships and privations, she became sick, and asked for straw to lay down on the planks where she slept, she was told by the chief of police, Mélnikof, that there was no straw for her. But for the food smuggled into her cell and the aid surreptitiously given to her by sympathetic common-criminal convicts in the same prison, she would undoubtedly have died before the meeting of the court appointed to investigate the case. After three months of this wretched existence she was tried by court-martial and sentenced to be hanged. Then, for another whole month, she lay under sentence of death, arguing with herself, through many long, sleepless nights, the question whether or not she should make known to the authorities her pregnant condition, which had not yet become apparent. She knew that an announcement of the fact that she was with child would, in accordance with the custom in such cases, secure a long reprieve if not a commutation of her sentence; but, on the other hand, life held no hope for her, and she believed that if she allowed herself to be hanged under such circumstances, the fact of her pregnancy, which would inevitably be discovered after her death, would intensify the feeling of horror that she hoped would be excited by the series of events which had led up to the catastrophe—would give to such events even greater publicity, and would inspire all lovers of humanity and justice with a deeper and bitterer hatred of the Government. The questions that tormented her most were first, whether, if she allowed herself to be hanged without revealing her condition, she would not be the murderer of her unborn child, and secondly, whether that child would die when she died, or would live for a time in her dead body. This last ghastly doubt seems to have been particularly harrowing to her in her morbid mental condition, but even in the face of such reflections she finally decided to allow herself to be hanged. Early in January, 1883, the Government, without reference to her condition, of which it was still ignorant, commuted her sentence to penal servitude for life and sent her with a returning party of common-criminal exiles to the city of Irkútsk.[4] Although it was mid-winter, she was not provided with a sheepskin overcoat, nor with felt boots, and she might have perished from cold on the road if the common criminals in the party had not taken pity upon her and furnished her with warm clothing at the expense of their own comfort. When she reached Irkútsk she was in such a condition that she had to be lifted out of her sleigh. As a result of this prolonged agony of mind and body, her child, a short time afterward, was born dead in the Irkútsk prison. When we left Siberia in 1886 she was still living. All that I know of her life since that time is that it has ended.

When one of my informants first knew Madam Kutitón-skaya she was a happy, careless schoolgirl in Odessa, and no

4. I was credibly informed, and in justice the fact should be stated, that this commutation of sentence was asked for by Governor Ilyashé-vich, whose life Madam Kutitónskaya had attempted. Whether he felt, upon reflection, some stirrings of pity and remorse, or whether he merely wished to make a showing of magnanimity in order to throw doubt upon the reports of his cruelty at the mines and break their effect, I do not know.

one would have ventured to predict that in less than ten years she would develop into a woman of such extraordinary energy, courage, self-control, and firmness of purpose. There are few things more remarkable in the records of heroism than the determination of Madam Kutitónskaya to allow herself to be hanged, with a child in her womb, in order that the horror of such an execution might stir the emotions of every man and woman who heard of it, and give wider publicity to the series of events of which it was the final outcome. Such, however, is the type of character that is forged in the furnace of oppression and tempered in the cold bath of solitary confinement.

The statements that I have made with regard to the events that led to the shooting of Governor Ilyashévich are based upon conversations with the political convicts who were actors in them, and upon three independently prepared accounts of manuscript of the escape, the pogrom, and the hunger-strike. The story of the attempted assassination, and of Madam Kutitónskaya's life in prison is from one of her letters, written after her arrival in Irkútsk. The brief transcript of her intentions, thoughts, and reflections, while lying under sentence of death in Chíta, was obtained from an exiled lady who had many long talks with her in the Irkútsk prison, and whose acquaintance I subsequently made. The whole story, in its main outlines, is known to political exiles throughout Siberia, and I heard it in half a dozen different places. All the efforts that I dared make to get at the Government's side of the case were unsuccessful. The officials to whom I applied for information—with a few exceptions—either manifested such a disinclination to talk that I could not pursue the subject, or else made preposterous attempts to deceive me. A young surgeon in the Irkútsk prison whom I questioned about Madam Kutitónskaya was so frightened that he got rid of me as soon as possible and never dared return my call. The *isprávnik* of Nérchinski Zavód, who went to Kará with some of the recaptured fugitives after the escape, described the political convicts to me as clever rogues who were not deserving of either sympathy or respect.

Most of them, he said, were "priests' sons, or seminarists who had been expelled from school." Lieutenant-Colonel Nóvikof, who was for three years or more commander of the Cossack battalion at the mines of Kará, assured me that the political convicts were mere miserable insignificant boys, without any definite aims or convictions; that out of one hundred and fifty of them that he had known at Kará only three or four had any education, and that Madam Kutitónskaya's attempt to assassinate Governor Ilyashévich was "a mere crazy freak"—that "she didn't know herself what she did it for." The attentive reader will see that I have had no difficulty in making my choice between such preposterous statements as these and the clear, coherent, and detailed narratives of the political convicts themselves. If my history of the Kará political prison is one-sided, it is simply because the other side either refused to give me information, or was too ignorant to state its own case with any show of plausibility.

How far from the real truth were the statements made to me by officials with regard to the character of the political convicts at Kará, I purpose to show by giving brief biographies of three or four of the men and women who took an active part in the series of events that I have tried to describe, or who were identified with the later history of the political prison. One of the ablest and most distinguished of them was Anna Pávlovna Korbá. She was the daughter of a Russian nobleman named Paul Mengart, and was born in the province of Tver, near Moscow, in 1849. She was carefully educated under the direction of her mother, a cultured and deeply religious woman, and at the early age of eighteen or nineteen she was married to a Swiss gentleman residing in Russia named Victor Korbá. Her beauty and accomplishments made her greatly sought after in society, her husband was wealthy and was proud of her social success, and for a time she lived the life of a woman of the great world. This life, however, could not long satisfy a young girl of bright mind and serious character, and in 1869, when she was only twenty years of age, she made an attempt to fit herself for something better. A school for the higher education of the daughters of the nobility was opened about that time in connection with a boys' college in St. Petersburg, and Madam Korbá at once enrolled as a student, with the intention of finally completing her education in one of the institutions for women at Zurich or in Paris. In 1870 her husband failed in business: she was forced to abandon the hope of finishing her collegiate training abroad, and a short time afterward went with her husband to reside in the small provincial town of Minsk, where he had obtained employment. Here she began her career of public activity by organizing a society and raising a fund for the purpose of promoting popular education and aiding poor students in the universities. Of this society she was the president. In 1877 the Russo-Turkish War broke out, and opened to her ardent and generous nature a new field of benevolent activity. As soon as wounded Russian soldiers began to come back from Bulgaria, she went into the hospitals of Minsk as a Sister of Mercy, and a short time afterward put on the uniform of the International Association of the Red Cross, and went to the front and took a position as a Red Cross nurse in a Russian field-hospital beyond the Danube. She was then hardly twenty-seven years of age. What she saw and what she suffered in the course of that terrible Russo-Turkish campaign can be imagined by those who have seen the paintings of the Russian artist Vereshchágin. Her experience had a marked and permanent effect upon her character. She became an enthusiastic lover and admirer of the common Russian peasant, who bears upon his weary shoulders the whole burden of the Russian state, but who is cheated, robbed, and oppressed, even while fighting the battles of his country. She determined to devote the remainder of her life to the education and the emancipation of this oppressed class of the Russian people. At the close of the war she returned to Russia, but was almost immediately prostrated by typhus fever contracted in an overcrowded hospital. After a long and dangerous illness she finally recovered, and began the task that she had set herself; but she was opposed and thwarted at every step by the police and the bureaucratic officials who were interested in maintaining the existing state of things, and she gradually became convinced that before much could be done to improve the condition of the common people the Government must be overthrown. She soon afterward became a revolutionist, joined the party of "The Will of the People," and participated actively in all the attempts that were made between 1879 and 1882 to overthrow the autocracy and establish a constitutional form of government. On the 5th of June, 1882, she was arrested and thrown into the fortress of Petropávlovsk, and some months later was tried before the Governing Senate upon the charge of being a terrorist. At the end of the trial she was asked if she had any last words to say in her own defense, and she replied as follows:

"I do not admit my guilt. I will, however, admit that I belong to the revolutionary party—the party of the Will of the People—and that I believe in its principles and share its views. As for an organization that chooses and prefers a path of bloodshed, I do not know of any such organization, and I doubt whether any such organization exists. Such a party may arise in time, if the revolutionary movement extends; but if I be living when the time comes, I will not belong to it. If the party of the Will of the People adopts the policy of terror, it is not because it prefers terrorism, but because terrorism is the only possible method of attaining the objects set before it by the historical conditions of Russian life. These are sad and fateful words, and they bear a prophecy of terrible calamity. Gentlemen—Senators, you are well acquainted with the fundamental laws of the Russian Empire. You are aware that no one has a right to advocate any change in the existing imperial form of Government, or even think of such a thing. Merely to present to the Crown a collective petition is forbidden—and yet the country is growing and developing, the conditions of social life are becoming day by day more and more complicated, and the moment approaches when the Russian people will burst through the barriers from which there is no exit."

The presiding judge, interrupting: "That is your personal opinion."

Madam Korbá, continuing: "The historical task set before the party of the Will of the People is to widen these barriers and to obtain for Russia independence and freedom. The means for the attainment of these objects depend directly upon the Government. We do not adhere obstinately to terrorism. The hand that is raised to strike will instantly fall if the Government will change the political conditions of life. Our party has patriotic self-control enough not to take revenge for its bleeding wounds; but, unless it prove false to the Russian people, it cannot lay down its arms until it has conquered for that people freedom and well-being. As a proof that the aims of our party are wholly peaceful, I beg you to read the letter written to Alexander III soon after the 1st of March.[5] You will see from it that we desire only reforms, but reforms that shall be sincere, complete, and vital."

Madam Korbá's last words did not soften toward her the hearts of her judges, and of course she did not expect that they would. She was found guilty, and was sentenced to twenty years of penal servitude with deprivation of all civil rights, and forced colonization in Siberia for life at the expiration of her penal term. At the date of my last advices from the mines of Kará she was still living, but she was greatly broken, and there was little probability that she would long endure the hardships and privations of penal servitude.

Among the male political convicts at the mines of Kará whose careers most interested me was Hypolyte Muíshkin. In the year 1864 a well-known author and political economist named Chernishéfski, whose famous novel, *What Is To Be Done?* has recently been translated into English, was tried in St. Petersburg as a revolutionist and banished to Siberia. He was at first sent to the Alexandrófski central prison, near Irkútsk, but ultimately he was transferred to the small town of Villúisk, in the sub-arctic province of Yakútsk, where he lived

5. The date of the assassination of Alexander II.

many years under the strictest police surveillance. When, in 1870, the modern revolutionary movement began, it was the dream of all the ardent young Russian revolutionists to rescue Chernishéfski from Siberian exile, and enable him to escape from the Empire to some place where he could continue his work unmolested. Several attempts were made to liberate him, but they all failed, and the project was finally abandoned as impracticable. In 1875 a young student in the Technological Institute at St. Petersburg named Hypolyte Muíshkin conceived the idea of going to Siberia in the disguise of a captain of gendarmes and presenting himself boldly to the *isprávnik* in Villúisk with forged orders from the gendarmerie directing him (Muíshkin) to take charge of the exile Chernishéfski and carry him to Blagovéshchinsk, on the Amúr River. Such transfers of dangerous political exiles were not at that time uncommon, and Muíshkin felt confident that he should accomplish his purpose. He went as a private traveler to Irkútsk, resided there several months, succeeded in getting into the corps of gendarmes as a subordinate officer, and in a short time made himself so useful that he was generally trusted and was given the freedom of the office. He provided himself with the necessary blanks, filled them up with an order accrediting him as a gendarme officer intrusted with the duty of taking the exile Chernishéfski to Blagovéshchinsk, forged the signatures, affixed the proper seals, provided himself with the uniform of a captain of gendarmes, and then resigned his position in the gendarmerie upon the pretext that he had received news that made it necessary for him to return at once to European Russia. He disappeared from Irkútsk, and as soon as he deemed it prudent to do so he set out for Villúisk, with the uniform of a gendarme officer in his satchel, and a forged order in his pocket directing the *isprávnik* of Villúisk, Captain Zhírkof, to turn over the exile Chernishéfski to him for conveyance to Blagovéshchinsk. Muíshkin was an accomplished conspirator, an eloquent talker, and a man of fine personal presence, and when he presented himself in the uniform of a gendarme officer to the *isprávnik* at Villúisk he was received at first with unquestioning deference and respect. He stated his business, and produced the order directing the *isprávnik* to turn over the distinguished exile to him for conveyance to Blagovéshchinsk. The plot came very near succeeding, and probably would have succeeded if Muíshkin had had money enough to bring with him two or three confederates in the disguise of soldiers or gendarmes and in the capacity of escort. It is very unusual for a commissioned officer to travel in Siberia without at least one soldier or Cossack to look after his baggage, to see about getting post-horses promptly, and to act generally in the capacity of body-servant. The absence of such a man or men was especially noticeable and unusual in this case, for the reason that Muíshkin was to take charge of an important and dangerous political offender. The absence of an escort was the first thing that excited the *isprávnik's* suspicion. It seemed to him very strange that a gendarme officer should be sent there after Chernishéfski without a guard of two or three soldiers to help him to take care of the dangerous prisoner, and the more he thought about it the more suspicious the whole affair appeared to him. After a night's reflection he decided not to turn over Chernishéfski to this gendarme officer without the sanction of the governor of the province, who resided in Yakútsk, and at breakfast the next morning he told Muíshkin that Governor Chernáief was his— the *isprávnik's*—immediate superior, and that without an order from the governor he did not feel justified in surrendering an exile of so much importance as the political economist Chernishéfski. He proposed, therefore, to send a courier to Yakútsk with Muíshkin's papers, and to await the return of this courier before taking any action.

"Very well," replied Muíshkin coolly. "I did not suppose that it would be necessary to obtain the consent of the governor before complying with the orders of the imperial police; but if such consent is indispensable, I will go to Governor Chernáief myself and get it."

When Muíshkin set out for Yakútsk, the *isprávnik*, whose

suspicions had meanwhile grown stronger, said to him, "It is not proper for an officer of your rank to travel about without any escort, and if you will permit me to do so I will send with you a couple of Cossacks." Muíshkin could not object, and the Cossacks were sent—the *isprávnik* instructing them that they were on no account to lose sight of this gendarme officer, because there was something suspicious about him, and it was not certain that he really was what he pretended to be. As soon as Muíshkin had gone, the *isprávnik* wrote a letter to the governor, apprising him of his suspicions, and sent it by another Cossack, with directions to get ahead of Muíshkin if possible and deliver it before the latter reached his destination. The Cossack overtook Muíshkin on the road, and in the course of conversation among the soldiers the fact transpired that the third Cossack had a letter from the *isprávnik* to the governor. Muíshkin knew then that the game was lost, and at the first favorable opportunity he attempted to escape by dashing suddenly into the woods. The Cossacks, in pursuance of their instructions, endeavored to keep him in sight; but he drew his revolver, fired at them, wounded one of them, and finally made his escape. For nearly a week he wandered around in the great primeval forests that border the river Léna; but at last, half dead from cold, hunger, and exhaustion, he was captured. After some months of imprisonment in Irkútsk he was sent under strong guard to St. Petersburg and was there thrown into the fortress of Petropávlovsk. For nearly three years he lay in a bombproof casemate of the Trubetskói bastion awaiting trial, and all that I know of this part of his life I learned from an exile in Siberia who occupied a cell in the fortress near him. This gentleman said that Muíshkin was often delirious from fever, excitement, or the maddening effect of long solitary confinement, and that he frequently heard his cries when he was put into a strait-jacket or strapped to his bed by the fortress guard.

In October, 1878, Muíshkin was finally tried with "the 193" before a special session of the Governing Senate. All of the

Anna Pávlovna Korbá

HYPOLYTE MUÍSHKIN

political prisoners brought to the bar on the occasion of this famous trial insisted that the public should be admitted to hear the proceedings, and that they—the prisoners—should be allowed to have their own stenographer. The Government declined to accede to either of these demands, and, as a consequence, most of the politicals refused to make any defense or to take any part in the proceedings. At the end of the trial Muíshkin, when asked if he had any last words to say, made a fiery speech denouncing the secrecy of the trial, and declaring that they did not desire nor expect to escape punishment, but thought they had a right to ask that they be tried in open court and that their case be laid before the people through the press. As soon as Muíshkin began to attack the Government he was ordered by the presiding judge to be silent, and when he refused, and insisted upon his right to be heard, the gendarmes were directed to remove him from the court-room. The last words he uttered before he was choked into silence and dragged out were: "This court is worse than a house of ill-fame; there they sell only bodies, but here you prostitute honor, and justice, and law!" For his original offense, aggravated by this outrageous insult to the court, Muíshkin was sentenced to ten years of penal servitude with deprivation of all civil rights, and was shortly afterward incarcerated in the central convict prison at Kharkóf. I have not space for even the briefest description of the sufferings of the political convicts in that prison. The story has been written by one of them and published surreptitiously in Russia under the significant title, *Last Words over the Coffin of Alexander II.* I hope sometime to translate and republish this document, and I need only say now that I have the names of six politicals who went insane in that prison during the short time that it was used as a place of confinement for such offenders. Muíshkin was put into a small cell in the lower story that had formerly been occupied by the distinguished political Prince Tsitsiánof. His courage and energy soon led him to meditate plans of escape, and before the end of the first year he had made a dummy to lie in his place on the sleeping-platform, and with only his hands and a small piece of board had dug a tunnel out under the prison wall, disposing of the earth that he removed by packing it into a space between the floor of his cell and the ground. He had also made himself a suit of clothing to put on in place of the prison costume after he should make his escape. Prince Tsitsiánof, who had occupied the cell before him, was a scientist, and during his term of imprisonment had been allowed to have some large maps. These maps had been left as old rubbish on the oven, and Muíshkin had soaked the paper off from the muslin on which they were mounted and had made out of the cloth a shirt and a pair of trousers. His preparations for escape were virtually complete, and he was only waiting for a favorable opportunity, when one of the prison officials came to his cell at an unusual hour to speak to him. Muíshkin happened to be down in his tunnel, while the dummy was lying in his place on the bed as if he were asleep. The official soon discovered that the lay figure was not the prisoner, an alarm was raised, the mouth of the tunnel was found, and Muíshkin was dragged out like a rat from its hole. He was then put into another cell, from which escape was impossible. At the expiration of two or three months, fearing that he was about to become insane, he determined to do something for which he would be shot. He asked and obtained permission to attend service in the prison church one Sunday, and while there contrived to get near the governor of the prison; and as the latter turned around, after kissing the cross in the hands of the priest, Muíshkin struck him in the face. For this offense he would, under ordinary circumstances, have been shot; but just at that time the attention of the Minister of the Interior was attracted to the Kharkóf central prison by the large number of deaths and cases of insanity among the politicals, and Professor Dobroslávin, a sanitary expert from St. Petersburg, was sent to the prison to make an investigation. He reported that it was not fit for human habitation, said that the cases of death and insanity among the political convicts were not surprising, and recommended that all the prisoners of that class be removed. In the light of this report it was presumed that Muíshkin was insane, or at least in an abnormal mental condition, at the time when he struck the governor of the prison, and he was not even tried for the offense. Shortly afterward he was sent, with all his fellow-prisoners, to the mines of Kará. While they were in the city of Irkútsk on their way to the mines, one of the party, a man named Leo Dmokhófski, died. All the convicts in the party were permitted to attend the funeral in the prison church, and at the conclusion of the brief services Muíshkin felt impelled to say a few words over the body of his comrade. He referred to the high moral character of the dead man and his lovable personality, quoted a verse from the Russian liberal poet Nekrásof, and said, "Out of the ashes of this heroic man, and of other men like him, will grow the tree of liberty for Russia." At this point he was stopped by the chief of police, and at once taken back to his cell. For making what was regarded as a revolutionary speech within the sacred precincts of a church, and in the presence of the "images of the Holy Saints of the Lord," he was condemned to fifteen years more of penal servitude. In talking to me about Muíshkin, some of his comrades described him as "a born orator who never made but two speeches in his life; one of them cost him ten years of penal servitude, and the other fifteen." Muíshkin himself said, after reaching the mines of Kará, that there was only one thing in his life which he regretted, and that was his speech over the dead body of his comrade Dmokhófski in Irkútsk. The world could not hear it, it did no good, it was merely the gratification of a personal impulse, and it added so many years to his term of penal servitude that, even if he should live out that term, he would be too old, when finally released, to work any more for the cause of Russian freedom.

Muíshkin was one of the first of the eight prisoners who escaped from the Kará political prison in April, 1882, and he was recaptured, as I have said, in the seaport town of Vladivostok, to which American vessels come every summer. In 1883 he was sent back to St. Petersburg, with a party of other "dangerous" politicals, and incarcerated in the castle of Schlusselburg. In the autumn of 1885, fearing that, as a result of long solitary confinement, he was about to go insane, he struck one of the castle officers, with the hope that he would be put to death. The experiment that had failed in the Kharkóf central prison succeeded in Schlusselburg. He was promptly tried by court-martial and shot.

On the 12th of November Mr. Frost and I left the mines of Kará forever, and with glad hearts turned our faces, at last, homeward. As we drove away, with Major Pótulof, from the Lower Diggings, two political convicts, in long gray overcoats, who were walking toward the prison at a distance of one hundred and fifty or two hundred yards from the road, saw and recognized us, and as we passed they stopped, removed their caps, and made toward us what the Russians call a "waist bow" —a bow so low that the body is bent at right angles from the waist. It was their last mute farewell to the travelers who had shown them sympathy and pity, and it is the last remembrance I have of the mines of Kará.

We spent that night in the house of the overseer of the Ust Kará prison, at the mouth of the river, and on the following morning remounted our horses for another ride across the mountains to Strétinsk. Major Pótulof opened a bottle of white Crimean wine after we had climbed into our saddles, and, pouring out a glassful for each of us and for himself, said, "Here's to the beginning of a journey to America!" We drank the stirrup-cup with bright anticipations of a return to home and friends, thanked Major Pótulof for his kindness and hospitality, promised to apprise him by telegraph of our safe arrival at Strétinsk, and rode away into the mountains.

CHAPTER TEN

Last Days in Siberia

MINUSÍNSK, WHERE WE MADE
our last stop in Eastern Siberia, is a thriving little town of
5000 or 6000 inhabitants, situated in the fertile valley of the
upper Yeniséi, 3200 miles from the capital of the Empire and
150 miles from the boundary-line of Mongolia. It corresponds
very nearly with Liverpool in latitude and with Calcutta in
longitude, and is distant from St. Petersburg, in traveling time,
about twenty days. Owing to the fact that it lies far south of
the main line of transcontinental communication it has not
often been visited by foreign travelers, and at the time of our
visit was little known even to the people of European Russia;
but it had particular interest for us, partly because it contained
the largest and most important museum of archaeology and
natural history in Siberia, and partly because it was the place
of exile of a number of prominent Russian liberals and revolutionists.

We reached the little town about half-past five o'clock in
the morning. The columns of smoke that were rising here and
there from the chimneys of the log houses showed that some,
at least, of the inhabitants were already astir; but as the close-
fitting board shutters had not been taken down from the windows there were no lights visible, the wide streets were empty,
and the whole town had the lonely, deserted appearance that
most Siberian towns have when seen early in the morning by
the faint light of a waning moon.

"Where do you order me to go?" inquired our driver, reining in his horses and turning half around in his seat.

"To a hotel," I said. "There's a hotel here, isn't there?"

"There used to be," he replied, doubtfully. "Whether there's one now or not, God knows; but if your high nobility has no friends to go to, we'll see."

We were provided with letters of introduction to several well-known citizens of Minusínsk, and I had no doubt that at the house of any one of them we should be cordially and hospitably received; but it is rather awkward and embarrassing to have to present a letter of introduction, before daylight in the morning, to a gentleman whom you have just dragged out of bed; and I resolved that if we should fail to find a hotel, I would have the driver take us to the Government post-station. We had no legal right to claim shelter there, because we were traveling with "free" horses and without a *padarózhnaya;* but experience had taught me that a Siberian post-station master, for a suitable consideration, will shut his eyes to the strictly legal aspect of any case and admit the justice and propriety of any claim.

After turning three or four corners our driver stopped in front of a large two-story log building, near the center of the town, which he said "used to be" a hotel. He pounded and banged at an inner courtyard door until he had roused all the dogs in the neighborhood, and was then informed by a sleepy and exasperated servant that this was not a hotel but a private house, and that if we continued to batter down people's doors in that way in the middle of the night we shouldn't need a hotel, because we would be conducted by the police to suitable apartments in a commodious jail. This was not very encouraging, but our driver, after exchanging a few back-handed compliments with the ill-tempered servant, took us to another house in a different part of the town, where he banged and pounded at another door with undiminished vigor and resolution. The man who responded on this occasion said that he did keep "rooms for arrivers," but that, unfortunately, the full

complement of "arrivers" had already arrived, and his rooms
were all occupied. He suggested that we try the house of one
Soldátof. As there seemed to be nothing better to do, away we
went to Soldátof's, where at last, in the second story of an old
weather-beaten log building, we found a large, well-lighted,
and apparently clean room which was offered to us, with
board for two, at seventy cents a day. We accepted the terms
with joy, and ordered our driver to empty the *pavóska* and
bring up the baggage. Our newly found room was uncarpeted,
had no window-curtains, and contained neither washstand nor
bed; but it made up for its deficiencies in these respects by of-
fering for our contemplation an aged oleander in a green tub,
two pots of geraniums, and a somewhat anemic vine of English ivy climbing feebly up a cotton string to look at itself in a
small wavy mirror. Of course no reasonable traveler would
complain of the absence of a bed when he could sit up all
night and look at an oleander; and as for the washstand—it
would have been wholly superfluous in a hotel where you
could go out to the barn at any time and get one of the hostlers
to come in and pour water on your hands out of a gangrened
brass teapot.

As soon as our baggage had been brought in we lay down
on the floor, just as we were, in fur caps, sheepskin overcoats,
and felt boots, and slept soundly until after ten o'clock.

A little before noon, having changed our dress and made
ourselves as presentable as possible, we went out to make a call
or two and to take a look at the place. We did not think it prudent to present our letters of introduction to the political exiles until we could ascertain the nature of the relations that
existed between them and the other citizens of the town, and
could learn something definite with regard to the character
and disposition of the *isprávnik*, or district chief of police. We
therefore went to call first upon the well-known Siberian naturalist, Mr. N. M. Martiánof, the founder of the Minusínsk
museum, to whom we had a note of introduction from the editor of the St. Petersburg *Eastern Review*. We found Mr.

Martiánof busily engaged in compounding medicines in the little drugstore of which he was the proprietor, not far from the Soldátof hotel. He gave us a hearty welcome, and said that he had seen references to our movements occasionally in the Tomsk and Irkútsk newspapers, but that he had feared we would return to St. Petersburg without paying Minusínsk a visit. We replied, of course, that we could not think of leaving Siberia until we had seen the Minusínsk museum, and made the acquaintance of the man whose name was so intimately and so honorably associated with it, and with the history of natural science in that remote part of the Empire. In Tomsk, In Krasnoyársk. in Irkútsk, and even in St. Petersburg, we had heard the most favorable accounts of the museum, and we anticipated great pleasure in going through it, and especially in examining its anthropological and archaeological collections, which, we had been informed, were very rich.

Mr. Martiánof seemed gratified to know that we had heard the museum well spoken of in other parts of the Empire, but said, modestly, that it might disappoint travelers who were acquainted with the great scientific collections of America and Europe, and that he hoped we would make due allowance for the difficulties with which they had to contend and the scantiness of their pecuniary resources. It was, as yet, he said, only the kernel or nucleus of a museum, and its chief importance lay in the promise that it held out of becoming something better and more complete in the future. Still, such as it was, we should see it; and if we were at leisure he would take us to it at once. We replied that we had nothing better to do, and in five minutes we were on our way to the museum building.

The Minusínsk museum, of which all educated Siberians are now deservedly proud, is a striking illustration of the results that may be attained by unswerving devotion to a single purpose, and steady, persistent work for its accomplishment. It is, in every sense of the word, the creation of Mr. Martiánof, and it represents, almost exclusively, his own individual skill and labor. When he emigrated to Siberia, in 1874, there was not a public institution of the kind, so far as I know, in all the country, except the half-dead, half-alive mining museum in Barnaül; and the idea of promoting popular education and cultivating a taste for science by making and exhibiting classified collections of plants, minerals, and archaeological relics had hardly suggested itself even to teachers by profession. Mr. Martiánof, who was a graduate of the Kazán university, and whose scientific specialty was botany, began, almost as soon as he reached Minusínsk, to make collections with a view to the ultimate establishment of a museum. He was not a man of means or leisure. On the contrary, he was wholly dependent upon his little drugstore for support, and was closely confined to it during the greater part of every day. By denying himself sleep, however, and rising very early in the morning, he managed to get a few hours every day for scientific work, and in those few hours he made a dozen or more identical collections of such plants and minerals as could be found within an hour's walk of the town. After classifying and labeling the specimens carefully, he sent one of these collections to every country schoolteacher in the Minusínsk district, with a request that the scholars be asked to make similar collections in the regions accessible to them, and that the specimens thus obtained be sent to him for use in the projected museum. The teachers and scholars responded promptly and sympathetically to the appeal thus made, and in a few months collections of flowers and rocks began to pour into Mr. Martiánof's little drugstore from all parts of the district. Much of this material, of course, had been collected without adequate knowledge or discrimination, and was practically worthless; but some of it was of great value, and even the unavailable specimens were proofs of sympathetic interest and readiness to coöperate on the part not only of the scholars, but of their relatives and friends. In the meantime, Mr. Martiánof had been sending similar but larger and more complete collections to the Imperial Academy of Sciences, to various Russian museums, to his own alma mater, and to the professors of natural history in several of the great Russian universities, with a proposition in every case to exchange them for such duplicates of specimens from other parts of the Empire as they might have to spare. In this way, by dint of unwearied personal industry, Mr. Martiánof gathered, in the course of two years, a collection of about 1500 objects, chiefly in the field of natural history, and a small but valuable library of 100 or more scientific books, many of which were not to be found elsewhere in Siberia. In 1876 he made a formal presentation of all this material to the Minusínsk town council for the benefit of the public. A charter was then obtained; two rooms in one of the school buildings were set apart as a place for the exhibition of the specimens, and the museum was thrown open. From that time forth its growth was steady and rapid. The cultivated people of Minusínsk rallied to Mr. Martiánof's support, and contributions in the shape of books, anthropological material, educational appliances, and money soon began to come from all parts of the town and district, as well as from many places in the neighboring provinces.

In 1879, only three years after its foundation, the museum contained more than 6000 objects, and on the shelves of the library connected with it there were 3100 volumes. At the time of our visit it had outgrown its accommodations in the schoolhouse, and had been removed to the building of the town council, where it occupied six or seven rooms and was still very much crowded. Its contents were classified in six departments, or sections, known respectively as the departments of natural history, ethnology, archaeology, rural economy (including farm and household implements and utensils), technology, and educational appliances. The department of natural history, which comprised the plants, rocks, and animals of the district, was the largest, of course, and the most complete; but to me the department of archaeology was by far the most important and interesting, for the reason that it contained a very remarkable collection of weapons and implements found in the *kurgáns* and burial-mounds of the Yeniséi valley, and extending in an unbroken series from the flint arrow-heads and stone celts of the prehistoric aborigines, down through the copper and bronze age, to the rusty pikeheads and chain-mail shirts of the Cossack invaders.

After leaving the museum we called with Mr. Martiánof upon several prominent citizens of the town, among them Mr. Lítkin, the mayor or head of the town council; Dr. Malínin, an intelligent physician, who lived in rather a luxurious house filled with beautiful conservatory flowers, and a wealthy young merchant named Safiánof, who carried on a trade across the Mongolian frontier with the Soyóts. I also called, alone, upon Mr. Známenski, the *isprávnik*, or district chief of police, but, failing to find him at home, left cards. About the middle of the afternoon we returned to Soldátof's, where we had dinner, and then spent most of the remainder of the day in making up sleep lost on the road.

It must not be supposed that we had become so absorbed in museums, archaeological relics, and Káchinski Tatars that we had forgotten all about the political exiles. Such was by no means the case. To make the acquaintance of these exiles was the chief object of our visit to Minusínsk, and we did not for a moment lose sight of it; but the situation there just at that time was a peculiarly strained and delicate one, owing to the then recent escape of a political named Máslof, and the strictness with which, as a natural consequence, all the other exiles were watched. The provincial procureur Skrínikof and a colonel of gendarmes from Krasnoyársk were there making an investigation of the circumstances of Máslof's flight; the local police, of course, were stimulated to unwonted vigilance by the result of their previous negligence and by the presence of these high officers of the Crown from the provincial capital; and it was extremely difficult for us to open communication with the politicals without the authorities' knowledge. In these circumstances it seemed to me necessary to proceed with great caution, and to make the acquaintance of the exiles in a manner that should appear to be wholly accidental. I soon learned, from Mr. Martiánof, that several of them had taken an active interest in the museum, had been of great assistance in the collection and classification of specimens, and were in the habit of frequenting both the museum and the library. I should have been very dull and slow-witted if, in the light of this information, I had failed to see that archaeology and anthropology were my trump cards, and that the best possible thing for me to do was to cultivate science and take a profound interest in that museum. Fortunately I was a member of the American Geographical Society of New York and of the Anthropological Society of Washington, and had a sufficiently general smattering of natural science to discuss any branch of it with laymen and the police, even if I could not rise to the level of a professional like Martiánof. I therefore not only visited the museum at my earliest convenience, and took a deep anthropological interest in the Káchinski Tatars, but asked Mr. Martiánof to allow us to take a Soyót plow, a lot of copper knives and axes, and half a dozen bronze mirrors to our room, where we could study them and make drawings of them at our leisure, and where, of course, they would be seen by any suspicious official who happened to call upon us, and would be taken by him as indications of the perfectly innocent and praise-worthy nature of our aims and pursuits. The result of our conspicuous devotion to science was that Mr. Martiánof kept our room filled with archaeological relics and ethnological specimens of all sorts, and, moreover, brought to call upon us one evening the accomplished geologist, archaeologist, and political exile, Dmítri Kléments. I recognized the latter at once as the man to whom I had a round-robin letter of introduction from a whole colony of political exiles in another part of Eastern Siberia, and also as the original of one of the biographical sketches in Stépniak's "Underground Russia." He was a tall, strongly built man about forty years of age, with a head and face that would attract attention in any popular assembly, but that would be characterized by most observers as Asiatic rather than European in type. The high, bald, well-developed forehead was that of the European scholar and thinker, but the dark-brown eyes, swarthy complexion, prominent cheek-bones, and rather flattish nose with open, dilated nostrils, suggested the features of a Buriát or Mongol. The lips and chin and the outlines of the lower jaw were concealed by a dark-brown beard and mustache; but all the face that could be seen below the forehead might have belonged to a native of any South Siberian tribe. As soon as I could get my round-robin certificate of trustworthiness out of the leather money-belt under my shirt, where I carried all dangerous documents likely to be needed on the road, I handed it to Mr. Kléments with the remark that although Mr. Martiánof had given me the conventional introduction of polite society, he could not be expected, of course, as a recent acquaintance, to vouch for my moral character, and I begged leave, therefore, to submit my references. Mr. Kléments read the letter with grave attention, went with it to one corner of the room, struck a match, lighted the paper, held it by one corner between his thumb and forefinger until it was entirely consumed, and then, dropping the ash and grinding it into powder on the floor under his foot, he turned to me and said, "That's the safest thing to do with all such letters." I was of the same opinion, but I had to carry with me all the time, nevertheless, not only such epistles but documents and letters infinitely more compromising and dangerous. After half an hour's conversation Mr. Martiánof suggested that we all come to his house and drink tea. The suggestion met with general approval, and we spent with Mr. and Mrs. Martiánof the remainder of the evening.

On the following morning we had our first skirmish with the Minusínsk police. Before we were up an officer in a blue uniform forced his way into our room without card or announcement, and in rather an offensive manner demanded our passports. I told him that the passports had been sent to the police-station on the day of our arrival, and had been there ever since.

"If they are there the inspector doesn't know it," said the officer impudently.

"It's his business to know it," I replied, "and not to send a man around here to disturb us before we are up in the morning. We have been in the Empire long enough to know what to do with passports, and we sent ours to the police-station as soon as we arrived."

My aggressive and irritated manner apparently convinced the officer that there must be some official mistake or oversight in this matter of passports, and he retired in confusion; but in less than ten minutes, while I was still lying on the floor, virtu-ally in bed, around came the inspector of police himself—an evil-looking miscreant with a pock-marked face, and green, shifty, feline eyes, who, without his uniform, would have been taken anywhere for a particularly bad type of common convict. He declared that our passports were not at the police-station and had not been there, and that he wanted them immediately. Furthermore, he said, he had been directed by the *isprávnik* to find out "what kind of people" we were, where we had come from, and what our business was in Minusínsk. "You have been making calls," he said, "upon people in the town, and yet the *isprávnik* hasn't seen anything of you."

"Whose fault is it that he hasn't seen anything of me?" I demanded hotly. "I called on him day before yesterday, didn't find him at home, and left him my card. If he wants to know 'what kind of people' we are, why doesn't he return my call in a civilized manner, at a proper time of day, instead of send-ing a police officer around here to make impertinent inquiries before we are up in the morning? As for the 'kind of people' we are—perhaps you will be able to find out from these," and I handed him my open letters from the Russian Minister of the Interior and the Minister of Foreign Affairs. He glanced through them, and then, in a slightly changed tone and manner, inquired, "Will you permit me to take these to show to the *isprávnik?*"

"Certainly," I replied; "that's what they are for."

He bowed and withdrew, while I went down to see the pro-prietor of the house and to find out what he had done with the passports. It appeared that they had been taken to the police-station at once, but that the police secretary could neither read them nor make anything out of them, and had stupidly or angrily declined to receive them; whereupon the proprietor had brought them back and put them away safely in a cupboard drawer. In the course of half an hour the inspector of police returned with the open letters, which he handed me without remark. I gave him the passports with a brief statement of the fact that his secretary had declined to receive them, and we parted with a look of mutual dislike and suspicion. We were destined shortly to meet again under circumstances that would deepen his suspicion and my dislike.

With the coöperation of Mr. Martiánof and Mr. Kléments we made the acquaintance in the course of the next three or four days of nearly all the political exiles in the place, and found among them some of the most interesting and attractive people we as yet had met in Siberia. Among those with whom we became best acquainted were Mr. Ivánchin-Písaref, a landed proprietor from the province of Yároslav; Dr. Martínof, a surgeon from Stávropol; Ivan Petróvich Belokónski, a young author and newspaper man from Kiev; Leonídas Zhebunóf, formerly a student in the Kiev university; Miss Zenaïd Zatsépina, and Dmítri Kléments. The wives of Dr. Martínof and Mr. Ivánchin-Písaref were in exile with them; both spoke English, and in their hospitable houses we were so cordially welcomed and were made to feel so perfectly at home that we visited them as often as we dared. Dr. Martínof was a man of wealth and culture, and at the time of his arrest was the owner of a large estate near Stávropol in the Caucasus. When he was banished his property was put into the hands of an administrator appointed by the Minister of the Interior, and he was allowed for his maintenance a mere pittance of fifty dollars a month. He had never had a judicial trial, and had never been deprived legally of any of his civil rights; and yet by order of the Tsar his estate had been taken away from him and he had been banished by administrative process, with his wife and child, to this remote part of Eastern Siberia. He was not allowed at first even to practice his profession; but this the Minister of the Interior finally gave him permission to do. Some time in December, 1885, a few weeks before we reached Minusínsk, a man knocked at Dr. Martínof's door late one night and said that a peasant who lived in a village not far from the town had been attacked in the forest by a bear, and so terribly mangled and lacerated that it was doubtful whether he could recover. There was no other surgeon in the town, and the messenger begged Dr. Martínof to come to the wounded peasant's assistance. At that late hour of the night it was not practicable to get permission from the police to go outside the limits of the town, and Dr. Martínof, thinking that he would return before morning, and that the urgency of the case would excuse a mere technical violation of the rule concerning absence without leave, went with the messenger to the suburban village, set the peasant's broken bones, sewed up his wounds, and saved his life. Early in the morning he returned to Minusínsk, thinking that no one in the town except his wife would be aware of his temporary absence. The *isprávnik*, Známenski, however, heard in some way of the incident, and like the stupid and brutal formalist that he was, made a report to General Pedashénko, the governor of the province, stating that the political exile Martínof had left the town without permission, and asking for instructions. The governor directed that the offender be arrested and imprisoned. Dr. Martínof thereupon wrote to the governor a letter, of which the following is a copy.

MINUSÍNSK, December 3, 1885

To His EXCELLENCY THE GOVERNOR OF THE PROVINCE OF YENISÉISK: On this 3d day of December, 1885, I have been notified of the receipt of an order from your Excellency directing that I be arrested and imprisoned for temporarily leaving the town of Minusínsk without permission. It seems to me to be my duty to explain to your Excellency that I went outside the limits of Minusínsk for the purpose of rendering urgently needed medical assistance to a patient who had been attacked by a bear, and whose life was in extreme danger as the result of deep wounds and broken bones. There is no surgeon in the town except myself to whom application for help in such a case could be made. My services were required immediately, and, in view of the oath taken by me as a surgeon, I regarded it as my sacred duty to go, the same night I was called, to the place where the injured man lay. I had neither time nor opportunity, therefore, to give the police notice of my contemplated absence. Besides that, in the permission to practice given me by the Minister of the Interior there is nothing to prohibit my going outside the limits of the town to render medical assistance. If, notwithstanding this explanation, your Excellency finds it necessary to hold me to accountability, I beg your Excellency to issue such orders as may be requisite to have me dealt with, not by administrative process, which would be inconsistent with section thirty-two of the Imperially confirmed "Rules Relating to Police Surveillance," but by the method indicated in the "Remark" which follows that section, and which provides that a person guilty of unauthorized absence from his assigned place of residence shall be duly tried. In order that such misunderstandings may not occur in future, I beg your Excellency to grant me, upon the basis of section eight of the "Rules Relating to Police Surveillance," permission to go temporarily outside the limits of the town to render medical assistance.

SERGE V. MARTÍNOF, M.D.

Governor Pedashénko did not condescend to make any direct reply to this letter, but merely sent the letter itself to the *isprávnik* Známenski with the laconic indorsement, "Let him be tried." Of course an offender in Russia cannot expect to be tried in less than a year after the accusation is made; and up to the time of our departure from Minusínsk the accused in this case was still waiting for arraignment. Since my return to the United States I have been informed by letters from Siberia that five years more have been added to Dr. Martínof's term of exile. Whether this supplementary punishment was inflicted upon him because he dared to save a poor peasant's life without the permission of the *isprávnik*, or merely because his behavior generally was that of a self-respecting Russian nobleman, and not that of a cringing slave, I do not know. When the end of an exile's term of banishment draws near, the local authorities are called upon for a report with regard to his behavior. If the report be unfavorable, an addition of from one to five years is made to his period of exile. Perhaps the *isprávnik* Známenski reported that Dr. Martínof was "insubordinate"; and very likely he was insubordinate. He certainly had grievances enough to make him so. One peculiarly exasperating thing happened to him almost in my presence. There is an administrative regulation in force in most Siberian penal settlements, requiring political exiles to appear at the police-station daily, semi-weekly, or weekly, and sign their names in a register. The intention, apparently, is to render escapes more difficult by forcing the exile to come, at short intervals, to the local authorities, and say, "I am still here; I haven't escaped." And as a proof that he hasn't escaped they make him sign his name in a book. It is a stupid regulation; it affords no security whatever against escapes; it is intensely humiliating to the personal pride of the exile, especially if the authorities happen to be brutal, drunken, or depraved men; and it causes more heartburning and exasperation than any other regulation in the whole exile code.

One morning about a week after our arrival in Minusínsk I was sitting in the house of Ivánchin-Písaref, when the door opened and Dr. Martínof came in. For a moment I hardly recognized him. His eyes had a strained expression, his face was colorless, his lips trembled, and he was evidently struggling with deep and strong emotion.

"What has happened?" cried Mrs. Ivánchin-Písaref, rising as if to go to him.

"The *isprávnik* has ordered Márya to come to the police-station," he replied.

For an instant I did not catch the significance of this fact, nor understand why it should so excite him. A few words of explanation, however, made the matter clear. Mrs. Martínof [Márya] was in hourly expectation of her confinement. I remembered, when I thought of it, that only the night before I had had an engagement to spend the evening at Dr. Martínof's house, and that he had sent me word not to come because his wife was ill. As it happened to be the day that all of the politi-

cal exiles were required to sign their names in the police register, Dr. Martínof had gone to the *isprávnik,* explained his wife's
condition, said that she was unable to go out, and asked that
she be excused. The *isprávnik* made a coarse remark about her,
which must have been hard for a husband to bear, but which
Dr. Martínof dared not resent, and said that if the woman was
not able to walk of course she could not come to the police-
station. This was Friday afternoon, and it was on the evening
of that day that Dr. Martínof sent word to me not to come to
his house on account of his wife's illness. It turned out, however, that her suffering was not decisive, and early the next
morning, by her husband's advice, she took a walk of a few
moments back and forth in front of the house. The *isprávnik*
happened to drive past, and saw her. He went at once to the
police-station, and from there sent an officer to her with a curt
note, in which he said that if she was able to walk out she was
able to come to the police-station, and that if she did not make
her appearance within a certain short specified time, he should
be compelled to treat her "with all the rigor of the law." The
poor woman, therefore, had to choose between the risk, on the
one hand, of having her child born at the police-station in the
presence of the *isprávnik* and his green-eyed assistant, and the
certainty, on the other, of having it born in one of the cells of
the Minusínsk prison. If her husband should attempt to defend
her, or to resist the officers sent to take her into custody, he
would simply be knocked down and thrown into a solitary-
confinement cell, and then, perhaps, be separated from her altogether by a sentence of banishment to the arctic region of
Yakútsk on the general and elastic charge of "resisting the
authorities." The stupid brutality of the *isprávnik*'s action in
this case was made the more conspicuous by the circumstance
that Mrs. Martínof's term of exile would expire by limitation
in about two weeks, and she would then be a free woman. Not
only, therefore, was her condition such as to render escape at
that time utterly impossible, but there was no imaginable motive for escape. Long before she would recover from her con-

finement sufficiently to travel she would be free to go where she liked. This made no difference, however, to the *isprávnik*. A certain administrative regulation gave him power to drag to the police-station a delicate, refined, and cultivated woman at the moment when she was about to undergo the great trial of maternity; and drag her to the police-station he did. I think that his action was the result rather of stupidity and senseless formalism than of deliberate malignity. The rules and regulations which control the actions of a petty Russian bureaucrat— as contradistinguished from a human being—require the periodical appearance of every political exile at the police-station. No exception is made by the law in favor of women in childbirth, or women whose term of banishment is about to expire; and the *isправnik* Známenski acted in the case of the wife just as he had previously acted in the case of the husband—that is, obeyed the rules with a stupid and brutish disregard of all the circumstances.

The two weeks that we spent in Minusínsk were full of interest and adventurous excitement. The *isправnik* was evidently suspicious of us, notwithstanding our open letters, and did not return our call. The green-eyed inspector of police surprised me one day in the house of the political exile Mr. Ivánchin-Písaref, and doubtless made a report thereupon to his superior officer, and it seemed sometimes as if even science would not save us. I succeeded, however, in establishing pleasant personal relations with the colonel of gendarmes and the Government procureur from Krasnoyársk, told them frankly all about our acquaintance with Kléments, Ivánchin-Písaref, and the other political exiles, as if it was the most natural thing in the world for us to meet them on account of our common interest in archaeology, anthropology, and the museum, and behaved, generally, as if it afforded me the greatest pleasure to tell them—the colonel of gendarmes and the procureur—all that I was doing in Minusínsk, and to share with them all my experiences. What reports were made to St. Petersburg with regard to us I do not know; but they had no evil results. We were not searched and we were not arrested.

Upon the advice of some of my friends in Minusínsk, I decided to get rid of all my notebooks, documents, letters from political convicts, and other dangerous and incriminating papers, by sending them through the mails to a friend in St. Petersburg. To intrust such material to the Russian postal department seemed a very hazardous thing to do, but my friends assured me that the postal authorities in Minusínsk were honorable men, who would not betray to the police the fact that I had sent such a package, and that there was little probability of its being opened or examined in St. Petersburg. They thought that the danger of losing my notes and papers in the mails was not nearly so great as the danger of having them taken from me as the result of a police search. The material in question amounted in weight to about forty pounds, but as packages of all sizes are commonly sent by mail in Russia, mere bulk in itself was not a suspicious circumstance. I had a box made by an exiled Polish carpenter, took it to my room at night, put into it the entire results of my Siberian experience—most of the dangerous papers being already concealed in the covers of books and the hollow sides of small boxes—sewed it up carefully in strong canvas, sealed it with more than twenty seals, and addressed it to a friend in St. Petersburg whose political trustworthiness was beyond suspicion and whose mail, I believed, would not be tampered with. Thursday morning about half an hour before the semi-weekly post was to leave Minusínsk for St. Petersburg, I carried the box down into the courtyard under the cover of an overcoat, put it into a sleigh, threw a robe over it, and went with it myself to the post-office. The officials asked no question, but weighed the package, gave me a written receipt for it, and tossed it carelessly upon a pile of other mail matter that a clerk was putting into large leather pouches. I gave one last look at it, and left the post-office with a heavy heart. From that time forward I was never free from anxiety about it. That package contained all the results of my Siberian work, and its loss would have been simply irreparable. As week after week passed, and I heard nothing about it, I was strongly tempted to telegraph my friend and find out whether it had reached him; but I knew that such a telegram might increase the risk, and I refrained.

On many accounts we were more reluctant to leave Minusínsk than any other town at which we had stopped on our homeward way, but as a distance of 3000 miles still lay between us and St. Petersburg, and as we were anxious to reach European Russia, if possible, before the breaking up of the winter roads, it was time for us to resume our journey. Thursday, February 4th, we made farewell calls upon the political exiles, as well as upon Mr. Martiánof, Mr. Safiánof, and Dr. Malínin, who had been particularly kind to us, and set out with a *tróika* of "free" horses for the city of Tomsk, distant 475 miles. Instead of following the Yeniséi River back to Krasnoyársk, which would have been going far out of our way, we decided to leave it a short distance below Minusínsk and proceed directly to Tomsk by a short cut across the steppes, keeping the great Siberian road on our right all the way. Nothing of interest happened to us until late in the evening, when, just as we were turning up from the river into a small peasant village, the name of which I have now forgotten, both we and our horses were startled by the sudden appearance of a wild-looking man in a long, tattered sheepskin coat, who, from the shelter of a projecting cliff, sprang into the road ahead of us, shouting a hoarse but unintelligible warning, and brandishing in the air an armful of blazing birch-bark and straw.

"What's the matter?" I said to our driver, as our horses recoiled in affright.

"It's the plague-guard," he replied. "He says we must be smoked."

The cattle-plague was then prevailing extensively in the valley of the upper Yeniséi, and it appeared that round this village the peasants had established a sanitary cordon with the hope of protecting their own livestock from contagion. They had heard of the virtues of fumigation, and were subjecting to that process every vehicle that crossed the village limits. The "plague-guard" burned straw, birch-bark, and other inflammable and smoke-producing substances around and under our *pavóska* until we were half strangled and our horses were frantic with fear, and then he told us gravely that we were "purified" and might proceed.

On Friday, the day after our departure from Minusínsk, the weather became cold and blustering. The road after we left the Yeniséi was very bad, and late in the afternoon we were overtaken by a howling arctic gale on a great desolate plain, thirty or forty versts west of the Yeniséi and about one hundred and fifty versts from Minusínsk. The road was soon hidden by drifts of snow, there were no fences or telegraph-poles to mark its location, we could not proceed faster than a walk, and every three or four hundred yards we had to get out and push, pull, or lift our heavy *pavóska* from a deep soft drift. An hour or two after dark we lost the road altogether, and became involved in a labyrinth of snowdrifts and shallow ravines where we could make little or no progress, and where our tired and dispirited horses finally balked and refused to move. In vain our driver changed them about, harnessed them tandem, coaxed, cursed, and savagely whipped them. They were perfectly well aware that they were off the road, and that nothing was to be gained by floundering about aimlessly the rest of the night on that desert of drifted snow. The driver ejaculated, "Akh Bozhemoi! Bozhemoi!" ("O my God! my God!") besought his patron saint to inform him what he had done to deserve such punishment, and finally whimpered and cried like a schoolboy in his wrath and discouragement. I suggested at last that he had better leave us there, mount one of the horses, find the road, if possible, go to the nearest settlement, and then come back after us with lanterns, fresh horses, and men. He acted upon the suggestion, and Frost and I were left alone on the steppe in our half-capsized *pavóska*, hungry, exhausted, and chilled to the bone, with nothing to do but listen to the howling of the wind and wonder whether our driver in the darkness and in such weather would be able to find a settlement. The long, dismal night wore away at last, the storm abated a little toward morning, and soon after daybreak our driver made his appearance with ropes, crowbars, three fresh horses, and a stalwart peasant from a neighboring village. They soon extricated us from our difficulties, and early in the forenoon we drove into the little settlement of Ribálskaya, and alighted from our *pavóska* after fourteen hours' exposure to a winter gale on a desolate steppe without sleep, food, or drink. When we had warmed and refreshed ourselves with hot tea in a peasant's cabin, we ate what breakfast we could get, slept two or three hours on a plank bench, and then with fresh horses and a new driver we went on our way.

The overland journey in winter from the boundary line of Eastern Siberia to St. Petersburg has often been made and described by English and American travelers, and it does not seem to me necessary to dwell upon its hardships, privations, and petty adventures. We reached Tomsk in a temperature of thirty-five degrees below zero on the fifth day after our departure from Minusínsk, renewed our acquaintance with the Tomsk colony of exiles, gave them the latest news from their friends in the Trans-Baikál and at the mines of Kará, and then continued our journey homeward. On the 22d of February—Washington's birthday—we reached Omsk, stopped there twenty-four hours to rest and celebrate, and then went on by what is known as the "merchants' short cut" to Tobólsk. We were again surprised in the vicinity of Omsk by the appearance of camels. We had of course reconciled our preconceived ideas with the existence of camels in Siberia during the summer, but we had never stopped to think what became of them in the winter, and were very much astonished one frosty moonlight night to see three or four of them drawing Kírghis sledges.

Beyond Omsk we began to meet enormous freight-sledges of a new type drawn by six or eight horses and loaded with goods from the Irbít fair. Some of them were as big as a cottage gable-roof with a little trough-shaped box perched on the summit for the driver, the merchant, and his clerk. The great annual fair at Irbít in Western Siberia is second in importance only to the world-renowned fair of Nízhni Nóvgorod, and is visited by merchants and traders from the remotest parts of northern Asia. The freight-sledges that go to it and come from it in immense numbers in the latter part of the winter cut up the roads in the vicinity of Tiumén and Tobólsk so that they become almost impassable on account of deep ruts, hollows, and long, dangerous side-hill slides. We capsized twice in this part of the route notwithstanding the wide spread of our outriggers, and once we were dragged in our overturned *pavóska* down a long, steep hill and badly shaken and bruised before we could extricate ourselves from our sheepskin bag and crawl out. Rest and sleep on such a road were of course almost out of the question, and I soon had reason to feel very anxious about Mr. Frost's health. He was quiet and patient, bore suffering and privation with extraordinary fortitude, and never made the least complaint of anything; but it was evident, nevertheless, that he was slowly breaking down under the combined nervous and physical strain of sleeplessness, jolting, and constant fear of arrest. When we reached Tobólsk on the last day of February, and took off our heavy furs in the little log hotel under the bluff to which we had been recommended, I was shocked at his appearance. How serious his condition was may be inferred from the fact that about midnight that night he crept noiselessly over to the place where I was lying asleep on the floor, pressed his lips closely to my ear, and in a hoarse whisper said, "They are going to murder us!" I was so taken by surprise, and so startled, that I snatched my revolver from under my pillow and had it cocked before I waked sufficiently to grasp the situation, and to realize that Mr. Frost was in a high nervous fever, due chiefly to prolonged sleeplessness, and that the contemplated murder was nothing but an hallucination.

In the course of the next day I made, under the guidance of the chief of police, a very superficial examination of two convict prisons, but did not find much in them that was of interest. I also visited the belfry where now hangs the first exile to Siberia—the famous bell of Uglích, which was banished to Tobólsk in 1593 by order of the Tsar Bóris Gúdenof for having rung the signal for the insurrection in Uglích at the time of the assassination of the Crown Prince Dmítri. The exiled bell has been purged of its iniquity, has received ecclesiastical consecration, and now calls the orthodox people of Tobólsk to prayers. The inhabitants of Uglích have recently been trying to recover their bell upon the plea that it has been sufficiently punished by three centuries of exile for its political untrustworthiness in 1593, and that it ought now to be allowed to return to its home. The mayor of Tobólsk, however, argues that the bell was exiled for life, and that, consequently, its term of banishment has not yet expired. He contends, furthermore, that even admitting the original title of the Uglích people three centuries of adverse possession by the city of Tobólsk have divested the claimants of all their rights, and that the bell should be allowed to remain where it is. The question, it is said, will be carried into the Russian courts.

Late in the afternoon I walked over to the little plateau east of the city where stands the monument erected in honor of Yermák, the conqueror of Siberia, and then, returning to the hotel, paid our bill, ordered post-horses, and proceeded to Tiumén, reaching the latter place on the following day.

A week's rest at Tiumén, with plenty of sleep and good food, and the inspiriting companionship of English-speaking people, so restored Mr. Frost's strength that we were able to start for St. Petersburg by rail Tuesday, March 9th. How delightful it was to move swiftly out of Tiumén in a luxurious railroad car only those can conceive who have traveled eight thousand miles in springless vehicles over Siberian roads.

We reached the Russian capital on the 19th of March, and as soon as I had left Mr. Frost at a hotel with our baggage, I called a *dróshky*, drove to the house of the friend to whom I had sent my precious box of notebooks and papers, and, with a fast-beating heart, rang the bell and gave the servant my card. Before my friend made his appearance I was in a perfect fever of excitement and anxiety. Suppose the box had been opened by the post-office or police officials, and its contents seized. What should I have to show for almost a year of work and suffering? How much could I remember of all that I had seen and heard? What should I do without the written record of names, dates, and all the multitudinous and minute details that give verisimilitude to a story?

My friend entered the room with as calm and unruffled a countenance as if he had never heard of a box of papers, and my heart sank. I had half expected to be able to see that box in his face. I cannot remember whether I expressed any pleasure at meeting him, or made any inquiries with regard to his health. For one breathless moment he was to me merely the possible custodian of a box. I think he asked me when I arrived, and remarked that he had some letters for me; but all that I am certain of is that, after struggling with myself for a moment, until I thought I could speak without any manifestation of excitement, I inquired simply, "Did you receive a box from me?"

"A box?" he repeated interrogatively. Again my heart sank; evidently he had not received it. "Oh, yes," he continued, as if with a sudden flash of comprehension; "the big square box sewed up in canvas. Yes; that's here."

I was told afterward that there was no perceptible change in the gloomy March weather of St. Petersburg at that moment, but I am confident, nevertheless, that at least four suns, of the largest size known to astronomy, began immediately to shine into my friend's front windows, and that I could hear robins and meadowlarks singing all up and down the Névski Prospékt.

I forwarded the precious notes and papers to London by a special messenger, in order to avoid the danger of a possible search of my own baggage at the frontier, and then sent our passports to the municipal police with the usual notification that we desired to leave the Empire. The documents were promptly returned to us with a curt verbal message to the effect that we could not leave the Empire "without the permission of the governor-general of Eastern Siberia." As that official was about four thousand miles away, and we could not possibly get the necessary permission from him in less than three months, there was obviously nothing left for us to do but make complaint at the United States legation. I called upon Mr. Wurts, who was then acting as chargé d'affaires, and told him that the police would not allow us to leave the Empire.

"Why not?" he inquired.

"I don't know," I replied. "They say that we must have permission from the governor-general of Eastern Siberia, and of course we can't get that in three months—perhaps not in six months."

Mr. Wurts wrote a polite note to the chief of the bureau of passports in the Foreign Office, asking for information with regard to the alleged refusal of the police to allow two American citizens to leave the Empire. I delivered the note in person, in order that I might take the bull by the horns and find out definitely what the matter was. The chief of the passport bureau, an Italian whose name I have now forgotten, read the communication attentively, looked scrutinizingly at me, crossed the room and held a whispered consultation with a subordinate, and then returning said: "Mr. Kennan, have you ever had a permit to reside in the Russian Empire before this time?"

"I have," I replied.

"Do you remember when?"

"Yes, in 1868."

"Will you be kind enough to tell me at about what season of the year?"

"It was sometime in the spring, and I think in March."

He touched a bell to summon a clerk, and said to the latter, "Find the permit to reside that Mr. George Kennan, an American citizen, took out in March, 1868."

The clerk bowed and withdrew. In three or four minutes he returned bringing the original permit to reside that I had taken out *eighteen years* before, and a printed schedule of twenty or thirty questions concerning myself and my life which I had then answered in writing. The chief examined carefully my earlier record as an officer of the Russian-American Telegraph Company, held another whispered consultation with a subordinate, and then, coming back to me, said, "There are certain informalities, Mr. Kennan, in your present papers that would justify us in keeping you here until we could communicate with the governor-general of Eastern Siberia; but if you will bring me a formal letter from the American Minister, asking that you be allowed to leave the Empire without regard to such informalities, I will give you the necessary permission."

I could not see how a formal letter from the diplomatic representative of the United States could cure the defects in a Russian document duly issued by authority of the Tsar, and properly stamped, signed, and sealed by the East Siberian authorities; but I was not in the habit of raising unnecessary questions in my dealings with the Russian police, and I had good reason, moreover, to say as little as possible about Siberia. I obtained the "formal letter" from Mr. Wurts, brought it to the passport bureau, declared that I was not a Jew, signed my name at the bottom of sundry blanks, disbursed various small sums for stamps, sealing-wax, and paper, paid an official for showing me what to do, received a document which I was directed to take to the police-station of the precinct in which I resided, brought back from there another document addressed to the passport bureau, and finally, after four days of going back and forth from one circumlocution office to another, received a little book, about as big as a religious tract, which certified that there was no objection, on the part of anybody, to my leaving the Empire. Three days later I was in London.

It was my intention merely to write a full report from there to the editor of the *Century Magazine*, and then return to European Russia and continue my investigation; but my companion, Mr. Frost, was taken dangerously ill as a result of the tremendous mental and physical strain of our Siberian experience, and I could not leave him for almost a month. He had borne the extraordinary hardships and privations of our eight-thousand-mile ride through Siberia with heroic fortitude and without a single murmur of complaint; but his strength had given way at last, chiefly as the result of nervous excitement and prolonged insomnia. He recovered slowly, but on the 13th of April he was strong enough to sail for the United States, and on the 16th I took out a new passport and returned with my wife to St. Petersburg. I spent four months in making the acquaintance of Russian liberals, revolutionists, and officials in St. Petersburg, Tver, Moscow, Nízhni Nóvgorod, and Kazán; visited the friends and acquaintances of many of the political exiles whom I had met in Siberia and delivered the letters that I had for them; called upon Mr. Vlangálli, assistant Minister of Foreign Affairs, General Órzhefski, the chief of gendarmes, and Mr. Gálkine Wrásskoy, the chief of the prison administration; inspected two of the large St. Petersburg prisons—the Litófski Zámok, and the House of Preliminary Detention—completed my investigation, so far as it seemed possible to do so, and finally returned to New York in August, 1886, after an absence of about sixteen months.